D1500013

HOW TO BE AUTHENTIC

HOW TO BE AUTHENTIC

Simone de Beauvoir
and the Quest for Fulfillment

SKYE C. CLEARY

ST. MARTIN'S
ESSENTIALS
NEW YORK

To Ali

First published in the United States by St. Martin's Essentials,
an imprint of St. Martin's Publishing Group.

HOW TO BE AUTHENTIC. Copyright © 2022 by Skye C. Cleary. All rights
reserved. Printed in the United States of America. For information, address
St. Martin's Publishing Group, 120 Broadway, New York, NY 10271.

www.stmartins.com

Designed by Steven Seighman

The Library of Congress Cataloging-in-Publication Data
is available upon request.

ISBN 978-1-250-27135-8 (hardcover)
ISBN 978-1-250-27136-5 (ebook)

Our books may be purchased in bulk for promotional, educational, or business
use. Please contact your local bookseller or the Macmillan Corporate and
Premium Sales Department at 1-800-221-7945, extension 5442,
or by email at MacmillanSpecialMarkets@macmillan.com.

First Edition: 2022

10 9 8 7 6 5 4 3 2 1

My philosophy must be from life.
—*Diary of a Philosophy Student, Volume 1*

CONTENTS

INTRODUCTION

BECOMING AN AUTHENTIC REBEL

I feel within me something tumultuous that frightens me, an intensity that exhausts me. But I accept the great adventure of being me.
—Diary of a Philosophy Student, Volume 2

"Just be yourself." The "just" makes it sound so simple. If it were simple, the instruction wouldn't be necessary. But as it turns out, it is necessary. We crave authenticity precisely because it is so painfully rare to find and difficult to achieve. In the end, we have to fight to become authentic. This book is meant to assist in the quest.

Authenticity has become a devalued currency, attenuated to the point of meaninglessness. The meaning of "Just be yourself" is anyone's guess. Leadership literature advises us on how to fake authenticity. It promises to reveal the "secrets" of authenticity, to help us get ahead at work. Oprah Winfrey says if she'd known authenticity was so profitable, she would have done it much sooner. Brené Brown, bestselling author of *The Gifts of Imperfection,* defines authenticity as "the daily practice of letting go of who we think we're supposed to be and embracing who we are." Letting go of who we're supposed to be sounds right, but how do we know who we are? To ensure our lasting happiness, we're supposed to embrace our true selves. But what is a true self, and do we even have one?

If we're going to use the word "authentic," it would be helpful to understand what it really means, and if it's something we can have or something we must do. We might wonder who has access to it, how we can get access to it, and how setting it as a target would affect our lives. Is rapper Lizzo authentic when she loves herself out loud and rejects other people's beauty standards? Or is authenticity more like the philosopher Angela Davis, who bravely speaks out against injustices such as sexism, wars, and prisons as she acts upon her beliefs? Perhaps we zero in on things that seem obviously inauthentic: the incessant lies of politicians, gossipy musings of co-workers and friends, and selfies by Instagram influencers beholden to filters. But if they are inauthentic, what makes them so?

French existential philosopher Simone de Beauvoir pointed to authenticity as a foundational element of the meaning of life. But she meant something very different by the idea than the familiar parade of platitudes about being true to a pure form of yourself. For Beauvoir, there is no fixed essence to our being, since we are always becoming something other than what we are today. For Beauvoir, "existence precedes essence," meaning that we exist first and then spend the rest of our lives creating who we are (our essence).[1] She thought that there is no "true self" to discover, but only a vibrant self that we create through our choices. In other words, we are creative nothings.

To become authentic means to create our own essence. It's the creation that is vital here. We don't discover ourselves, we make ourselves. Authenticity is a way of expressing our freedom: to realize and accept that we are free; to be lucid about what we can and can't choose about ourselves, our situation, and others; and to use our freedom as a tool to shape ourselves. Our selves are not the product of a chain of impersonal causes and effects. Creating ourselves is an art form—the act of intentionally choosing who we become.

Authenticity is a poetic quest, a continuous process of self-creation and self-renewal, with unique rhymes and rhythms, verses and stanzas, muses and missteps. There are no particular rules or prescribed goals to guide us in our style. We have to fashion authenticity for ourselves. And it's how we compose it that matters.

* * *

Although authenticity is a quest, it's not a solo one. Authenticity isn't something you do, or even could do, on your own for two key reasons. One, there is an ethical dimension to Beauvoir's understanding of authenticity. We are always in the world with other people, interacting with them, with some awareness of what they want for us and what we want for them. Sometimes others uplift. Sometimes others obstruct. Either way, our lives are inextricably bound with others. And two, we can discover aspects of ourselves in others' stories, even, and perhaps especially, in the mistakes and delusions. Becoming more aware of ourselves, others, and our possibilities for growth fortifies us along our quests for fulfillment.

Authenticity is about forging our own paths, but it doesn't mean we get to do whatever we like. For Beauvoir, freedom without responsibility is meaningless. Responsibility means acknowledging that we are interconnected, and that we live situated in a particular time and place. Beauvoir—more so than any other philosopher—is unique in helping us navigate this tension between riding our own freedom and maneuvering through a world filled with others trying to do the same.

Beauvoir wrote, "One's life has value so long as one attributes value to the life of others, by means of love, friendship, indignation, compassion."[2] Love, friendship, and compassion are fairly standard on people's lists of important things. But indignation is not. She means indignation against injustices in the world. This is why compassion for others is essential to authenticity and it's also where rebellion comes in—rebellion against oppression and rebellion for every person's right to freely create their own lives.

In the lead-up to World War II, Beauvoir tended toward pacifism, but upon seeing the spread and horrors of fascism, she realized the importance of humanism, solidarity, and resistance. She lived through Nazi-occupied Paris. Her life partner, Jean-Paul Sartre, spent nine months as a prisoner of war. Many of her friends mysteriously disappeared. Beauvoir launched a resistance group but later disbanded it because people in other resistance groups started getting arrested and vanishing. In 1939 she wrote, "History took hold of me, and never let go thereafter."[3] The ethics of authenticity also never let her go.

Beauvoir captures the ethical dimension of authenticity with the idea of "intersubjectivity," that is, the mutual recognition and respect for one another's freedom. In one of her most provocative essays, "Must We Burn Sade?," Beauvoir examined the possibilities of intersubjectivity in sexual sadism. The Marquis de Sade was an eighteenth-century libertine who enjoyed violence, sexual cruelty, and performing acts of torture.

Beauvoir saw Sade as an example of someone who was authentic in the sense that he created his own rules, was uninhibited by social mores, and was passionate about writing and sadism. But he wasn't authentic from an existential perspective because he confused power and freedom. He turned scandal into a duty, ignored social inequality, robbed his victims of their freedom by turning them into passive objects of his desires, and his actions were tyrannical.

The implication of Beauvoir's thinking here is that egoism such as Sade's might feel to you as true to yourself. But this way of living overlooks the interconnectedness of our existences. Authenticity isn't a selfish, inward-only quest. There's a moral dimension to authenticity because we coexist with others. Existential freedom entails a responsibility to others because we share the same human condition.

A common objection to existentialism is that if we're free to choose our values, if becoming authentic is about embracing and exercising our freedom, and if nothing stops us from exploiting others, then what reason is there to act ethically? As Fyodor Dostoyevsky suggested in *The Brothers Karamazov*, if God is dead—if there is nothing external to guide our actions—then anything goes. Beauvoir wrestled with this conflict and worked hard to build an ethics based on freedom. Her sustained argument against the "anything goes" attitude is one of the reasons that she is unique amongst the existential philosophers.

Across her work—from her earliest novels to her late autobiographies to her massive philosophical books and many philosophical essays—she sketched the possibility of an authentic life that recognizes our relationships to others. After all, authenticity involves courageous honesty with ourselves. Authenticity beckons us to see ourselves with clear eyes. And when we look closely at ourselves, we discover all the ways we depend on others. We discover the ways we enrich one another's lives, or become obstacles to them and their projects.

So how can you become authentic in Beauvoir's existential sense? Strive to be a creative rebel with a cause. The cause is freedom itself. To become authentic we must free ourselves from oppression as well as self-imposed chains. We lock ourselves in with patterns of fear, ponchos of anxiety, and the longing to fit in. We put on masks for other people, and we often mask parts of our being from ourselves, parts of ourselves that we're not entirely comfortable with. Authenticity frees us to remove those masks we use to protect ourselves. It allows us to pursue an open future of our choosing.

When we stand up and put our very being at stake, taking a risk to do what we think is right, we create ourselves—we *make* ourselves into creative rebels. To take this kind of courageous action—to become these kinds of courageous selves—is exhilarating. But this quest takes effort. We must think twice. Act without automatically accepting other people's expectations about what we should do. Act with the awareness that we are enmeshed with each other's lives. Act by taking responsibility for who we become.

*   *   *

I encountered Simone de Beauvoir in the unlikeliest of places. I was sitting in a four-hour evening lecture for my MBA program, listening to my professor describe the intricacies of corporate governance. As heads began to sag and attention wandered, the pace of the professor's speech quickened. The pitch of her voice rose as she pivoted into a new subject.

"At work, how free are you *really*?" she asked. My head snapped back to its steadier state. "What a strange question," I thought. What does freedom have to do with boardroom mechanics? She went on to speak passionately about Simone de Beauvoir, Jean-Paul Sartre, and their defense of freedom, authenticity, and taking responsibility for the choices we make. She talked about how organizations like to create the illusion of freedom, but the only freedom most people have at work is to put up with the given conditions or to quit. We're expected to think independently—"outside the box," as they say—but doing so is rarely rewarded. Now she had my full attention.

The existentialists advocated creating your own values, she continued, but at work we're pressured to conform to the values of the company or risk not being a "team player." We're regulated in the name of organizational culture and hired based on whether we're deemed to be a "good fit." Regardless of performance, this practice clashes with the existential idea that we're always becoming and changing—often in unexpected and unpredictable ways. I felt light-headed. I hadn't had time to eat dinner before class, but it wasn't that. Something about this lecture was dizzying.

I'd heard of the French existentialists Simone de Beauvoir and Jean-Paul Sartre, although I didn't know much beyond superficial facts. I knew that Beauvoir had energized a wave of feminism with her 1949 book *The Second Sex*—a radical manifesto that challenged women's oppression. I knew she was as famous for her personal life as she was for her ideas—for socializing in Parisian jazz clubs and cafés with the intellectual elite and having a scandalous lifelong relationship with Sartre, a philosopher and womanizer.

Beauvoir's life and philosophy were a far cry from the distressingly clichéd situation I'd found myself in. Professionally, I was accomplished but burnt out, lost. At twenty-seven, I'd built a successful career as an international equity arbitrage trader managing my own portfolio of stocks and currencies. After six years on Wall Street, I had returned to Australia when my H-1B work visa ran out and set up my own desk at home, trading on American and European stock markets from Sydney.

Within a year, I was exhausted from being a financial vampire: up all night, staring at the Bloomberg screens, sucking money from market inconsistencies. The dot-com bubble had burst and computer algorithms tightened spreads, meaning greater risks for fewer rewards. As I saw it, an MBA would be my ticket back to the land of the living and a new career. I didn't know what I would pivot to. Initially I flirted with journalism, but found myself at a boutique management consulting group for a few years while I started my PhD part-time.

Meanwhile I was in an intellectually and professionally stifling relationship with a person who didn't understand my ambition. And everywhere I turned I encountered pressure to settle down.

People gave me books with titles like *The Rules: Time-tested Secrets for Capturing the Heart of Mr. Right*. It was clear what expectations society had for me, an unmarried woman pushing thirty: find love, get married, have babies, and live happily ever after. I suspected this formula for a happy life was a lie.

Existential philosophy came into my life at a moment when I needed to hear about it—when I was hungry to hear about it. With matrimony and fertility—or the glaring absence of both—banging on my door, and with the weight of conformity closing in on me, existentialism, with its talk of freedom, responsibility, and anxiety, was an awakening, or an invitation not to sleepwalk through the rest of my life.

Being existentially conscious, like being yourself, is deceptively difficult in the adult world. I have found Beauvoir's philosophy to be a deeply compelling way to think about how we should live and love, and about how we can become authentic in meaningful ways, in a world that is constantly tempting us to sell out—for a job, for acceptance by friends, for a social media profile—and to fill our voids with selfies and superficial status symbols.

Beauvoir galvanized me because she was ambitious and spritely and vivacious. She was dazzlingly intelligent but didn't seem to care, and she was glamourous but didn't seem to try. She was passionate about philosophy and pushed back against her parents who wanted her to pursue something more sensible like library studies. Beauvoir's family wasn't wealthy. Beauvoir didn't have a dowry and so she had to get a job, but she wanted to work anyway because she didn't want to be dependent on anyone but herself. She had a lifelong boyfriend (Jean-Paul Sartre) but she loved other people too. And I found her philosophy to be more nuanced than that of her male contemporaries. Beauvoir argued, for example, that context matters. Being a woman means you're in a different situation than the ones men find themselves in, and that makes a difference to the choices available to you.

I was disillusioned with my life. I felt boxed in by other people's expectations of me. I wanted to know how Beauvoir saw the world, and how she might see the world if she were in my shoes. I didn't want to do exactly as she did, but I wanted to try to figure out how she looked at situations, how I too could bring as much awareness as possible to my choices and the meaning of them. I wanted to create myself, but to become fortified by her philosophizing about authentic ways to do so. I thought studying Beauvoir's ideas could help me find a way out of that boxy feeling. So I embarked on a quest to understand Beauvoir's philosophy of authenticity, kept on questing, and this book is about what I've found so far.

*   *   *

Who was Simone de Beauvoir? Beauvoir was a French philosopher, novelist, and activist. Beauvoir was born in 1908, grew up in Paris, and studied philosophy at the Sorbonne—at a time when women had only recently been allowed to receive the same education as men. She voraciously read writers such as Karl Marx, Rosa Luxemburg, Edmund Husserl, Martin Heidegger, Søren Kierkegaard, Gottfried Wilhelm Leibniz, and Georg Wilhelm Friedrich Hegel. And she studied alongside fellow students who, like her, became some of the greatest French intellectuals of their era. These people included Jean-Paul Sartre, Maurice Merleau-Ponty, and Simone Weil.

Beauvoir was the ninth woman and youngest person to be awarded the *agrégation*, France's highly competitive and well-respected teachers' qualification by examination, from the École Normale Supérieure.[4] She has become one of the most famous and widely read philosophers of all time. American playwright and writer

Lorraine Hansberry suggested that "*The Second Sex* may very well be the most important work of [the twentieth] century . . . And the world will never be the same again." Sarah Bakewell described *The Second Sex* as "the most transformative existentialist work of all," and when Beauvoir died, French philosopher Élisabeth Badinter announced, "Women, you owe her so much!"[5] Beauvoir's novel *The Mandarins* won the Prix Goncourt, the most prestigious award in French literature, in 1954.

But Beauvoir resisted the label of "philosopher."[6] She was skeptical about joining what she saw as an elitist tradition that required obsessive efforts to create a "lunacy known as a 'philosophical system'"—as other philosophers, including Sartre, did.[7] She was more interested in living attitudes and practical existential solutions.[8] This is one reason why she also wrote novels, a play, and autobiographies.

The Second Sex begins with questioning the definition of a woman.[9] The answer, Beauvoir found, was so complicated that she spent almost one thousand pages in historical and philosophical analysis. This massive work took her just over a year. Such industriousness earned her the nickname "Castor," which means "beaver" in French. It's also a joke about "Beauvoir" sounding to French ears like the English "beaver."[10] (It's unclear if it was also a sexual reference. Beauvoir did not say how she felt about the nickname, but she didn't seem to have a problem with it.)

As she beavered away on *The Second Sex* in the 1940s, Beauvoir became acutely aware of the inequalities between the sexes. She realized her luck in being able to pursue an education and a teaching career—although her family struggled to send her to good schools and she studied very hard. She had choices that most women did not because of her intelligence and middle-class whiteness. And Beauvoir was able to capitalize on her privilege. She said: "No; far from suffering from my femininity, I have, on the contrary, from the age of twenty on, accumulated the advantages of both sexes."[11]

In an interview in the 1970s, Beauvoir talked about how writing *The Second Sex* transformed her views:

> [A working woman such as a secretary] could not sit in a café and read a book without being molested. She was rarely invited to parties for "her mind." She could not establish credit or own property. I could. More importantly still, I tended to scorn the kind of woman who felt incapable, financially or spiritually, to show her independence from men. In effect, I was thinking, without even saying it to myself, "if I can, so can they." In researching and writing *The Second Sex* I did come to realize that my privileges were the result of my having abdicated, in some crucial respects at least, my womanhood.[12]

One of the central themes underpinning Beauvoir's philosophy is that we are thrown into the world and create our being through our choices. If we're prevented from choosing, then that's oppression; if we choose to give up our freedom, then that's a moral failure.[13] *The Second Sex* became a two-volume investigation of how both oppression and women's acceptance of it have shaped women's situation as secondary to men, as they most certainly were in terms of opportunities and status when she was writing in the 1940s, and as they often still are today.

Beauvoir's most revolutionary idea is also her most well-known: "One is not born, but rather becomes, woman."[14] The meaning of this sentence has been debated ever since the book was first published, but mostly it is taken to mean that although sex is biological, gender is socially and culturally constructed—although Beauvoir didn't specifically use the term "gender" in *The Second Sex*.[15] In Beauvoir's view, you become a woman as a result of the social pressures to be and act in particular ways. These social pressures include the ways you are brought up, the expectations of people in your social circles, and even internalized pressures to conform with a stereotype. The forces are enough to inculcate you into certain ways of behaving, being, and even looking.

However, the biological fact of having a womb does not mean that a woman's primary role in society is to be a domestic worker and a man's primary role is to be a breadwinner. Beauvoir argued that such flawed logic—which overemphasizes the biological and reduces women to babymakers—has been used to keep women socially and culturally (and, by extension, financially) subordinate to men.

Another interpretation of the sentence "One is not born, but rather becomes, woman" is that we are not *made* into women, but we have the potential to *make ourselves* into women. Beauvoir's concern in *The Second Sex* was with both dimensions: understanding how external forces pressure us into conforming to traditional concepts of women, and the freedom we have to create ourselves. *The Second Sex* concludes with an urgent call to action for women to challenge their oppression, to embrace their freedom, and to live authentically by pursuing self-chosen projects and careers.

Beauvoir became famous for redefining a woman's role—not just theoretically, but in the way she seized this attitude in her everyday life. She grew up as a dutiful Catholic daughter and dreamed of becoming a nun. But she did not stick long with Catholicism. Beauvoir abandoned the conventional trajectory expected of a woman, such as getting married and having children. Yet she was so in tune with the experiences of other women that she was able to share ideas about choosing either conventional or alternative life paths and living them authentically, in freedom and power, not by default or lack of other options.

Beauvoir wrote *The Second Sex* in 1949, when French women had only just won the right to vote (in 1944). France lagged significantly behind universal suffrage in New Zealand (1893—the first nation to allow it), the United States (1920), and the United Kingdom (1928). During World War II, out of necessity, women had occupied many roles traditionally assigned to men. The battle for the right to vote started well before World War II. But after the war, feminists resumed the battle to demand greater equality in the workplace and at home.

The disruption of World War II created opportunities to form solidarities to challenge traditional conceptions of women's places in society. And a new wave of feminism emerged in Europe, North America, and elsewhere, ushering in far greater access to education, to birth control through contraception, and later, to no-fault divorce than had been available before the war. These and other rights were crucial for women to be able to take control of their own destinies.

In 1975 Beauvoir said that she was pleased that her work had resonated with so many women and activists—including feminist icons Betty Friedan, Gloria Steinem, and Kate Millett. Beauvoir didn't start a feminist movement, but philosopher Julia Kristeva credits Beauvoir with clarifying, crystallizing, and accelerating the feminist revolution of the mid-twentieth century better than anyone else.[16] Beauvoir's work mobilized people to fight for the right for women to control their bodies, to access professional and political worlds, and to transform bonds between the sexes.

* * *

Beauvoir's time was very different than ours in many ways. She lived through two world wars, and she lived without Wi-Fi, social media, and streaming television. But one of the reasons Beauvoir's thinking remains timely is that she was writing at an exceptionally bleak and politically tumultuous period. We still face uncertainties about life, not only politically, but also existentially: the abyss of a world with no clear meaning haunts many of us. Neatly packaged recipes, whether delivered by religion, family, society, or our leaders, remain highly suspect. Often it seems like we're sliding into a post-truth realm. We need to think critically about our lives, and Beauvoir can help us do this. I have written this book to disclose what we can learn from Simone de Beauvoir's philosophy to help us see our lives with lucidity and live authentically.

In existentialism, and particularly Beauvoir's existentialism, there are no strict rules. The existentialists couldn't even agree on a definition of their philosophy. Existentialism is better characterized by themes such as personal experience, freedom, authenticity, responsibility, individuality, anxiety, death, passionate engagement, concrete action, and figuring out the meaning of life for ourselves.

Existentialism rose to prominence in the 1940s with the work of not only Beauvoir and Sartre, but also Karl Jaspers, Gabriel Marcel, Martin Heidegger, Maurice Merleau-Ponty, Albert Camus, and others. One of the reasons existentialism became popular was because they acknowledged the importance of individual freedom, collective responsibility, and the absurdity of a world in which the barbarity of war is possible.

With a series of essays and lectures as the Nazis withdrew from France at the end of World War II, Beauvoir and Sartre launched what she called an "existentialist offensive."[17] Turning to Beauvoir, I'm mounting a new chapter in the existentialist offensive against superficial self-help and quick-fix promises. I don't prescribe rules, nor do I guarantee results. Instead, I provide a starting point to help reveal and understand the tyrannies of other people's demands on us and the chains we impose on ourselves, in the name of love, duty, or any other strings of excuses we offer up to avoid responsibility for our freedom.

An existential way of thinking is not a life hack. It isn't a prescription for winning at life. It's not an armchair philosophy. Existentialism is about recognizing that it is up to each individual to create her own meaning and values in life, by engaging in the world, by pushing back against oppressions that threaten to limit our possibilities, and by getting out there and doing things—not just contemplating what you might do. A strong part of Beauvoir's message is that other people are a condition of our existence. And if we value freedom for ourselves, we must value it for other people. It's self-deception to think otherwise.

Beauvoir has been criticized for looking at the world through white, middle-class glasses. It's true that she failed to meaningfully address some issues, especially racism, and so we do need to turn to the wisdom of other thinkers to address these gaps. We should incorporate a deeper analysis of racism that includes structural racism and considerations of intersectionality—by listening to bell hooks, Audre Lorde, Gayatri Spivak, and others who speak from personal experience to reveal the power dynamics of society. Yet Beauvoir did much to reveal the structural patterns of oppression and freedom. She was deeply concerned about material inequalities, which is why she focused on issues including sexism, ageism, and classism.

We live in a world broken by racial and economic inequality, the coronavirus pandemic, climate change, and natural disasters, in which we need to rethink our interconnectedness and our attitudes toward ourselves and one another. Beauvoir provides some ways to think about our situation in this messed-up world, where so much is damaged and awful and where it can be hard to see the beauty of our lives. Many people are fighting injustices and pushing for change, but many are struggling, mired in ambiguity and insecurity, at loose ends for what to do, whether and what to change, and how best to take action.

Beauvoir's existentialism enables us to forge ourselves into responsible beings who are capable of transforming our shared world for the better. Some of the powerful cognitive tools she gives us, as we shall see, include learning what we can and can't control, selecting and dedicating ourselves to future-oriented goals, taking others into account when we make decisions, and being honest with ourselves about life's tensions and ambiguities.

This book isn't a Twelve Rules for Authenticity step-by-step manual.[18] It is an introduction to the philosophy underpinning authenticity and an exploration of how the quest for authentic fulfillment has enriched the lives of real women. I'll share examples of some of the successes and failures that Beauvoir, other women, and I have experienced in striving toward authenticity.[19] As you will discover in this book, mine is undoubtedly a faltering quest toward authenticity. But my quest continues, and it is guided by Beauvoir's thinking above all others—except, most important, my own. To be true to Beauvoir's insights we must set out on our own quests, not follow hers.

I'm writing this book because Beauvoir's thinking about authenticity changed my life for the better. I think Beauvoir's philosophy can change your life too—or you can change your own life if you take its central message to heart. Beauvoir's philosophy can help us understand the challenges of living, as well as the need to keep making choices about ourselves and what we value. We can learn by taking heed of her philosophy, and by extending it to meet the particular demands of life today.

* * *

"It isn't easy to be sincere," one of Beauvoir's characters reflects in her novel *The Mandarins*. This captures something of the difficulty of "just being yourself." How do we express ourselves, convey the flavor of life's moments and attitudes, interpret the swirling of stories of our lives intertwined with friends, enemies, and lovers—and do so authentically?

This book is about these tensions—between how we create ourselves, how other people influence how we create ourselves, how we influence other people creating themselves—and how we might collectively recreate the world to orient ourselves toward authenticity. The structure of this book is partly inspired by *The Second Sex,* which addresses facts and myths about being a woman and some particular lived experiences.

Part I of this book discusses some of the central aspects of being human: existential perspectives on what we can and can't control, some of the ways femininity is configured and regulated, and how adolescence is a process of revealing the power of human choices to shape the world.

Part II explores how tensions between ourselves, others, and our world play out in some specific human situations. We create ourselves in relationships with friends and lovers through intersubjectivity and reciprocity. Marriage and parenthood burden many people with the weight of tradition and others' demands, but we can, through our choices, start to reshape our world so that these life paths do not crush our freedom. The process of aging calls for us not to give up on continuing to create ourselves, and to create a world that neutralizes discriminatory gazes. Death shapes our lives in profound ways because it provides the urgency to create meaning.

Part III focuses on choosing projects: how to evaluate which projects will support us in our quests for fulfillment and which are likely to lead us astray. Narcissism (self-importance), mysticism (self-denial), and the pursuit of happiness can be distracting, but rebellious projects are the key to freeing ourselves and others from self-sabotage and oppression so that we're free to shape our lives and our world in authentic ways.

When I refer to something—such as relationships, living, or happiness—as "authentic," what I mean is *authentically meaningful.* I'm talking about whether the way of being, doing, choosing, acting, relating, or becoming, is *infused* with authenticity, that is, with authentic intentions; intentions that aren't selfish choices, but which acknowledge the person who is making them and the situation they are in.

This book isn't a comprehensive overview of Beauvoir's philosophy. I have been selective, concentrating on themes and strategies that I see as particularly relevant to our lives today. This book draws on both Beauvoir's ideas and her life—not only because at times her very existence was an act of rebellion—but also because she described her life and reflected on her situations philosophically. She prompts us to do the same. She shared astounding levels of intimate details in her letters, diaries, memoirs, and elsewhere. All these aspects of her public persona can help us to understand her thinking.

As a philosopher, I've been trained to avoid looking at how thinkers lived; it shouldn't matter who a philosopher was or how they behaved, only that they arrived at the correct conclusion in an argument. What is supposed to matter is only their ideas, and the arguments and the evidence they give to support their conclusions. If we're talking about something abstract like the philosophy of mathematics, the person writing about it is not so relevant. Does it make a difference to Gottlob Frege's philosophy of mathematics, for instance, that he was an anti-Semite? Probably not.

However, when we're talking about the human condition, these things matter a great deal, and it seems worthwhile committing this "biographical fallacy." Of course, telling you how you might live is different from living a life yourself. But Beauvoir's choices and actions—her successes and her failures—are both fascinating and enlightening about what it meant for her to become authentic. She continually struggled against other people's conceptions about how she was supposed to live and act, and she recommends this struggle to us, too. Looking at her life can help us anticipate some of the challenges we might face.

Why is Beauvoir so important? The philosophical canon is filled with voices of men, who write with certain sets of assumptions, prejudices, and lenses. Women who have not been allowed the same education, who were born into lives of oppression, or into other underprivileged situations, have different perspectives and experiences to philosophize from. Many women have more options today than in Beauvoir's era—especially white western women, of which I am one—and yet we still face challenges that men do not.

In 2021, as I'm writing this, the Equal Rights Amendment in the United States—guaranteeing equal legal rights regardless of sex—has not been fully ratified. Also in 2021, Texas banned most abortions after about six weeks of pregnancy, before most women even know they're pregnant. The United States Supreme Court has, at the time of writing this, left the decision in place. Author bell hooks wrote, "So many words of love offered us by great men fail us when we come face to face with reality."[20] Given our less-than-ideal reality, women need to push back more than ever. I hope the examples I offer in this book will encourage people to do just that.

One of Beauvoir's several autobiographical books opens with the question: Why am I me and not one of billions of other possibilities? She finds it astonishing that she should be in this particular life. "If I had not been born no question would have arisen: I have to take the fact that I do exist as my starting point."[21] The comment "I am not myself today" is a throwaway one. But we can also do a double take and deconstruct it seriously. It raises real issues, like what, how, or why we are who we are, and what we should do about it once we find out.

Jean-Paul Sartre once said that he was not himself authentic but pointed the way for others. Likewise, I don't claim to have achieved authenticity. But from the moment that Beauvoir's existential philosophy fissured the assumptions about the life I was living, I have attempted to orient my life in authentic ways. I have (mostly) made choices for myself, rather than letting them be made for me. I don't always know when decisions I make are authentic or not—sometimes it only becomes clear after I've leapt into a choice. And I make plenty of mistakes.

But authentic living isn't judged by whether you are successful or not. Authenticity flowers in making intentions and in following through with actions. Authenticity is a process of boldly embracing our freedom, resolutely striding into life, and creating our essence and the world around us. When we set off on a quest to live authentically, we affirm freedom for ourselves and others. We create a world worth living in.

But an authentic life is also about directing yourself toward an ideal that can never be achieved. It's always ongoing. It is a never-quite-there-yet way of being. Authenticity is a receding goal, like snow that liquefies as soon as it caresses your skin. And if you think you have achieved authenticity, it's certain you have not. Authenticity is not like a certification you can hang on your wall. Authenticity is an adventure, not an end point in itself.

So why bother chasing such an elusive goal? Because *not* striving for authenticity is tantamount to metaphysical malnutrition. Because not striving for authenticity starves the part of our being that reaches beyond our given situation. For Beauvoir, the quest for authenticity is the difference between being and non-being. If you don't strive to create yourself, you risk becoming a passive object that the world and society act on without your consent.[22]

Existentialism is not a set of practices, but a language to think through life's challenges. It is not a philosophy to subscribe to, but a platform of knowledge and understanding from which we each must leap.[23] Where we leap *to* is up to each of us to decide for ourselves. Beauvoir's existentialism is demanding. It's not therapy and it might not bring relief or comfort, but it might just help us become more attuned to living purposefully, thoughtfully, and with vitality. Authenticity won't guarantee our happiness, but we're guaranteed to miss out on authenticity if we aren't willing to pursue this courageous path. And I have come to believe that true happiness cannot be achieved through any other means.

PART I

FORMATIVE YEARS

EXISTENTIAL INFRASTRUCTURE

As soon as we accept a human perspective, defining the body starting from existence, biology becomes an abstract science.

—The Second Sex

After the United States presidential election in 2016, I over-heard a woman say, "I'm glad a man won. Women are just too emotional to be president." This is one example of the persistent myths about women's capabilities: that having a woman's brain and hormones means that you're prone to hysteria and incapable of taking on senior roles in most public and private realms, or that people in senior roles should not behave like women (whatever that means).[1] Beauvoir wrote extensively about myths—what she often refers to as "mystifications"—about women. Mystifications are false ideas about who we are and what we're supposed to be. Mystifications are a problem because they are illusions that get in the way of authenticity.

One of these mystifications is the assumption that people have inbuilt essences that define them in an absolutist way—for example, that women are emotional and men are rational, which enables men to be better presidents and leaders than women.[2] The assumptions we make about being human can add up and ossify into rigid and oppressive structures. It's important for us to understand our situations so we can consider what's determined by our environment and what's within our control. You may have heard of the Serenity Prayer: "God, grant me the serenity to accept the things I cannot change, courage to change the things I can, and wisdom to know the difference." Beauvoir was an atheist and didn't subscribe to the Serenity Prayer, but she did attempt to untangle facts about the human condition from myths. And distinguishing between things we can't control and things we can is incredibly tricky because webs of assumptions, biases, and prejudices get tangled up with the facts about what it is to be human.

Modern science is exploring and sometimes unraveling some of these complexities, such as between free will and determinism. There is some evidence to suggest that although there are parts of our being that are determined, we seem to be able to override our impulses, and perhaps even train our brain to create new pathways.[3] Even if some of our brain is determined, what's interesting from an existential perspective is our window of freedom.

Making mistakes about what we can and can't control leads to all kinds of problems, such as warped images of ourselves and others, which limit our possibilities. In order to create better and clearer opportunities to shape our own futures and essences, we need to expose the mystifications and how they operate. We can only live authentically if we are accurate about what we can and can't control and then pursue our lives with as much awareness as possible. Unfortunately, patriarchal culture constantly seeks to subvert a woman's capacity to live authentically.[4] Fortunately, patriarchal culture does not wholly prevent authenticity either because our lived experiences are not completely defined by our situations.

*   *   *

An "existential infrastructure," as Beauvoir calls it, can help us to expose common mystifications and make sense of our situations.[5] Beauvoir describes the nature of human existence as both freedom and facticity. "Freedom" is a movement toward being, but also a never-attaining, open-ended way of existing. "Facticity" is the given—or unchosen—facts of our lives, including our parents, the bodies and brains we're born with, other people, and where we exist in relation to others.

Beauvoir teaches us that we are our facticity (bodies and situations) but we are also transcendence (our goals and intentions). We live free lives by transcending our facticity: holding ourselves in question, making definitive choices, striving toward our goals, and concretely engaging ourselves in the world. This is the foundation of the existential idea that "existence precedes essence," which means that we are cast into the world and then each of us must figure out who we will become.

Yet we all are born into different situations with different bodies. We grow up in different environments. We are socialized in different ways. Ethical problems arise when we are cut off—or we cut ourselves off—from our freedom, such that we become mired in our facticity. Being stuck in our facticity is what Beauvoir calls "immanence." Exercising our freedom is transcendence. (And by transcendence, I mean transcendence *of* facticity.)

To live authentically, we must transcend our facticity into the future, freely pursuing self-chosen goals, or what Beauvoir often refers to as "projects." Human existence involves us spontaneously *projecting* ourselves into the world. We set up goals in our life, and we project ourselves toward them. Projects are activities that bring coherence, meaning, and justification to our lives. Any activity can count as a project—a career, a passion, a hobby, a home, a social or creative work—but to be authentic, these activities need to reflect our own choices and support collective freedom.

The opposite of authenticity is inauthenticity, sometimes called "bad faith," which (in an existential sense, as opposed to a legal one) means to deny one's own or others' freedom. People in bad faith may wish their life were otherwise but do nothing about it, fail to confront the truth of their lives and situations, or deny their responsibility for their actions.[6]

Beauvoir's collection of short interwoven stories *When Things of the Spirit Come First* sketches a series of case studies in bad faith. The character Chantal presents a glittering and glamorous image of herself to others, which is entirely fake. Bad faith exists in her failure to confront the truth of her life and her lies to try to manipulate how others see her. Her inner monologue and diary reveal the chasm between her private and public lives.[7]

Bad faith isn't only about misrepresenting oneself to others, but also annihilating oneself for others. Another character Marcelle dreams of surrendering herself to great love. Her bad faith reveals itself in her obsession with being a dutiful and supportive wife at all costs and transforming her passivity and tolerance of bad sex into false virtues: "She took every one of Denis's piercing thrusts with passionate submission, and to make his possession of her the more complete she let her consciousness glide away into the night."[8]

It's also bad faith to deny responsibility for our lives, such as when we believe that our choices and the consequences of our actions don't matter. Denis makes commitments, like marrying Marcelle, but promises don't bind him. He believes that things just happen to us, we have no real choices in our lives, and all we can do is submit blindly to fate.

The characters in *When Things of The Spirit Come First* show that, as Beauvoir wrote in *The Second Sex*, "Inauthenticity does not pay."[9] Marcelle cowers in her abusive relationship with Denis. Denis flounders in despair and depression. The story closes with Marguerite, Marcelle's sister, grieving that her loved ones "will die without ever having known or loved anything real."[10] By contrast, when we face the world authentically—welcoming our freedom, seizing responsibility for our choices, refusing to annihilate ourselves before delusions and false idols—the world reveals exhilarating possibilities.

One way to think about Beauvoir's existential infrastructure—facticity, transcendence, freedom, and bad faith—is as follows: facticity is being born into an English-speaking family, while transcendence is choosing to study French. Though you will never be a native French speaker—because you can't change the fact of where you were born—you can transcend beyond your English-speaking facticity. You might diminish your own freedom, through bad faith, if you were to discount your own ability to learn French on the basis of throwaway excuses such as being "too old" or "not smart enough." Or you can exercise your freedom toward becoming fluent in French. When you learn a language, you create yourself as a bilingual person: a person who is reaching toward being bilingual. If you are forbidden to learn or are told you're not capable, or if basic resources to learn (such as library books and the internet) are denied to you, then the ways you can exercise your freedom shrink.

One might argue that it's bad faith to suggest that there are external limitations on our freedom. But to ignore limitations entirely is like a scene in a horror movie where a torturer chops off a captive's feet and then says they are free to go. It's the same with meritocracy and white privilege: working hard doesn't always lead to success for many people because of systemic racist obstacles.

If you don't have the power to act on your freedom, then it's a shallow notion of freedom. You have to be *free from* oppression in order to be *free to* reach for authenticity. This means that it is bad faith *not* to acknowledge the structures that prevent people from exercising their freedom. Beauvoir's philosophy is so powerful because she recognizes that human existence is a complicated mix of tensions between freedom and facticity. We can't control our facticity, but to be free is to be able to control our lives by transcending the situations that we're thrown into.

* * *

People don't arrive in the world tabula rasa, with absolute freedom. While we have to create our essence from scratch and invent our lives as we would compose a poem, we're not writing on a blank sheets of paper suspended in a vacuum. The world we are born into contains a moiling mass of human history and on top of it is heavy-duty societal and cultural architecture. These structures form the background of our creations and frame our movements toward authenticity.

Beauvoir argued that one of the primary features of our social and cultural architecture is the mystification that women are the second sex. Women are defined in relationship to men, who are defined as the universal. Men have assumed the essential role (Subject) while women have taken on the inessential role (Other).[11] "Other" is capitalized when a person's subjectivity is denied, when they are treated as an Other *only* and not a subject *also*.

In Beauvoir's view, this process of "othering"—of defining people in relation to and in contrast with others—is profoundly human. Othering has always happened and continues to happen, among people of different origins, races, religions, abilities, classes, ages, and sexual preferences, for example. The effects are much more drastic for people who experience othering on multiple dimensions. The question Beauvoir puts forth in *The Second Sex* is: Why are women so often men's Other? Why have women submitted to men so reliably? Why have the relations between the sexes so consistently failed to be equal? How have men oppressed women so effectively?[12]

Humans are both subjects for themselves and objects for others. For Beauvoir, as for Sartre, humans are being-for-themselves, while objects such as rocks are being-in-themselves. The key difference is that a human is conscious, that is, a human being is a transcending consciousness who can question themselves and overcome their facticity. A rock is not. We come to recognize our being-*for*-others when we realize that we are objects for other people. We are not self-conscious around a rock but we are with another person. Ideally, we might achieve being-*with*-others, that is, solidarity and friendship.

There is a tension for each of us between being-for-ourselves and being-for-others: defining ourselves as we wish and realizing others judge us as well. Focusing too much on being-for-yourself is self-centered and other people will very likely find you intolerable. Focusing too much on being-for-others at the expense of being-for-yourself turns you into a doormat, and you risk losing yourself.

Oppression reduces people to being-in-themselves, like the rock, and denies their claim to being-for-themselves. Oppression downgrades people to objects, denies their subjectivity, and excludes them from being-with-others in reciprocal ways. Women have been Other to men, not only economically because they were dependent on men, but also existentially, and this dynamic has generally worked in men's favor.

As a person asserts themselves in the world to understand their being, they come up against obstacles: against a subway that's running late, against other people trying to squeeze into the train car in rush hour, or against their own needs and desires such as hunger and free Wi-Fi. Objects in the world can either be abstract and remain foreign to me, such as the delayed train, or they can be objects that passively submit, such as a juicy peach that I can possess, consume, and destroy. When we treat Others as objects, we contradict their experience as another free consciousness with a robust being-for-themselves.

There are two key implications to Beauvoir's philosophy here. One, when we oppress another, we treat them as an object to be possessed, consumed, or destroyed, instead of treating them as an authentic subjectivity in themselves. And two, interactions with objects like peaches don't give me any deep understandings about myself. To begin to understand ourselves, we need other people. Only other freedoms, other subjectivities, can disclose aspects of our being that we can't see on our own.

Jean-Paul Sartre suggested this dynamic, this pull away from being-for-oneself and toward being-for-others, meant that "hell is . . . other people!"[13] Beauvoir recognized that others can just as easily be friendly as hostile, depending on how each person approaches an encounter. To relate authentically to another is to be friendly because it calls for reciprocal acknowledgment of others as subjects, transcending the desire to possess and control one another, continually overcoming the compulsion to make ourselves the center of our own universes, and treating each other with respect and generosity. Authentic relationships, for Beauvoir, are the best things humans can achieve.[14] The risk is that we never know if another person will reciprocate in a relationship, romantic or platonic. While we can't choose whether other people will cast us as Other, we can choose how we treat other people.

*   *   *

The mystification of the "eternal feminine" is one way that some have tried to solve the tension between being-for-themselves and being-for-others and to avoid the risk and vulnerability of authentic relationships. The eternal feminine is an idealized image of women as essentially being-for-others: unthreatening, generous, companionable, saintly, and subservient. Beauvoir noted that the Virgin Mary is the pinnacle of the eternal feminine.[15]

When Beauvoir wrote that one becomes a woman, she meant that it's mostly civilization that habituates women to conform to the mystification of the eternal feminine. "Habituates" is the right word: Women learn how to live within the expectations of their roles, and they are constantly tutored in the expectations of the eternal feminine. Women's subservience is written into the deepest cultural scripts that continue to dictate modern behavior.

Creation myths in many Christian, Jewish, and Islamic traditions play to the mystification of the eternal feminine. Genesis 2 asserts Eve was created for Adam, designed to be his submissive companion. Adam came first and as such, his presence in the world was primary and Eve's was secondary. Mystifications such as these set a precedent that men are the standard of the world, the universal humankind, the creators, while women are handy, nice-to-have sidekicks. In existential terms, Adam is the essential being while Eve is the inessential. She is his complement, a subservient (but untrustworthy) Other created from him and for him.

For Beauvoir, one of the main ways the mystification of the eternal feminine frustrates relationships between the sexes is that men want women to be Other. Men attempt to constrain women's facticity—so that women are secondary to men's primacy—to the point of enslavement. Still, there's no way that women's transcendence can be fully bridled, which frustrates men who want to control women.[16] These conflicts come about because men want what isn't theirs (women's freedom). Such delusions go some way to explaining why men have been so obsessed with controlling women's bodies and stifling women's voices.

Beauvoir challenged reductive and restrictive mystifications such as the ideal of the eternal feminine and was punished for not conforming. Upon publication of *The Second Sex*, when Beauvoir was forty-one years old, she received a deluge of praise and hate. Beauvoir had written openly about women's experiences, including detailed discussions of taboo topics such as menstruation, puberty, sex, lesbians, and women's oppression.

Some readers were ardent admirers of her candor and bravery. Others were scandalized that she revealed so many intimate secrets about women's bodies. Some people criticized her for not revealing enough about the diversity of women's experiences—in particular, not focusing on women of color. Beauvoir said the torrents of coarse slurs and snickers, particularly from men, were violent and spiteful: "Unsatisfied, frigid, priapic, nymphomaniac, lesbian, a hundred times aborted, I was everything, even an unmarried mother. People offered to cure me of my frigidity or to temper my labial appetites."[17]

The philosopher Albert Camus, winner of the 1957 Nobel Prize in Literature and once a friend, said that she humiliated French men.[18] Some condemned her writing as pornography. In later memoirs, recounting the reception of *The Second Sex*, Beauvoir pointed out the double standards that applied to her: while it's normal for men to discuss women's bodies, when women talk about it, they're branded as indecent. Beauvoir recalled, "One might almost have believed that Freud and psychoanalysis had never existed. What a festival of obscenity on the pretext of flogging me for mine!"[19]

The Second Sex clearly touched a vulnerable nerve for men and exposed many of their insecurities: that they might not deserve their superiority over women; that they aren't as great in bed as they had hoped; and that women do not need them for sexual satisfaction. Some feared the book would help women to realize that they don't have to tolerate men's bad behavior.

In an unfinished 1957 commentary on *The Second Sex*, Lorraine Hansberry recalled the ambivalent reactions to Beauvoir's book in the United States. American men, Hansberry observed, took *The*

Second Sex more seriously than American women. Men interested in equal rights admired Beauvoir's book. Some men disagreed with Beauvoir but respected the work enough to attack it for what Hansberry described as "its formidable solidity and undeniable brilliance." Some women revered the book too. Hansberry knew of a playwright-actress who, to the horror of the male director, read *The Second Sex* aloud to her colleagues, "indoctrinating" them in between curtain calls. Other women read the book diligently, seeing their "liberation" and calls for *"égalité, fraternité, liberté—pour tout le monde!"* within its pages. Yet many women, even intelligent and feminist women, were cool toward *The Second Sex* and criticized it for being too harsh on marriage and motherhood or too preoccupied with sex. Hansberry recounted, "I have seen clear thinking, crisp American types of women (women intolerant and contemptuous of the more blatant codes of a male supremacist universe) puzzling briefly and inadequately over the work and then dismissing it."[20]

The Vatican apparently deemed *The Second Sex* too dangerous to dismiss and added it (along with *The Mandarins*) to the (now defunct) index of banned books in 1956.[21] Sometimes any publicity is good publicity: *The Second Sex* sold incredibly well. Around 55,000 copies were printed within the first five months, which is a lot for any book, let alone a philosophy book in 1949. The book has since been translated into around forty languages and millions of copies have been printed.[22]

Still, Beauvoir was in a privileged position. For many women the cost of not conforming to the eternal feminine—male standards of what a woman should be—is mortally dangerous. Many people who don't fit the cisgender and heterosexual model are facing lethal challenges. Black women in America have always suffered under worse conditions than most white women from the time they were slaves and their bodies not their own. While white women may sometimes be treated as objects, Black women literally were objects, and the legacy of that white gaze still exists today.

* * *

Biological mystifications often get in the way of progress. Biology is commonly used to explain differences between the sexes. Male and female animals are defined in terms of their role in reproduction, though there are exceptions. Comparing ourselves to animals can give us information about some biological processes of living creatures. But our biology tells us nothing about the *meaning* of being human.

Existentialism offers its own answer about what makes humans unique: non-human animals act instinctively while humans transcend. In *The Second Sex*, Beauvoir argued that humans take risks to overcome our natural condition, stretching beyond our given situations, and looking for meaning in our lives.[23] (Non-human animals think and feel and create social bonds, but as far as we know, they don't philosophize.) To be human is to transcend the facts of our existence through our actions to create meaning.

Beauvoir wrote, "As soon as we accept a human perspective, defining the body starting from existence, biology becomes an abstract science."[24] Biology defines the facts of our lives, but not the meaning of life. Meaning comes from how we live, what we do, and how we act. We create this meaning with our choices, choices we make from the position of having the sex organs we find ourselves with, choices we make while navigating the human social world which has assigned certain values to certain sex organs.

Of course, biology can create complexities and tensions between facticity and freedom. Bodies sometimes get in the way of living full and rewarding lives. In my twenties, menstrual cramps brought so much pain that during breaks at work I'd curl up in the fetal position under my desk or on the nearest bathroom floor. For many women, menstruation is inconvenient if not agonizing, childbirth is excruciating if not mortally dangerous, and breastfeeding is exhausting if not grueling.[25] Nevertheless, with technology, birth control, and medication, all these can be more easily managed. For me, either birth control pills or a single codeine tablet each month completely erased my pain.

What defines us is not simply what sort of body we have. What's important is what we do with our particular body, and what we're allowed and enabled to do with it. The problem for women is that the meanings of our bodies—the meanings of our biology—have been mostly dictated by men in power on the basis of a mystification. The biological mystification is often used to justify discrimination, but biology can't account for socialized value systems.

Beauvoir points to psychoanalytic theories as another potential mystification that obscures authenticity. The idea that women think differently because of their "female brains" is contentious but widespread. Beauvoir blames psychoanalysts such as Sigmund Freud for sprouting this idea. Freud famously thought most of women's problems came from not having a penis—an idea that says a lot more about Freud than it does about women. Freud didn't examine a wider context of why men rose to dominance, for instance, or the effect of social and economic structures, or the role of choice and values.

Freud and psychotherapist Alfred Adler described children as being torn between identifying with the father or mother, between the masculine and feminine. Beauvoir maintains that this theory is a mystification, and a more accurate explanation of childhood turmoil is that girls are torn between exercising their freedom and being a "good girl." Good girls conform to the eternal feminine. Good girls do what they are told, speak only when spoken to, make themselves pretty, don't take up too much space, and always smile.

Beauvoir points to historical materialism as still another mystification that gets in the way of authenticity, specifically Friedrich Engels's idea of *homo economicus*. *Homo economicus* is the notion that tools (like materials and technology) have shaped the means of production and, consequently, the organization of society and the division of labor between the sexes. Homo economicus is based on the idea that in the Stone Age, men were suited for hunting, while women were suited for using smaller tools such as spades in the garden and weaving implements. Later, with the development of the plow, agriculture intensified, and some people enslaved Others to cultivate fields and established private properties to manage slaves. Men worked with bigger tools, which created more profit and thus became more valuable—by superficial and limited financial measures—than the work women did to maintain homes and care for families.

One of the most famous historical studies of inequality, Gerda Lerner's *The Creation of Patriarchy* (1987), gels with this idea. Lerner dated the creation of patriarchy to a process during the period between 3100 BC to 600 BC. Inequality rose with agriculture, Lerner contended, as men took control of land and women's bodies (and children) as economic resources, which were then consolidated with private property.[26]

Private property and inheritance laws cemented the inequality, encouraging women to be dependent on men because they had little to no rights over any wealth. These laws institutionalized the patriarchal family and the idea that women were assets. Over time, the oppressive relationship between men and women became a habit. Men continued transcending—inventing, creating, realizing, and risking themselves—and turning these activities into values associated with masculinity. Most women were caught in the facticity of their animal nature—caring for and providing food for themselves and others—and blocked from creating their essence in ways that were authentic to them.

Beauvoir points to two key historical factors that transformed women's situations in the twentieth century: freedom from reproduction and freedom to participate in production. Technology rendered physical differences between men and women, for the purpose of work, largely obsolete. Birth control opened up possibilities for many men and women to free themselves from large families or parenthood—although this still varies greatly by culture and class. Some privileged women didn't need to work, but women who did paid work were doubly oppressed: even when they were granted the right *to* work, they weren't granted rights *at* work. They were paid less, given more boring work, and faced discrimination and sexual harassment.

These historical developments reinforced male domination over women. However, Beauvoir argued that such theories as homo economicus are superficial and abstract because they don't explain how tools alone were a sufficient means to shift society from communitarianism to individualism. They don't explain exactly how private property caused women's oppression, nor why the division of labor was based on subjugation instead of friendship.

While differences in bodies are biological, differences in power are cultural. Though many have justified men's domination as natural simply because "it's always been this way," this message is an obfuscation and a means of oppression. It's like saying that people have always died of diseases so we shouldn't look for cures and vaccines, and that's absurd. Beauvoir urges us not to confuse the verb "to be" when it is used about women in sentences like "Women are docile." "To be" does not mean *ought*, it means "to have become."[27]

Although we can't control our biology, psychology, or history, we can control—or at least we should be able to control—how we structure the workplace and jobs and use technology to overcome historical inequalities in the division of labor. To reduce people to only their facticity is oppressive, immoral, and dehumanizing. It's human to want to stretch beyond the given. To be human is to put being into question, to seek reasons to live, to justify oneself. Put simply: to transcend.

* * *

Freud's theories have largely been discredited.[28] But biological, psychological, and historical theories still operate effectively in contemporary culture, perpetuate damaging mystifications, and thwart authentic living. In the *New York Times* best-selling *Sapiens: A Brief History of Humankind*, Yuval Noah Harari agreed with Beauvoir (although he doesn't mention her) that roles, rights, and duties allocated to men and women are cultural, not biological. But he also insisted that there is probably a biological reason why men have dominated women, even though he readily admits that there is no evidence of this.

Harari pointed out that while it's true that on average men are more muscular, women are stronger than men in many other ways, such as resisting hunger, disease, and fatigue.[29] Moreover, there is little—and sometimes inverse—correlation between social power and muscles. Those who rise in the ranks of political, religious, and legal leadership have rarely been the most buff and fit, let alone the most successful.

Some theories propose men are dominant because they're more aggressive—the assumption being that more testosterone makes men more hostile. Yet it's not at all clear that men are more aggressive than women. Some studies have found that women are more aggressive than men, although men are far more likely to inflict injury.[30] Harari notes that while aggressive soldiers probably help win wars, leading armies is more about stamina, organization, manipulation, cooperation, and imagining situations from the enemy's perspective. And there's no evidence that men are better at those skills than women.

Still other popular theories claim that men have had to compete with other men to procreate with women, and women need protective men who are going to stick around for the pregnancy and first few years of the child's life. But there's no reason why women would have had to rely on men for anything other than sperm. Species of animals such as elephants, lions, spotted hyenas, and bonobos form matriarchal societies where females support each other in childrearing while the males fight amongst themselves. Still, non-human animals don't dictate how humans should organize our social systems.

In Beauvoir's existential terms, pushing women toward destinies that aren't the result of their free, authentic choices—by discouraging them from male-coded roles—cramps their attempts to live authentically. So when does stereotype indoctrination start? Very, very early. By age six, children are already starting to believe that girls are less intelligent than boys and less suited to science, technology, engineering, and mathematics (STEM) subjects, even though girls outperform boys in grades and standardized tests.[31] A counterargument could be that even if men are not better suited to STEM on average, there are some men who excel more at it than most women; but the evidence for this is also rickety.[32]

Theories that purport that men are naturally better at STEM are inherently sexist because they ignore socioeconomic and cultural factors that pointedly discourage young women from pursuing careers in STEM. Silicon Valley is a notoriously unwelcome place for those who don't fit the mold. STEM subjects are still perceived as a masculine pursuit, but that is because of the ways men have valued them—not because of inherent biological differences. Beauvoir explained: "In creating universal values—by which I mean mathematics, for example—men have often left their specifically masculine, male, virile stamp on them . . . in a very subtle and devious way."[33]

A key step toward equal opportunity—the right for each person to be important and relevant—so that everyone can assume themselves authentically, is to untangle the mess of values that says men should be masculine and women should be feminine. Values such as mathematics and science should, Beauvoir noted, be properly assigned as *universal* values. We can't change value systems overnight, but it's important to keep challenging mystifications of values because they can change and when they do, it will be revolutionary.

*   *   *

In my junior year of college in Australia I joined the university's Army Reserve regiment. I didn't look like the type of person you would imagine signing up to the army. I enrolled with the hope of earning money, having a completely new experience, and making friends. My first day trying to deconstruct a rifle—an old hunk of metal of the type that were used in World War II—was the opposite of fun.

Having never touched anything more serious than a water pistol before, I left with scrapes, blisters on my fingers, and aching arms. But I wasn't easily deterred. During my training, many incredible teachers and mentors (mostly men) encouraged and supported me. Most of the women who started the training with me dropped out over the years, and I became a token woman. I was proud of myself because I completed exactly the same training and tests as the men, even though they were physically bigger and stronger than me.

At twenty, I became a lieutenant. One of my roles was as a platoon commander. On boot camps, I was in charge of thirty new recruits, teaching them skills such as navigation. At the beginning of one training course, I introduced myself to a full-time army sergeant, around twice my age, who would be reporting to me. I held out my arm for a handshake. He didn't shake it; he looked me up and down, burst out laughing, and walked away. As I said, I didn't look like an army person. I ignored it, focused on my job, and did it well. At the end of the course, he said he had misjudged me and apologized for being disrespectful. I might have believed his apology was sincere if it weren't for the fact he then asked me out on a date. (I declined.)

On another boot camp, at the end of a week in the bush spent digging holes and filling them up again, patrolling through thick scrub, and sleeping under plastic bivouacs, it was time for a fifteen-kilometer (nine-mile) route march. We were headed back toward the barracks, each with a twenty-eight-kilogram (sixty-two-pound) pack and webbing. It was long and it was tough, but I had done it many times before with a full pack and webbing. As we lined up in formation, an order came down the hierarchy that all women were to load their backpacks into the trucks and march without them. Only the women.

My insides roiled with fury and adrenaline. Shaking in my dusty boots, with green and brown camouflage cream smeared on my face, in a stinky uniform drenched in days of sweat and dirt, doing my utmost to keep my composure, I spoke with my superior. I told him women were capable of doing the march too and should be held to the same standard as men.

He was a lovely, kindly middle-aged man, who could have been outraged that an indignant young woman was questioning his orders, but extended his generosity to explain that it was about health and safety because the weather was too hot, something something something. The order for women to drop their packs was more deeply entrenched than the whim of my superior: the advice had come from medics (I don't remember whether they were men or women). But my orders were final: if I didn't follow instructions, I was told I might face court-martial proceedings.

Some people gave me supportive looks and stood close to me in solidarity. But it was the military. Disagreeing with authority had serious consequences. "Why do you care so much?" one person whispered, and another: "Why aren't you glad we don't have to do that?" Had the directive been changed at my request, some of the women would have been furious. I didn't want other women to be angry with me. And I didn't want to be a martyr.

Defeated, I dropped my pack. The shame weighed more heavily than any baggage could, making it doubly difficult to compose myself as a leader in front of dozens of curious eyes. Every step along those fifteen kilometers, I suppressed tears of humiliation, anger over how I had been treated differently, and a feeling of failure for having obediently stepped in line with what I was told to do, to keep the peace.

One might think that I should have been relieved that I was held to a lower standard than men. If an easier path is offered to you, why shouldn't you take it? Beauvoir knew about the temptation to settle for easy solutions. Skirting our freedom is tempting because it's easier to avoid the anguish of transcending. But dodging our freedom makes us passive, prey to others' freedoms.[34]

I didn't know about Beauvoir and her ideas at the time, but I cared because we all passed the same physical tests. I knew I could do it. I wanted others to know I could do it. I wanted new recruits to know that I was a legitimate leader, and that women could be legitimate leaders.

The orders weren't in my control. My biology as a woman wasn't within my control. My choice should have been clear: follow the order or don't follow it and accept the consequences. In retrospect, Beauvoir's philosophy has helped me to understand that there is something crucial missing from this either/or interpretation of my situation on the march: the orders were sexist. The assumption underlying the order was that women's biology means they are not as strong as men and therefore should be required to do less. The view also claims that women need to be protected, and if need be, against their will.

Beauvoir also taught me that the existential issue I faced on that sandy march in the Australian outback was that I was being othered. Othering reduces people to brute stereotypes and overlooks the fact that each person is so much more than a fixed essence can capture. I was reduced to my immanence (the facts of my body). My alleged female fragility was prioritized over my will to do my job and my desire to have the same access to possibilities as men. I was treated as an Other that needed to be protected from herself.

For Beauvoir, we are what we do. Our acts measure who we become.[35] The "act" in this example was the march with packs. Men were given the opportunity to measure themselves and to be measured by others. Women were denied the same opportunity to seek growth and self-knowledge, to challenge themselves, and to discover their capabilities. I was, in effect, being told that my judgment about my capabilities was wrong.

Many factors—such as the facticity of each recruit's body, their goals, or their willpower—mediated the difficulty of the march, not their sex. Some of the recruits were better equipped for marching physically, others were better equipped psychologically. It wasn't possible to determine that the march with packs was too hard for women but achievable for men. When a male recruit was struggling mid-march, I offered to carry his pack. He thought about it and ultimately said no. I understood: to be perceived as weaker than a woman would have been humiliating and too great a price to pay.

I still think about what I should have done differently on that march. Should I have refused to put down the pack? Should I have petitioned for the men to be required—or at least given the option—to put down their packs too? Should I have launched a campaign to challenge sexist rules? Had I had the courage and patience, I could have done all of the above. Instead, I transcended the military altogether and was free to pursue career paths that didn't limit me (at least so explicitly) simply for being a woman.

Mystifications about women's capabilities are among the reasons why women are still paid less than men for the same work: because often women aren't perceived to be as competent as men. It's one of the reasons why many women aren't listened to: It's assumed that they don't know what's best for them; they can't be trusted to think rationally because their brains are designed to prioritize procreation; decisions need to be made for them; and their opinion isn't valid. Our culture continues to relentlessly reinforce these mystifications.

* * *

Feminism has benefited a privileged few. But in many ways even feminism conforms to the rules men have created and supports the institutional status quo. It valorizes individual success, holding out the elusive ideal of "balance" while blaming those who fail. For those superwomen who do strive to have it all, one of Beauvoir's characters in her novel *Misunderstanding in Moscow* suggests,

> They have some sort of career, they claim to dress well, to engage in sports, look after their house perfectly, bring up their children very well. They want to prove to themselves that they can be successful at all levels. And, in fact, they spread themselves too thinly, they succeed in nothing.[36]

While this is a dramatization—many women succeed in many things—it does highlight the ongoing dilemma that women face: feminism has not sufficiently acknowledged the structures that thwart success, it has widened the intersectional gap between the privileged and the exploited, and it pays only lip service to collective justice and equality.[37]

We don't know what Beauvoir would have thought about our current situation, but I suspect she would have been painfully disappointed with the "progress" we have made. In the United States, an American is sexually assaulted every sixty-eight seconds and ninety percent of them are women.[38] Worldwide, more than one in every three women have experienced physical or sexual violence.[39] Females are more than twice as likely as males to be victims of human trafficking.[40] Family members kill twice as many women as men and more than four times as many women are killed by an intimate partner as men.[41] Women are more likely to live in poverty than men because on average they earn less and their jobs are less stable.[42] Women of color are particularly at risk because they face more structural barriers in the workplace and bear the physical and emotional brunt of racial violence.[43] Fewer—far fewer, pathetically fewer—women than men run companies and countries, and even fewer women of color.[44]

For many women, mystifications compound in multiple ways. Some women, particularly privileged white women, have escaped or overcome most of the obstacles Beauvoir analyzed. But many women face the same obstacles and greater, compounded challenges. Beauvoir is, to an extent, guilty of the same mistakes that we see in early American feminism where activists fought for suffrage and rights for white women and then didn't bother to keep fighting for women of color.[45] Some white feminists continue to neglect women of color.

Before we go any further with Beauvoir's philosophy, it's important to take a detour to look at a few of the critiques about her work. Some people argue that Beauvoir focused too much on the obstacles that hold mostly white, privileged women back and didn't go far enough to acknowledge how age, class, race, and other differences intersect to create more extreme oppression—or to use Kimberlé Crenshaw's famous term: intersectional oppression.

Philosopher and activist Angela Davis argued that analyses such as Beauvoir's undervalue the complex ways that oppression intersects. Davis points out many examples of racial, sexual, and class oppression, such as that historically white men couldn't be charged with raping Black women—because Black women are assumed to be consenting seducers—and that white women very often treat Black men unjustly.[46]

White women still do: consider Amy Cooper, a white New Yorker who, in 2020, called the police on Black birdwatcher Christian Cooper, saying she felt threatened by him when he asked her to leash her dog in a zone that required it. And white men still do too: consider Oklahoma police officer Daniel Holtzclaw who in 2016 sexually assaulted at least thirteen African American women. He targeted vulnerable women with criminal histories in poor neighborhoods because he thought no one would take their claims seriously.

Another criticism of Beauvoir is that she was wrong to set sex as the fulcrum of oppression because there are many other factors that shape a person's freedom and facticity. While bell hooks admired Beauvoir as an intellectual, hooks also criticized Beauvoir for not paying enough attention to intersectionality: "While Beauvoir separates issues of class, race, and gender—a perspective that distorts the true reality of human being—I continually insist that we cannot understand what it means to be female or male without critically examining interlocking systems of domination."[47]

Some criticize Beauvoir for discounting her whiteness. In *Against White Feminism* (2021), attorney, human rights activist, and author Rafia Zakaria argued that not all women face the same disadvantages because white women benefit from whiteness. Zakaria said that Beauvoir should have known about how much worse the situation was for women of color, and not to have done so obscures their suffering.

And some criticize Beauvoir for failing to unpack white women's racism. English professor Kathy Glass argued that Beauvoir overlooks white women's tendency to marginalize women of color, their reluctance to empathize with them, and their hesitance to include them in political struggles. However, Glass also argued that Beauvoir's philosophy does contain a "coalitional possibility" because it rejects fixed essences and identities which are often the basis of oppression.[48]

It's true that Beauvoir's analysis does not refer to all women in all situations and she did not discuss women of color as a central demographic in her analysis. It is difficult to imagine oneself in another's shoes, let alone to speak for others, but Beauvoir's critique of privileged women—who gatekeep the patriarchy and uphold oppression via economic exploitation—was radical for her time.

Moreover, Beauvoir recognized her privilege and knew that many women faced more difficult hurdles than white western women such as herself. In *The Second Sex*, Beauvoir explicitly acknowledged that women, especially privileged white women, were tethered to their oppressors more tightly than to one another.[49]

Beauvoir also acknowledged the pervasiveness of racism in America. She deeply admired Richard Wright's work and cited his memoir *Black Boy* to illustrate how much harder it is for Black Americans to get on to the same playing field as struggling white people, let alone the same playing field where white people flourish.[50] (Although notably she referenced a Black male author.)

Beauvoir also recognized the maltreatment of women in rural areas that reduces them to "beast[s] of burden."[51] She was similarly concerned with the exploitation of sex workers and the appalling conditions of their work.[52] Beauvoir also pointed out how men often infantilize oppressed people, telling them what to think and how to behave and punishing them for deviating.[53] And Beauvoir was troubled by the way that patriarchal societies pit underprivileged people against one another, which curbs solidarities and entrenches oppression.

In later interviews, Beauvoir became aware of a broader range of oppressions. She recognized that the class struggle wasn't going to automatically emancipate everyone, saying, "Of course, the oppression of women takes on different forms, according to class. There are women who are victims on both fronts: working women who are themselves workers' wives."[54] Literary scholar Meryl Altman argues that Beauvoir was attuned to intersectional oppression, but Beauvoir's version of it focused on material exploitation.[55]

I have wrestled with critiques by women of color of Beauvoir and whether I should write at all because, as a white middle-class woman, I don't want to soak up the moral oxygen by claiming that my struggle should be the only one that matters. There are perspectives I don't have and simply can't fully grasp because I haven't experienced them myself. My whiteness affords me a degree of privilege and power that many people don't have, even if I still struggle to overcome patriarchal oppressions.

Yet, saying nothing because I was born white—a fact of my existence that I can't change—doesn't help anyone and it certainly wouldn't be authentic of me. To discredit mild injustices means that we are edging closer toward accepting larger injustices. So I decided to put my voice and privilege to good use, to include the criticisms of women of color, and to aim to write in a respectful way that acknowledges their pain. I believe that one's own suffering and limitations can serve as a starting point to empathize with people who would perceive my life to be a vacation. Beauvoir's mantra is that every one of us has a responsibility to challenge our own particular set of oppressions—a daily act of taking stock and action.

Beauvoir's analysis did not resonate with all women in all contexts. She wrote *The Second Sex* at a time when information was not nearly as widespread as it is now. There were bound to be errors and limitations. Yet her analysis did, and still does, resonate with many people.[56] Many of the hurdles that she pointed to are pervasive enough to warrant revisiting her philosophy—as long as we acknowledge that some people face greater obstacles than others.

It's important to examine the nature of a variety of obstacles because this investigation helps us better understand lived experiences. We find ourselves in a world that's already brimming with meanings and structures that others have created. Seeing the patterns in our struggles helps us to figure out ways to reach beyond them.

And many obstacles are not only "women's" problems. Some men also face similar obstacles, especially those who present themselves and act in ways that stray from traditional masculine patterns of being in the world. Although Beauvoir's focus was middle-class, white, western European women, her ideas provide a framework for social justice more generally. Her dictate to be present and to act is a guideline for all women to fight injustice against themselves and others.

*   *   *

Human existence is much more complicated than appeals to biology, psychoanalysis, historical materialism, or other interpretations would suggest. Many theories, interpreted through the male lens, obscure the reality of what we can and can't control and create mystifications that keep many people oppressed. Beauvoir's aim was to take all of human reality into account, acknowledging that we are more than our biology, more than a collection of body parts flung about by hidden sexual impulses or different brain wiring, and more than our collective history. These elements are at play, but they only take on

meaning when we consider how people live in their concrete existences, blended in situations and caked in values. While you can say
that someone is good or lacking in particular skills, or acted in virtuous or unethical ways, you can't define who a person is by pointing
to their body or reproductive functions, or to use Beauvoir's term, by
pointing to their facticity.

It has always been difficult for women to transcend, that is, to
control their own quests in life. The twenty-first century brings
new challenges to women who want to live authentically, as we
will see in the rest of this book. Some people say inequalities are
the result of life choices, but Beauvoir shows that there is much
more going on than this. The weight of mystifications traps many
people, shifting the architecture of the world, making it easier for
some people to grasp and climb, and making it exceedingly difficult for others to live authentically. This infrastructure frames our
experiences and although we can't change what came before us, we
can smash old mystifications and create new authentic narratives.

Perhaps some worry that their world will be worse off when we
respect other people as living beings with all their flaws, but they
shouldn't be concerned. In Beauvoir's view, human experience is
deeper and more exciting when it is free from lies and deception, and
when we can clearly understand what's within our control and what
isn't. In an ideal world, we would accept one another—and would
accept ourselves—as authentically engaged freedoms. In Beauvoir's
view, living less constricted lives would be better for everyone because intersubjective relationships are rich, intense, adventurous, and
best of all, truthful.[57]

It's much easier to drop the backpack and take the uncompli-
cated path, to faint and sigh softly into a knight's protective and
oppressive arms, but then we're not really living. Beauvoir teaches
us that when we can live in freedom—free from comforting, anes-
thetizing, and prostrating mystifications such as the ideal of the

eternal feminine—we will be able to seize our lives authentically. And even if we can't break free from all these mystifications, we must still strive for authenticity in spite of them.

The way we're brought up shapes our understanding of how to set out on our quests for authentic fulfillment because our collective human history, expected destinies, and mystifications condition our earliest years and underpin who we are permitted and forbidden to become. In *The Second Sex*, Beauvoir shows that one of the most insidious ways that mystifications manifest is through cultural traditions and social forces that tear at children, pushing and pulling them in different directions and channeling them into pre-reflective styles of thinking.

GROWING UP

One is not born, but rather becomes, woman.
—The Second Sex

One day my four-year-old said to me, "Mommy goes to yoga and Daddy goes to work." I took a deep, calming breath, trying to keep the heartbreak and indignation from seeping into my voice, before explaining that Mommy and Daddy both go to yoga and both of them also go to work. It is impossible to know what led him to this assertion—perhaps it was something he picked up at preschool—but what's certainly true is that society overwhelmingly imposes gender schemas onto us without our being fully cognizant of it. The issue, then, is what hope does anyone have of grasping for authenticity if they are hurled into an infrastructure that they didn't choose?

Beauvoir argued that as girls grow up, they're trained to be inauthentic. They are groomed to be "for men," implicitly taught that their body is a passive object of desire to be presented for men's gaze, and that their role is to please others, sit down, and watch quietly while the men go about their activities. To be a woman is to accept this restrictive form of femininity. It's confining for men, too, because they're trained to appear tough and strong, to smother any hint of vulnerability. To be a man is to accept this restrictive form of masculinity. The outcome of living in the midst of these mystifications is that all too many women develop unwarranted inferiority complexes and all too many men develop unwarranted superiority complexes, and everyone wallows in inauthenticity.

The fundamental existential idea that "existence precedes essence" means that there is no gendered personality or nature or identity that we're born with. It also means children do not contain the people they will become. There is no fixed essence that blooms from a seed within growing bodies. Humans are "natural-born existentialists" because freedom isn't something that we *have* or *gain,* freedom is what we *are.*[1] And although babies are unreflective and oblivious to their freedom, Beauvoir suggested that we are free even if we aren't cognizant of it.[2]

In her 1947 book *The Ethics of Ambiguity,* Beauvoir proposed that being cast into the world is the original fact of human existence. Children find themselves thrown into a world of seriousness, that is, a world that they didn't choose, that has been created without them, and that imposes values, customs, and languages they didn't select. Children are beholden to caregivers who appear as omnipotent. Their caregivers' attention to them has the power to make children realize that they exist and that they are subject to others' value judgments. Children care deeply whether their caregivers judge them as angel or demon, hero or failure. Caregivers shape children's notions of good and bad through reward, punishment, and education.

Children's lives are mostly lived in a state of dependence and ignorance. This is not necessarily bad. A carefree childhood is healthy, and it can be a time of security. Children in healthy environments realize that their actions don't have much of an impact on the world, and feel themselves to be free without being weighed down by responsibility.[3] This is one of the reasons that some people, who had healthy, happy childhoods, get nostalgic about those times of blissful innocence. Then as children grow, they are expelled from the warmth of their caregivers' arms.

Since children don't choose their world, they escape the anxiety of responsibility, and this makes them, in Beauvoir's words, "metaphysically privileged."[4] In her view, children can't be considered morally responsible until they can understand that they are decision-making beings whose lives are a synthesis of the past, present, and future. This happens around adolescence. Until then, children's freedom is generally exercised within the boundaries that other people have created.

Babies all go through the same early stages: they are born, they are fed milk, they are weaned—not only from breasts or bottles, but from caregivers carrying and moving them. The body is the lens through which humans first learn about themselves and their situation, discovering themselves as subjects who can choose their actions and as objects to the gaze of caregivers and teachers.

This development is not gendered. There is no difference in babies' engagement with the world at birth that's determined by their sex. Children initially learn through their eyes and ears and touch, not sexual organs. Beauvoir explained, if adults think they see indications of feminine destiny in girls such as passivity and empathy, as opposed to reason and action in boys, it's because adults impose their own lenses and training on girls.

The nature versus nurture debate still rages, but psychologist Barbara Rothman's research supports Beauvoir's stance on acculturation. Gender socialization is well underway even in the baby stage: girls' hands are often described as delicate, tiny, and clingy, while boys' hands are fists with "firm grips." Speaking with women who knew the sex of their fetus as well as those who didn't, Rothman found that gender stereotyping even starts in the womb. Women with male fetuses used words such as "strong" and "vigorous," like "a saga of earthquakes" to describe the movement they felt during pregnancy. Women with female fetuses rarely used these terms. In contrast, only female fetuses "squirm" and were described in the negative using "not" in terms such as "*not* violent, *not* excessively energetic, *not* terribly active." Women who didn't know the sex of their fetus used similar words but without any gendered pattern.[5]

The findings of neuroscientist Gina Rippon also lend support to Beauvoir's analysis. Rippon proposed that there is scant evidence for structural sex differences in babies' brains. Most studies find either no difference or the sample sizes are too small to make any meaningful conclusions. Baby brains, Rippon argues, are more like "cerebral sponges" that soak up cues from their early environment and are adaptable. But stereotyping from birth puts people into what Rippon calls "biosocial straitjackets, a form of 'brainbinding.'"[6] What's important from Beauvoir's perspective is that the way children are brought up influences whether they leap courageously into transcending or shy away from it—and the problem is that brainbinding pushes boys to leap in and girls to shy away.[7]

Consider a riddle that demonstrates brainbinding: A father and his son are in a car crash. The father dies. The son is rushed to the hospital. The doctor walks in and says, "I can't operate on this child because he is my son." How is that possible? (If you haven't heard this "riddle" before, stop and think about it for a moment.) I first heard it posed to a group of women in which one of three guessed the right answer.

I later posed it to a group of my own friends. Two fathers in a same-sex relationship? Was the child adopted? Was the father who died a priest? The doctor is transgender? All of these are possibilities. While it's true that the riddle primes people psychologically to think about men, the simplest answer—that the doctor is a woman and the mother of the child—eludes many (even feminists), and reveals implicit biases about women's roles.

In *The Second Sex*, Beauvoir observes that boys are coached toward freedom and girls are coached to be secondary to male freedom.

Boys are encouraged to be active, sporty, to confront others, and to test themselves against others, in combat with others. For boys, Beauvoir argued, there is no conflict between what he does and what he is supposed to be, between what's expected of him and his will for self-affirmation—as long as he sticks to the script of masculinity, which is restrictive in many ways.

Boys are encouraged to assume their freedom and to assert themselves for themselves, while girls experience a strong conflict between their will to self-affirmation and expectations placed on them. This conflict creates more obstacles along girls' paths than boys'.[8] Beauvoir acknowledged that people of color and marginalized people face this type of conflict in incomparably severe ways. The Black and very poor twenty-year-old protagonist in Richard Wright's novel *Native Son* (1940) grasps himself as an autonomous subject, but he experiences himself in a strange world where he is Other and where many possibilities are closed to him. He knows that the color of his skin will prevent him from ever flying in a plane and reaching the sky.[9]

While white boys are seen as boys, Black boys are perceived as older and more threatening, othered to a degree where their gender becomes a particular sign of threat. Consider Michael Brown, and Trayvon Martin, Tamir Rice. White men murdered these boys because they were Black.

And consider Black Olympic gymnast Simone Biles who in 2021 accomplished moves that judges allegedly deemed too dangerous for women so they punished her performance with a low score.[10] Although a few men have completed the feats in competition, Biles hit her head against an artificial ceiling that tells women that they should not be too magnificent.

The bounds are beginning to change. In 2019, the UK banned advertisements that depicted gender stereotyping. Authorities banned a cream cheese advertisement that showed men letting their babies be whisked away on a conveyor belt, implying that fathers were incompetent caregivers. A Volkswagen ad was also banned because it showed men in adventurous roles, such as being astronauts and para-athletes, and women in passive roles such as sitting with a stroller and sleeping. Books such as the Yasmin series by Saadia Faruqi and Hatem Aly are showing girls in a wide range of diverse roles such as builders, explorers, soccer stars, fashionistas, and chefs. Films such as Disney's *Brave* (2012), *Frozen* (2013), and *Moana* (2016) are challenging stereotypes about girls and their interests. And films such as Pixar's *Luca* (2021) are showing boys in nuanced roles, such as being vulnerable to others, forming friendships, and rejecting toxic masculinity.

Initiatives like these challenge gender stereotypes, and they are a move in the right direction. But they are so minuscule and inadequate to foster the real transformation that we desperately need. The world still appears differently for girls and boys in the stories we tell, in how we police appearances, and in how we regulate activities.

These differences continue to relentlessly instill inferiority in girls. For example, classic fairytales such as Cinderella, Snow White, Sleeping Beauty, and Rapunzel teach us that girls wait quietly—even unconsciously—to be saved, while boys fight dragons and witches to rescue them. Beauvoir acknowledged that these stories condition boys and girls alike.[11] Traditional fairytales were created by men for men to idealize themselves as heroes.

Appearances are policed. One of my son's teenage babysitters had very long hair and when she went to get it cut, the stylist refused because he said girls should have long hair. She left the salon in tears and wet hair. During the COVID-19 quarantine, my son decided he didn't want his hair to be cut, despite people constantly commenting on how long it was—including me. I had to catch myself in the unconscious patterns of brainbinding.

Clothing is still policed by gender. In a short film titled *Not*

My Responsibility (2020), singer-songwriter Billie Eilish pointed out that no matter what she wears, she's criticized harshly. Disapproving gazes judge her body relentlessly. The stringent, contradictory judgments and moral values imposed on women's appearances bind them. Essayist Lisa Selin Davis argues that American children are more gendered now than in the past. Around the nineteenth century (and earlier), boys played with dolls and wore dresses. In the 1970s, boys' clothing was marketed to girls, but "girlish" clothing for boys is still a highly niche market. Masculine girls are labeled tomboys, and feminine boys are called sissies. Being like a girl is an insult; being like a boy is empowerment. Boyhood was opened up to girls, but girlhood is still not socially acceptable for boys. Davis suggests that this policing is so strong and subtle that by age three, children are already conforming to stereotypes. In a statement that echoes Beauvoir's sentiment, Davis said that, "If we stop falsely labeling traits masculine and feminine and embrace ambiguity, there would be a lot less distress."[12]

Emotions are also policed. "Boys don't cry," so the trope goes. And getting angry is not ladylike. Neutral women's faces are inaccurately classified as "resting bitch face" because, neuroscientist Lisa Feldman Barrett argued, people see more negativity in women's faces than in men's. Women are meant to be happy and the lack of a smile on a woman's face is assumed to be an emotional response such as anger or disapproval. When women do get angry, they're perceived as bitchy or crazy; when men get angry—and even kill people—they're "just having a bad day."[13] And it's much worse for women of color.[14]

* * *

In *The Second Sex*, Beauvoir attempted to define what a woman is. She considered some possible answers: Having a uterus? Ovaries?

Wearing skirts? No. Some females are criticized for not being womanly enough even if their anatomy is female. We use gender terms like "women" not only to describe sex but also to evaluate people, as in: "You are not a real woman." But sex organs also don't provide a clear-cut, descriptive definition of what a woman is.

What does this attempt to define womanhood mean for people who do not conform to the sex binary? After all, not every person can fit neatly into either male or female categories, and there is still major disagreement about the basis on which we should distinguish between a male and female person.

Beauvoir's views about the relationship of biology and gender are ambiguous. On the one hand, she noted that sexual organs indicate a person's anatomy at birth, but do not tie them to a destiny. On the other hand, she emphasized that we can't deny the facts of our bodies and situations.[15] A person born with female sex organs who becomes a woman will have a different set of experiences than a person born with female sex organs who transitions. In *The Second Sex*, Beauvoir wrote, "Rejecting feminine attributes does not mean acquiring virile ones; even a transvestite cannot turn herself into a man: she is a transvestite."[16]

Because Beauvoir believed that each of us is a unique synthesis of our past, present, and future intentions, she thought there was a meaningful difference between being born with male, female, or intersex sex organs. She also suggested that in sport, biological sex provides a clear demarcation between groups:

> In sports, the goal is not to succeed independently of physical aptitudes: it is the accomplishment of perfection proper to each organism; the lightweight champion is as worthy as the heavyweight; a female ski champion is no less a champion than the male who is more rapid than she: they belong to two different categories.[17]

Nevertheless, there are two reasons why I think Beauvoir's ideas support trans-inclusionary feminism. The first is philosophical: We have already seen that Beauvoir wrote that one *becomes* a woman, suggesting that not all people born with female sex organs are destined for womanhood. This famous quote also implies that not all people born male become men, and that people born without female (or male) organs may potentially become women (or men)—although Beauvoir didn't specifically take her philosophy in this direction.

Given the sexist limitations that girls discover as they grow up, Beauvoir thought it shouldn't be surprising that many girls despair of being female and, presumably, that many boys despair being male. Greater equality between the sexes, as well as acceptance of different forms of gender expression, might help with some of this despair.

But Beauvoir's understanding of biology also makes room for gender freedom. She thought that biology determines our situations—the facticities that we cannot control—but our bodies do not control our gender destinies. Beauvoir emphasized the ways we can transcend our facticities, reaching beyond our given biology and situation. Technology and medicine are allowing people to transcend in ways that were previously thought impossible. Birth control and abortion allow people to make intentional choices about pregnancy, rather than being trapped by biological processes. Science helps people to pursue goals and lives that were once limited by infirmities. Why shouldn't we embrace the ways medical science can help people to transcend beyond the sex organs they were born with?

For Beauvoir, we can't change or erase the past—we drag it around with us like a ball and chain—but at the same time, our past does not determine our future. Being born in a certain situation or biology does not mean we have to confine ourselves to our past bodies if there are possibilities to transcend them. Conceived in this way, Beauvoir's philosophy gives us tools to understand gender transitioning as an exercise in becoming authentic. Transgender people reorient their situation and aspects of their lives—which historically have been taken to be inescapable destinies—in new, creative, and meaningful ways.

The second reason I think Beauvoir's ideas support trans-inclusionary feminism is because of the way Beauvoir talks about a neighbor in both an autobiography and her first novel, the psycho-drama *She Came to Stay,* published in 1943. The neighbor, Beauvoir wrote, is "a hermaphrodite, legally male, with breasts, a beard, both male and female sexual organs, and hair on the chest," and dresses as a woman.[18] Of course, this person wasn't transgender, but Beauvoir spoke with compassion about the torment that this person experienced because they didn't fit into binary sex categories. The neighbor was always in tears because Hitler's government exiled them, they lived in poverty, they liked men but men weren't interested, and they had spent time in a German concentration camp.

Beauvoir made no explicit judgments about transgender people, but was clearly sympathetic to their struggles, and acknowledged that discrimination against them is oppression. Beauvoir condemned all oppression and supported people's freedom to choose how to transcend their facticity, as long as they don't trample on others' freedom. And it's overwhelmingly the case that transgender people are egregiously discriminated against and abused.[19]

So, then, what is a woman? For Beauvoir, we can't say what a woman is because there is no definitive concrete answer. There's no essence to which women can be reduced. There is no feminine nature or masculine nature. Women cannot be reduced to hormones and sexual organs because there is an entire social context, multifarious facticity, and lived experience in which women are raised. A person with a female history will be situated in a context, facticity, and with experiences that are different to a person with a male history, even if they both project themselves into the future as women.

Like men, women are transcending consciousnesses. Unlike men, women are relentlessly and unfairly pushed into the role of Other.[20] Beauvoir said that even privileged women (including herself) could not completely escape the female condition.[21] We are all shaped by the choices we make against the backdrop of our sexed and gendered bodies and we are delusional—in bad faith—if we think that we aren't.

*   *   *

Beauvoir disagreed with Freud that girls' problems stem from penis envy. In Beauvoir's view, many problems spring from children witnessing how people with penises are treated differently. Girls are socialized to think of themselves as doll-like objects with the purpose of pleasing others. This fosters an inferiority complex, which can be frustrating, if not devastating and harmful.

Beauvoir does tend to overemphasize the symbolic meaning of the penis. For example, she assumes that boys standing up to urinate implies transcendence and girls sitting down represents immanence.[22] Yet even if we reject this analysis of peeing, we can still accept Beauvoir's point that a person's perspective of the world can be very different depending on what body parts they have—or are expected to have.

Puberty exacerbates the differences between girls and boys even further because, in Beauvoir's view, adolescence is when children start to face adulthood and the freedom and responsibility that come with it. Puberty is both an awakening to the world and an anxiety-inducing crisis in which adolescents find themselves swimming without the floaties of caregiver protection in a world of moral choice.

According to existentialists, humans are both being and nothingness, meaning that we exist (as human *beings*) but we are also incomplete (we are *nothing* because at every moment we lack our future being). Adolescence is a time when the lack at the heart of being and the universe, void of inherent meaning, calls to each of us to give our world meaning. Some children become aware of this angst before they reach puberty, but in adolescence it becomes a concrete reality as their bodies change and they become more independent. In adolescence, people question the meanings that were spoon-fed to them as children and begin to forge their own meanings.

Growing up requires breaking away from childhood servitude and ignorance, but Beauvoir proposes that girls and boys are called to do this differently. Boys' futures are consistent with their childhood and the values they have been taught: how to be assertive, be daring, and push their limits. Girls are called to femininity, that is, alterity, passivity, docility.

Adolescent boys coincide with themselves because they are more easily able to reach toward the people they set out to be. But adolescent girls face, in Beauvoir's words, a harrowing quandary between being feminine and becoming "properly human."[23] They are torn between the human desire to surge forward into the future, establishing themselves as autonomous subjects, and the social pressure to dilute themselves into objects and to smile while putting themselves second to other people.

As political theorist and feminist Iris Marion Young contends, girls are neither encouraged nor given opportunities to practice and develop bodily skills in the same way that boys are. Boys are taught "I can," girls are taught "May I?" Girls are instructed to be timid, neither too awkward nor too strong. The result is that girls are caught in a self-fulfilling prophecy of underestimating their capacity, not putting their whole being and energy into tasks, and then failing. This cycle undermines their trust in their bodies and reinforces misguided beliefs that girls can't perform to the same level as boys. Hence the insult: "You throw like a girl."

*　　*　　*

During puberty, girls go through an alienating metamorphosis in which their bodies can escape them, ripping them from themselves and their desires, hurling them into a realm beyond their existence toward the traditional feminine destiny of marriage, maternity, and mortality. Menstruation is often still treated with shame and secrecy.

Beauvoir was horrified when, in her tweens, her body was thrown into pubescent tumult. She would dread getting out of bed in the morning. The thought of growing breasts disgusted her. Discovering herself bleeding during the night mortified her. She was relieved when her mother told her what it was and ashamed when her father joked about it.[24]

Beauvoir's father had showered her with praise when she was a child, saying, "Simone has a man's brain; she thinks like a man; she *is* a man," but through adolescence, everyone still infantilized her.[25] As her younger sister grew prettier and more elegant, Beauvoir felt that her father was disappointed and held her perceived ugliness against her.

The security of Beauvoir's childhood crumbled away and she found herself facing the ambiguity of adulthood. She rebelled against her parents' unjustified and seemingly arbitrary decisions. She resisted them telling her what her "duty" was, their proclamations about what's done and what's not, and their attempts to impose their will on her. She was torn between telling the truth and doing what girls are expected to do, such as keeping their opinions to themselves. She discovered her parents were fallible, but they could still pull at her heartstrings and weigh her down with guilt. As their gaze shifted from protection to suspicion, she felt tormented with self-doubt.[26]

Just as girls reach the age of ambition, independence, and intellectual confidence, the pressure to conform to classic femininity—to make themselves appealing and desirable for men—intensifies. Women are encouraged to mask their natural bodies with cosmetics, accessories, dyes, and clothes that emphasize some curves and shrink others. It is exhausting and time-consuming to maintain.[27]

My adolescent pressures were slightly different, but not dramatically so. I also faced the ubiquitous pressure to monitor my body for the pleasure and demands of others. People relentlessly commented (and still comment) on my weight, bombarding me with contradictory messages: "Eat!" but also when I ate: "You'd better watch yourself! You'll balloon!" I went through various phases of having no interest in eating and purging food. The bile would burn my esophagus, make my teeth ache and my eyes puffy, but it gave me a glowing complexion.

Beauvoir explained that self-harm is an understandable but inauthentic mechanism that some girls use to cope with their sexual destiny as passive prey to the male gaze. Self-mutilation—cutting, burning, or in the case of one of Beauvoir's friends, slicing her own foot with an axe to avoid going to a party—constitutes a sadomasochistic revolt: sadistic because she enjoys torturing her body and masochistic because the pain gratifies her. She affirms that no one can harm or hate her more than she can harm and hate herself. But, for Beauvoir, self-injury is inauthentic because although the behaviors reveal a protest against her objectification, the practices also expose that she accepts herself as flesh condemned to submission. I wouldn't mutilate myself if I didn't think of myself as an object that can and should be mutilated.[28]

Beauvoir doesn't fully explain self-harm. For example, she doesn't say anything about why men and boys self-harm too. The relation between self-harm, policing, and obsessive self-control is a tight one, one that I don't fully understand, and one that I am sure will not disappear anytime soon in our contemporary culture. But Beauvoir's account goes some way to explaining the tensions I faced as a teenager and my desire to manipulate my body for others.

Perhaps I could get over the policing of my body had it not been for my hair. "Clean up that scruffiness with a swanky haircut," my father said. "Shave your legs," school friends said. "Shave your armpits," my mother said. "Here's my aesthetician's number. She's great with thick eyebrows," older friends said. "Shave everywhere," boyfriends said. It was just like Camille Rainville's poem "Be a Lady, They Said," which Cynthia Nixon recited in a 2020 viral online video detailing the ruthless and contradictory messages that attempt to regulate women's bodies and behavior and punish women no matter what they choose.[29]

As a young woman I found it demoralizing that the natural body could be such an object of shame, indecency, and inadequacy. But I succumbed to the pressure: I plucked, shaved, epilated, waxed, lasered, and suppressed tears of pain. So much writhing in the name of conformity, in the hope of becoming a silky object worthy of social validation, infantilized into a prepubescent shell.

I suspected I was failing myself, but I didn't have the courage to incite a hairy rebellion toward authenticity. Nowadays, when I see women with hair peeking out from under their arms, I realize that I have internalized sexism to such an extent that my initial reaction is still surprise—though it is followed quickly by a deep admiration for the fact that they have been able to brush off sexist socialization in a way that I still struggle with.

It's unclear whether Beauvoir shaved, but it's unlikely. In an interview she said that as a little girl, "I deliberately neglected my appearance because it was associated with my parents and their conventional way of life."[30] During the war, she mostly wore a turban because she preferred to spend what little money she had on food instead of hair products.

I am a white woman with what I always thought was dreadfully boring, mousey brown, dead-straight hair. Only now can I appreciate how I (and Beauvoir) escaped a different sort of torment. I was never discriminated against for my hair, as women of color are. Black women overwhelmingly find they need to change their natural hair to fit in at work—or risk being sent home for something that has nothing to do with their job performance. Because of their hair they are often perceived as less professional and competent, although standards and norms vary by industry.

Black schoolchildren often face detention or suspension when their natural hair, or styles such as braids or dreadlocks, are deemed (typically by white administrators) not to fit school policies. Such grooming rules are designed to center white people's hair as the norm, displaying a pernicious, racist beauty bias, and they demand a high mental and physical price from people of color.[31]

It's no wonder many children have trouble adjusting and finding balance with the myriad judgments and expectations they face for their appearance. Beauvoir pointed out that every person deals with the conflict between internal and external expectations differently. Some shy away from thinking about the tensions and get lost in seriousness and busyness. Some young women turn into masochists because in annihilating themselves, in making themselves objects, they become fascinating idols for the gaze of others. Some girls don't question their objectification; they continue to take for granted the values they inherited. Some become narcissistic, indulging in the cult of the self; others turn to friends for support, escape, and self-esteem; some explore their sexuality. Then there are those who rebel, attempting to assert their autonomy, to control their world, and to feel powerful. Transgressing offers the voluptuous thrill of risking freedom, but the catch-22 is that defiance will reinforce her as an object—this time as an object of shame and blame instead of admiration and praise.

* * *

While it's traumatic for women to be trained in inferiority, it's also detrimental for men. Women's inferiority means men's existence is not founded positively, on their freedom, but negatively, upon the Other's lack of freedom—and that's nothing to be proud of.[32] As author Ijeoma Oluo argued, this unearned superiority harms everyone: "The rewarding of white male mediocrity not only limits the drive and imagination of white men; it also requires forced limitations on the success of women and people of color in order to deliver on the promised white male supremacy."[33]

This phenomenon of unwarranted superiority is also teaching men to hide their fears. bell hooks argued that the patriarchal system teaches men to suppress vulnerabilities, fragilities, and feelings of hurt and to transform frustrations into anger and domination. This maneuver hurts their relationships and often correlates with abuse and assault. It also shortchanges men from living healthy emotional lives.[34]

Prevailing gender norms can endanger men's physical well-being too. Consider the COVID-19 pandemic. Studies have repeatedly found that men are significantly and consistently less likely to wear masks, more likely to catch coronavirus, less likely to see a doctor about symptoms, and more likely to die from it—and these attitudes are all related to beliefs about masculinity.[35]

It's not only men regulating masculinity. When then presidential candidate Joe Biden tweeted a video of himself putting on a mask with the caption, "Masks matter. They save lives," a conservative political commentator retweeted it with the caption, "Might as well carry a purse with that mask, Joe."[36] These comments imply that wearing masks—which involves being protective of oneself and others—is weak, feminine, and emasculating. This attitude traps men and women alike in sexist and self-sabotaging tropes.

Children face a rift between self-determination and being determined by others. Beauvoir manages to hold some women accountable (mostly white, privileged women) for reinforcing this rift, while she acknowledges that marginalized people are not complicit in the same ways. The difference in situations between white women and people of color, according to Beauvoir, is that Black women and men "endure their lot in revolt—no privilege compensates for [their situation's] severity—while for the [white] woman her complicity is invited."[37]

In other words, marginalized people have submission forced on them, whereas women are enticed toward sacrifice and vassalage. For privileged women, their submission is still a choice, but one that's stained with manipulation. The costs, consequences, and allurements of submission vary drastically depending on specific situations. While siren songs such as patriarchal protection tempt privileged women (sirens aren't always female), women of color are offered no such compensation. Many women of color don't get any real choice because systemic inequalities ensure there is never a question of them being able to choose their own fate. Adolescence is an indoctrination in the options and costs of submission and rebellion.

*   *   *

Unreflectively conforming to a destiny that is already laid out is one way to relieve the responsibility of creating our own futures. But this option is bad faith. It is "bad" because it amounts to sheltering in the shadow of others, locking ourselves into an infantile state, and being dishonest about who we are, namely free.

The existential caregiver must create a springboard for children to create themselves authentically: accomplishing themselves as autonomous, taking their future confidently into their own hands, facing the world with lucidity and courage, and exercising their freedom in responsible and self-affirming ways, without degrading themselves or others into objects. In Beauvoir's words: "And that is exactly what makes for the touching character of maternal love, properly understood. We must know that we never create anything for the other except points of departure, and yet we must want them for ourselves as ends."[38]

There are lots of explanations for the differences in the ways children grow up. But when we step back from all the subtleties, it's clear: from the moment a baby is born, cultural forces are at work channeling children into specific roles. The channels vary drastically between women, depending on class, race, age, disability, ethnicity, sexual orientation, and gender.

In Beauvoir's novel *Les Belles Images*, the protagonist Laurence, a mother, says, "Bringing up a child doesn't mean turning it into a pretty picture."[39] Yet overwhelmingly this is what caregivers try to do. The existential challenge is how to bring up and socialize children in morally healthy ways; we must recognize the impulse for social performance without railroading children and teenagers into other people's expectations.

The painful process of pubescent schisms can be overcome when we support adolescents in becoming both carefree and wise, pursuing projects that are harmonious with their interests, and freeing themselves from the dead weight of other people's rigid demands. We must create opportunities for all children to reach into an open future and choose their life paths for themselves. This existential freedom can enable children to overcome their inferiority and superiority complexes, and it will support them in becoming authentic. Unlearning is hard to do, but the ideal is for every person to feel confident on their quests for fulfillment, proud of who they are, and excited about who they are choosing to become.

Beauvoir teaches us that while we can't change when and where we were born, nor whom we were born to, the choices we make within those situations are vitally important for authentic living. To fulfill ourselves, we need other consciousnesses, and an authentic friend can be a safe portal toward authenticity. Friends can stretch one another toward new possibilities with support and confidence. An authentic friend—whether rivalrous or intimate or any complexity in between—can help us cope with the turbulence of growing up and beyond.

PART II

SITUATIONS

FRIENDSHIP

*The moment you acknowledge my conscience, you know
that I acknowledge one in you too. That makes all the
difference.*

—She Came to Stay

For Beauvoir, friendship is not only possible and important—it is
also the key to authenticity. Friendship is central to what she calls
an "authentically moral attitude."[1] But friendships support authenticity only when they are constructive and challenging. Although
friendship requires reciprocal recognition, according to Beauvoir,
friendship does not need to be reciprocated in the same ways or to
the same extent to be authentic.

Beauvoir refers to reciprocal recognition as "intersubjectivity."
Intersubjectivity describes the moment in which I discover that the
universe doesn't revolve around me. I come to see that other people
exist, and that their inner lives are as real and vibrant as my own.[2] Reciprocal recognition means that although each person is a subject and
other people are objects to them, each person is also an object to other
people's perspectives, and we must come to recognize and accept this.

To participate in intersubjectivity, we must become less self-
centered and less egoistic. This may seem obvious, perhaps, but

acting on it means transforming the way we relate to others. This pattern is at the very core of an existentialist friendship—a reciprocal, cooperative, and constructive relationship—and it serves as the template for all variations of authentic relationships.

Existence is a constant tension between projecting ourselves into life and making space for others. Other people are vitally important in our quest to create ourselves because we recognize and affirm our existences through interactions with others. In the absence of others, when we're left perfectly alone, we risk misinterpreting ourselves and the world around us.

In Beauvoir's novel *She Came to Stay*, the two main characters Françoise and Pierre discuss how vital intersubjectivity is to living meaningfully:

> "The moment you acknowledge my conscience, you know that I acknowledge one in you, too. That makes all the difference."
>
> "Perhaps," said Françoise. She stared in momentary perplexity at the bottom of her glass. "In short, that is friendship. Each renounces his pre-eminence. But what if either one refuses to renounce it?"
>
> "In that case, friendship is impossible," said Pierre.[3]

Friendship that creates the conditions for an authentically moral attitude is not easy. As we have already seen, being conscious, according to Beauvoir, necessarily entails othering: I am me and definitively not you. This realization can be either hostile or friendly. That's the rub. *She Came to Stay* opens with a quote from Hegel that illustrates this dynamic: "Each conscience seeks the death of the other."

Hegel argued that becoming self-conscious involves being recognized by other people. The problem is that other people sense us in ways that we cannot sense ourselves, meaning that part of our being is opaque to us and transparent to the other. If one of the goals of life is to know ourselves as completely as possible so that we can become fulfilled, then knowing what other people think of us—how they hear and see us, how they relate and respond to us—is important too.

Ideally others would just say what they think of us, but we can't know if they are telling the truth, and so full knowledge is a futile and impossible goal. But people still try and the attempt can fuel psychological power battles to recover that knowledge—that fragment of being—that others hold. Hegel said this dynamic results in a bitter mortal struggle.[4] This is Hegel's master–slave dialectic: When two people meet, one tries to dominate the Other. If both hold their confrontation with each other equally, they form a reciprocal relation—although it could be either antagonistic or amicable. However, if one succeeds in dominating the Other, it becomes a relationship of oppression.

This might sound overblown. Not everyone perceives other people's opinions as a theft that they need to fight to reclaim. But in practice, it's not completely outrageous. Very often people do care about other people's perceptions and want to control the impression they leave on others.

Imagine meeting someone. You're conscious of how you appear to them. You want them to think well of you—or at least not to think poorly of you. You wonder what they think of you. You imagine yourself from their perspective. And you size the other person up too, passing judgments and forming opinions. The more you care about them, the more you care what they think of you. The more you want them to think well of you, the more you want to control what they think of you. This type of relationship can quickly descend into one steeped in possessive tensions.

Anne, the protagonist in Beauvoir's novel *The Mandarins*, is talking to a man at a party when he tells her that other people have warned him about her. She tries not to care about what others have said. She wrestles with her desire to know: "But the glances, the looks, the stares of other people, who can resist that dizzying pit?"[5]

Certainly, it's unhealthy to be completely dependent on other people's opinions, but not to care at all, not to take others' views into account whatsoever, is to potentially ignore abiding insights about who we are. (To live in the sealed bubble of one's own self-reflection is also the hallmark of a narcissist, but more about self-sabotage later.) The tension between wanting to know and not being able to know others' opinions about us can be incredibly frustrating.

She Came to Stay illustrates a deeply inauthentic friendship. The novel depicts Hegel's master–slave dialectic in action. It shows how wanting to control another's view provokes psychological sadomasochism because this kind of domination objectifies the Other and disrespects their subjectivity. In the story, the beautiful and capricious Xavière comes to stay in Paris with her friend Françoise and Françoise's husband, Pierre. Xavière is wildly jealous of Françoise and Pierre's relationship, wanting to have each of them all to herself. When Pierre becomes obsessed with Xavière, Françoise feels alienated and sleeps with Xavière's boyfriend, Gerbert. (Xavière and Gerbert were on a break, but still.)

Xavière raids Françoise's desk, she finds a letter from Gerbert with incriminating details, and she is furious. Françoise feels unbearably guilty. She is desperate to talk to Xavière, but Xavière ghosts her. Beauvoir wrote,

> Behind Xavière's maniacal pleasure, behind her hatred and jealousy, the abomination loomed, as monstrous and definite as death. Before Françoise's very eyes, yet apart from her, existed something like a condemnation with no appeal: detached, absolute, unalterable, an alien conscience was rising. It was like death . . . [6]

While their friendship is complicated by sex, it illustrates how power struggles compromise authentic friendship. And it's not only the high drama of complex open relationships that inflame such clashes. Recently a friend went to a party without me and afterward she said, "We talked about you a lot!" I desperately wanted to know more. That burning curiosity characterizes the dynamic of wanting to reclaim perspectives of my being that were lost to my friend. Was she complimenting me? Or was she exercising power over me by flaunting the fact that she was privy to knowledge that I didn't have? She didn't offer to share. In asking her to tell me, I would have risked the submissive position in our relationship. It would have acknowledged her dominance on the basis of the power that her secrets held over me.

For Beauvoir, as for Hegel, the twist is that a submissive person holds more power than you might expect, since it is only because of their subjugation that the other can dominate. My friend's power depended on me caring about what was said at the party. So, the master needs the submissive person more than the submissive person needs the master. Clearly my friend has power over me since I'm still overthinking it, wondering what secrets she holds, and wanting to manage her impression of me. But that power play—of my friend brandishing the power of her knowledge over me, and my refusing to formally bestow that power upon her—clouds our ability to relate authentically to one other.

In *She Came to Stay*, Xavière and Françoise are also both caught in power games. Xavière wants Françoise to be at her beck and call. Françoise refuses and is eventually driven to murder because she cannot stand how her friend Xavière condemns her. This conflict—between wanting to control the other and letting go—needs to be overcome to create authentic relationships.

This tension also characterized Beauvoir and Sartre's open relationship, which Beauvoir said was, at its core, a deep friendship.

Sartre exercised the ability to sleep around more than Beauvoir did, but he still relied on Beauvoir's permission. Their unique agreement counted on both of them to be active and willing participants. Some read the arrangement as Beauvoir repressing her desires for Sartre's benefit.

However, it's possible that Beauvoir instigated the open relationship because although Sartre loved to seduce, he didn't care for sex, and couldn't satisfy her.[7] Beauvoir wrote to another lover, Nelson Algren, about Sartre: "Love was not very successful. Chiefly because [Sartre] does not care much for sexual life. He is a warm, lively man everywhere, but not in bed. I soon felt it, though I had no experience; and little by little, it seemed useless, and even indecent, to go on being lovers."[8] In an effort to overcome jealousy, Beauvoir and Sartre agreed to a pact of transparency. They would tell each other intimate details of their relationships with their "contingent" lovers—meaning secondary or ancillary to Beauvoir and Sartre's "essential" relationship.[9]

While *She Came to Stay* is fiction, it is not only fiction: the novel is based on Beauvoir and Sartre's real-life relationship with Olga and Wanda Kosakiewicz—who were merged into Xavière's character in the novel. Beauvoir dedicated the novel to Olga, who was one of Beauvoir's students. Olga was impetuous, disarming, charming, and infatuated with Beauvoir. Beauvoir wrote, "Her feelings toward me quickly reached a burning intensity, the full implications of which I took some time to appreciate."[10]

Olga touched Beauvoir's heart and, according to biographer Hazel Rowley, they also became lovers.[11] Beauvoir found the relationship was intoxicatingly delightful—until Sartre became infatuated with Olga. But when Olga insisted on a platonic friendship with Sartre, obsessive cycles of jealousy and resentment seethed amongst the friends. Beauvoir recalls the power that Olga, impetuous and childlike, had over Sartre and how Sartre struggled with not having the upper hand:

> In the face of her opposition Sartre, too, let himself go, to the great detriment of his emotional stability, and experienced feelings of alarm, frenzy, and ecstasy such as he had never known with me. The agony which this produced in me went far beyond mere jealousy: at times I asked myself whether the whole of my happiness did not rest upon a gigantic lie.[12]

To console himself after failing to seduce Olga, Sartre successfully pursued her sister Wanda. Sartre said Wanda was no more than a consolation prize: "The woman I loved had turned me down, so I got her spitting image, younger yet . . . Wanda was only twenty-two! Great for my ego."[13]

The "gigantic lie" that concerned Beauvoir was whether she occupied as essential a place in Sartre's heart as he did in hers. She thought their deep friendship was on an equal footing, but she had her doubts. Her concerns were not misplaced. Sartre clearly found it easier to embrace polyamory than Beauvoir, but his freedom came at the cost of transparency.

Though they were supposed to be strictly honest with each other, Beauvoir and Sartre often lied to others—such as about with whom they were each spending time—to avoid having to deal with the discomfort of sharing awkward truths. Sartre told another lover that he did not always share the whole truth with Beauvoir. In an interview he admitted that he lied to all his lovers, "*Particularly* to the Beaver" (Beauvoir).[14] But Sartre did not claim to be authentic. While Sartre had a philosophical problem with lying to oneself (bad faith), he had no theoretical issue with lying to others.[15]

It was neither the first nor the last time Beauvoir and Sartre grappled with feelings of jealousy and desires to control their lovers, but Beauvoir later admitted that the murderous ending of *She Came to Stay* was a mistake.[16] Although the chaos with Olga, Wanda, and Sartre rankled her, she regretted that she implied murder was an authentic way to deal with conflict. The saga of *She Came to Stay* shows that the way we relate to one another is more often a failure of reciprocity that explodes in conflict instead of flourishing into authentic friendship.

* * *

Solitude is valuable when it is freely chosen, but many people do not have the choice, and many are lonely. Social media can help people keep in touch with friends, but it can also exacerbate the feeling of isolation. The COVID-19 pandemic reminded many of how important in-person contact is, and proved that people are willing to risk their lives (and other people's) to avoid loneliness.[17] Loneliness has been classified as an epidemic and as dangerous to our health as smoking fifteen cigarettes per day.[18] As science writer Lydia Denworth said, "People think all the time about competition and survival of the fittest, but really it's survival of the friendliest."[19]

In 2018, the United Kingdom appointed a Minister for Loneliness tasked with addressing the loneliness epidemic. In 2021, Japan appointed one in the face of widespread social isolation that intensified with the COVID-19 pandemic. The Japanese have a name for one who dies alone: *kodokushi*, which became used widely after a sixty-nine-year-old man was discovered three years after his death. His utility bills were being automatically deducted from his bank account, and when his savings ran out, authorities came knocking at his apartment door. All they found was his skeleton, his body long stripped dry by maggots and beetles.[20]

Of course, no one makes friends for the health benefits. We make friends because most of us are social beings who enjoy other people's company. But it's worth noting, friendship is existentially priceless. We need solitude to cultivate independence, freedom, creativity, and serenity. But at times, being alone amounts to a living death—silent, final, and unspeakably dark. It was one of the things Beauvoir loved about her life with Sartre: he helped to protect her solitude and prevented her from feeling lonely. Because they lived independently, she had all the comforts of a partner without the oppressive obligations that can come with cohabitation.[21]

When loneliness turns into a mass phenomenon, people become primed for vulnerabilities to propaganda, conspiracy theories, and totalitarian domination.[22] When we're lonely, our thinking becomes isolated. Loneliness severs us from other people who can challenge us, open up possibilities and critiques that we don't see on our own, and help us question whether we're living authentically.

An everyday example: I can jog on my own, but I do a lot better when I run with an authentic friend. When one of us is struggling, the faster friend doesn't rub it in the slower friend's face. Occasionally the faster friend will prance around like a springbok to make the slower friend laugh when they're tired. Sometimes the faster friend will run ahead if they're working on their own time. But usually we will run beside each other, supporting each other with encouraging words like "Good pacing!" When one friend's shoelace comes undone the other is there to tell them before they trip. We are both ready to help if one falls or gets bitten by a snake (a risk when running in Australia, but it hasn't happened to me yet).

An inauthentic friend would be concerned exclusively with themselves, using me as a tool to make themselves feel better at my expense, such as gloating or making fun of me if they run faster. Destructive power games are a good indicator that a relationship is not worthy of being called an authentic friendship. I might still consider this person a friend. I might still hold this person in my circle of care, making them more than an acquaintance, but I would not call them an authentic friend. I would, however, nurture the possibility of transforming our situation into an authentic friendship.

The gaze of an authentic friend helps us better understand where we have room to improve. Authentic friends can be trusted for constructive and thoughtful criticism, whether it's checking our behavior when we metaphorically overstep or literally improving our stride while running, as is the case in my example of jogging with my friend. I need a friend to see aspects of myself that I can't see alone. I will come to a deeper understanding if I can discuss my behavior with another who cares about my well-being. It's still up to my friend and I each to decide what's right for our individual bodies, but being with one another—especially where we can compare our behaviors, habits, and techniques in person—helps us to learn from and through each other.

* * *

Inauthentic friendships stagnate in power games. Authentic friendships rise above them. One of the most authentic relationships of Beauvoir's life was with Elizabeth Lacoin ("Zaza" Mabille in Beauvoir's memoirs). Beauvoir and Zaza met as children. They were both exceptionally intelligent, academically competitive, and quickly became friends. Teachers called them "the two inseparables."[23]

They would talk about books, school, teachers, and the world. At a piano recital, after playing a piece her mother thought was too difficult, Zaza stuck her tongue out at her mother. Beauvoir was overwhelmed with respect for Zaza's confidence and contempt for authority: "For me this exploit surrounded her with a halo of glory . . . I was completely won over by Zaza's vivacity and independence of spirit."[24] Zaza boosted Beauvoir's confidence because Beauvoir saw herself through the eyes of someone she admired and identified with, instead of through her parents' imperious gaze. The friendship rescued Beauvoir from feelings of loneliness and helped her to recognize that her life was worth living.

With Zaza, Beauvoir discovered that great friends can assure each other of personal worth, make one another feel whole, heard, and valued, provide a structure and framework for their lives, and help better to understand oneself and another. It is exhilarating to be respected and recognized by a friend, to find comfort through shared suffering and empathy, to challenge each other with new ideas and insights, and to discover the world together.

While people of both sexes are capable of friendship, Beauvoir hypothesized that friendships with women were deeper than those with men because women are socialized to share more.[25] While at first glance this sounds like a gender stereotype or oversimplification, there is ample research that supports this idea. Sociolinguist Deborah Tannen found that girls and women talk to one another more than boys and men—more often, at greater length, and about more personal things—which creates opportunities for both intimacy and heartache.[26]

Beauvoir learned from Zaza's friendship that it is sometimes enough to be jubilant over the other's existence and said: "Joy, joy! Immense friendship, like my heart, which will not end."[27] The friendship did end when Zaza died in 1929 at age twenty-one, probably of meningitis or encephalitis. Beauvoir was devastated and—perhaps because she idealized her memory of Zaza—the friendship became a prototype for her idea of authentic relationships.

While we do not know how long Beauvoir and Zaza's friendship would have lasted, or how it would have ended if it were not so tragically cut short, it seems to have sparked the idea for Beauvoir that an important element of friendship is freeing one another from the self-imposed strictures that threaten to keep us from becoming authentic. While Françoise and Xavière trapped one another in possessiveness, Zaza's friendship helped free Beauvoir from being a dutiful daughter, and Beauvoir's friendship helped Zaza challenge Catholic bourgeois indoctrination (at least intellectually, if not practically). The difference between the two friendships is intersubjectivity. Although Beauvoir and Zaza were academically competitive, they rose above their rivalry to a level of mutual respect.

Yet reciprocity need not be equal in terms of how people perceive each other. Zaza was not quite as ecstatic about Beauvoir. At age eighteen, during a midnight conversation in their pajamas under a pine tree in a garden, they talked for hours about the past. "I loved you," Beauvoir told Zaza, referring to when they were younger—although her feelings had not waned. In her memoirs, Beauvoir recalled that Zaza was surprised and shared that none of her friends, including Beauvoir, were important to her.[28] In *Inseparable*, Beauvoir's novel based on her relationship with Zaza, Beauvoir suggests that she long suspected she was not as important to Zaza as Zaza was to her. In the novel, Beauvoir describes her pain and sadness that Andrée (based on Zaza) had no idea how Sylvie (based on Beauvoir) felt.

Asymmetrical friendships are not unusual. A study in 2016 found that fifty-three percent of friendships are reciprocal, meaning that if you wrote a list of your friends, only half of them would name you on their list. People aren't always good at knowing who their friends are because the mere thought that one might not be likeable challenges one's self-worth.[29] And what matters is not how many friends we have, but the quality of those relationships.

Sometimes people live in a state of ignorance about who their friends are. Asymmetrical friendships tend not to be discovered as quickly or starkly as we discover non-reciprocal romances. Learning that someone you consider a friend does not consider you a friend can be hurtful. Beauvoir came to terms with this. She didn't need Zaza to love her back because she admired her so much and was so thrilled to be Zaza's friend.[30]

When Beauvoir was thirty-eight, she found herself in a converse position. Beauvoir's friend Violette Leduc sent her a manuscript that said in no uncertain terms that she was passionately in love with Beauvoir. Beauvoir responded that she found it strange to be so precious to another, that Leduc's feelings were based on a mirage and would wear off quickly, and that Beauvoir was neither flattered nor bothered by it.

Many people would find such a relationship to be untenable. But, as in her friendship with Zaza, Beauvoir insisted that the difference in feelings between herself and Leduc did not preclude them from having an authentic relationship. Beauvoir thought of Leduc as an equal. They respected and trusted each other. Their authentic relationship was based on intellectual and emotional intimacy, sympathy, understanding, and moral amity.[31]

Authentic friendship is not a transaction, it's not instrumental, and there is no rule that it needs to be equal in terms of what people put into or get out of it. Of course, there needs to be some kind of reciprocity for there to be a relationship, but in an authentic friendship, the reciprocity means recognizing the other as a free subject.

The Latin poet Ovid wrote, *Si tempora erint nubila, solus eris,* which translates to something like: "when the storms arrive, you will find yourself alone." One interpretation of this is that success attracts friends, failure repels them. And if these are the sorts of superficial people who you find yourself with, then take that as a clear sign that your relationship is based on people treating you like an object and their priority is getting what they can out of you.

Moreover, if friendship is based purely on pleasure and profit, then you're missing out on meaningful connections that persist through tough times and challenges and allow for consolation, sadness, and grief. In her semi-autobiographical novel *The Bell Jar*, Sylvia Plath described an incident after a banquet and film screening in New York City, where she and her peers ate caviar and avocado halves stuffed with crab. It gave them food poisoning. "There is nothing like puking with somebody to make you into old friends," Plath wrote.[32] Shared experiences and adversities— whether they are cheerful like parties or horrific like holding one another's hair back while vomiting—are most certainly ways of creating deep bonds of friendship.

Yet giving up self-importance is what makes authentic friendship so hard: surpassing the desire to control others requires us to stop chasing the part of our being that only others see. And that requires being open and vulnerable to others, which makes friendships dangerous too. Vulnerability does not always pay: the closer friends are, the more they see through one another's eyes, and the more power they have over each other.

Beauvoir admired Jane Austen's class-conscious literature, which depicted a range of friendships. Austen's 1815 novel *Emma* illuminates Beauvoir's point about authentic friendship. The beautiful and wealthy protagonist Emma Woodhouse is a terrible friend to the poor, unsophisticated, and suggestible Harriet Smith. Fancying herself a brilliant matchmaker, Emma manipulates Harriet into refusing a marriage proposal from Robert Martin, with whom Harriet is in love, and stokes her hopes in men of higher social ranking, all of whom are in love with Emma. Thanks to Emma's interference, Harriet is humiliated and heartbroken multiple times.

A Beauvoirian reading of this story is that Emma's possessiveness and controlling behavior preclude authentic friendship with Harriet. Emma becomes an authentic friend when she renounces her self-important attitude, that is, the assumption that she knows better than others what's good for them. She realizes the mess she has made, and goes to Robert to salvage his relationship with Harriet. It is at that point that Emma throws out the golden rule (do unto others as you would have them do unto you) and instead lives by the platinum rule (do unto others as they want done unto themselves). This latter rule invites us to treat the other as a subject in themselves—even if we disagree with them.

Authentic friends make space for each other, respect each other's views, and accept differences of opinion. That's how friends transcend Hegel's vicious master–slave dialectic. Often people look for sameness in friends because it makes them feel secure and keeps life peaceful. However authentic friendship is not a matter of becoming similar or of being tolerant. Authentic friendship beckons us to keep our hearts open and our minds welcome to challenges, to having our being called into question.

The authentic friend, Beauvoir wrote, "is both an object wrenching her to the limits of herself and a witness who restores that self to her."[33] One way to think about this is like a bungee cord: authentic friendship stretches you in new, exciting, energizing, and scary ways, but also supports you and keeps you safe because you are recognized for who you are and not for what you can do for each other.

In a day and age when relationships are challenged by clashing political views, often expressed over social media, it's worthwhile to keep in mind cultural theorist Leela Gandhi's argument that the best kind of friendship is a type of cosmopolitanism in which people connect on a plane of social inclusion, respecting differences between us. Gandhi bases her idea on the ancient Greek idea of *philoxenia,* meaning friendliness to strangers. When solidarities are ambiguous, she wrote, "a utopian mentality shows the way forward to a genuine cosmopolitanism: always open to the risky arrival of those not quite, not yet, covered by the privileges which secure our identity and keep us safe."[34] Gandhi emphasized the notion that Beauvoir hinted toward: that friendships need not be equal and that it is not the label of "friend" that's important, but the attitude with which we approach one another.

*   *   *

In 2018, I taught a three-week course on the philosophy of love to a group of incarcerated men.[35] Part of my role at a university was to support a program that ran philosophy classes in this prison. My job included organizing training sessions for volunteers—ranging from undergraduate philosophy students to activists to senior tenured professors. We listened to formerly incarcerated students whose experiences learning philosophy had inspired them; heard from people who had taught philosophy in prison; learned about Augusto Boal's "Theatre of the Oppressed" techniques, and practiced the activities. (Boal's techniques are an attempt to break down some of the hierarchies in the classroom by creating a space where everyone has the opportunity for dignity and agency, and to enable freedom of thought, ideas, expression, and sharing opinions. I did the training too.)

When I arrived, the classroom was warm and stuffy but clean and bright with long fluorescent white lights on the ceiling and tall thin windows nestled between impossibly thick walls. Fifteen men in beige jumpsuits glided in. The two teaching assistants and I jumped up and shook their hands with enthusiasm and welcoming smiles, which I suspect only thinly veiled our nervousness. The men settled into the circle of chairs that we had set up in a scrambled attempt to bring Boal's techniques to life. We wanted to create a safe, judgment-free, non-hierarchical space, a space that was bracketed off from the daily experience of incarceration for three hours.

While I did not assume that all of this could be achieved by moving around a few chairs, we had been trained to do what we could with limited resources to at least suggest that the classroom was a space where people who are objectified at every moment of their lives are empowered to step forward as subject—however fleetingly. I did not know what the students in my class were imprisoned for. I wasn't allowed to ask and they were not allowed to tell me.

The reasoning behind this logic was that people would be better able to relate to one another on a basis where they are momentarily free from their past and where it would not matter what they had or had not done. I knew I could never entirely grasp what was going on in the students' lives. I didn't know anything about them or their backgrounds, but as facilitators, we focused on teaching and listening to their philosophical discussions, trying to simulate a mood of intersubjectivity in that specific, albeit highly limited, realm.

In front of long windows looking toward gleaming towers, with staff in black flak jackets passing silently on the other side of the glass wall, we talked about the female philosopher Diotima of Mantinea. Diotima was a central figure in Plato's *Symposium,* written around 385–370 BC. In *Symposium,* a group of men have a party, get tipsy on diluted wine, and eulogize about love. It is a work of fiction, but many assume it was based on real events and real people, with Diotima possibly being a pseudonym for a real woman in Ancient Greece. Although Diotima does not appear in person in the scene—only men were allowed at symposia—the celebrity of the evening, Socrates, lectures the group about his discussion with her.

Diotima describes to Socrates a staircase of knowledge on which passionate attraction to one person is petty and low. In order to understand true beauty, we need to overcome lust and move to a higher step by recognizing beauty in all bodies, then beauty of all minds, until we reach the truth of beauty itself at the top of the stairs. "If you ever saw that," Diotima tells Socrates, "it would seem to be on a different level from gold and clothes and beautiful boys and young men . . . if someone could see beauty itself, absolute, pure, unmixed, not cluttered up with human flesh and colors and a great mass of mortal rubbish . . ."[36]

In Plato's view, knowledge of such beauty leads to *eudaimonia*—well-being and flourishing—which the ancient Greeks thought was the goal of life. The best kinds of relationships are those where people can guide one another in ascending this staircase. They educate one another, discuss virtue, help one another to flourish, and explore what a good person should do. This is what the ancient Greek philosophers thought to be the key features of a great friendship.

"What do you think?" I asked the class. The room fell silent. Some students slumped back in their chairs, others leaned over the handouts. Some looked like statues, pondering. Others fidgeted. I waited a little longer, relaxing into the hush. A student raised his hand and asked, "What does she mean, 'beautiful boys and young men'?"

"Was Socrates *gay*?" chimed another. A sea of wide eyes gaze upon me. I explained that while it is true that some male relationships in Ancient Greece involved sex, carnal knowledge was generally frowned upon. In *Symposium*, Socrates coolly turns down the advances of Alcibiades who is a young and sexy—in his own opinion, at least—politician who, drunk and heartbroken, crashes the end of the party.

Normally, however, Greek men had to be very careful about their relationships. If the younger was seen to accept money or favors, they risked being charged with prostitution.[37] "Platonic" mentor-mentee affiliations were encouraged over erotic ones, and the ancient Greeks such as Plato and Aristotle referred to this kind of friendship as *philia,* or fraternal love.

"It's like us brothers in here," said one of the incarcerated men, a natural philosopher and teacher, always willing to translate from academic into more accessible language. "We help each other. We support each other. We look out for each other," he continued. A few heads nodded cautiously in understanding. "Like a bromance?" asked another student. The class burst into laughter.

"Yes, exactly!" I tried to say without laughing because it was so spot on. While Diotima is mostly referring to male friendships, she does suggest that women are equally capable of establishing intellectual relationships with men. Not only does Diotima tell Socrates that the path to knowledge of true beauty is open to both men and women, but also *she* is the one schooling the venerable Socrates— one of the wisest men in the history of western philosophy—about this staircase of knowledge. She quips, "Even you, Socrates, could perhaps be initiated in the rites of love I've described so far [but] I'm not sure you could manage this."[38]

We discussed whether Diotima's idea of friendship is a good one. Most of the students agreed that not all friends can live up to such lofty ideals—nor should they be expected to. Some students considered friendship to be a hierarchy, others as a continuum of emotional distance between intimacy and indifference. One student admitted to having once experienced a rare virtuous friendship such as Diotima describes, where both were deeply invested in the other's flourishing. He did not say how he lost that friend, but he told us that by the age of eleven, after losing everyone he had ever cared about, he got a tattoo that said, "Love don't love me."

Authentic friendship, Beauvoir wrote, is based on freedom, that is, "when it does not depend on any outside command, when it is lived in sincerity without fear."[39] The students were not free or fearless. It would be presumptuous to claim that any of us could have been completely sincere given the stifling circumstances on the other side of the glass wall. Most of the students were underprivileged men of color, some of whom told me they did not finish high school.

As a privileged white woman, if I said or did something wrong, the worst that would happen was that I would be asked to leave the premises and never return, and would have put the teaching program at risk. If they messed up, they risked humiliation at best, and solitary confinement and lengthened sentences at worst. They had some choice: whether to come to the class, to be engaged, or to be friendly. But ultimately they had extremely limited options. Given the circumstances and power differentials, anything approaching true reciprocity or intersubjectivity would have been impossible— but we were open to the risk of each other, and it felt friendly to me.

In their student evaluations and in person, the students said that reading and discussing philosophy provided them an invaluable experience, one that allowed them to stop thinking about being locked up, and to use their brain in ways that they had not been able to for a long time. One student said it was the first time in a long time he felt a sense of escape from his daily life. Another said that he could not remember the last time that anyone asked his opinion about anything. Many said they loved the "free thinking" and challenging discussions. They said it helped them to listen to one another, to be more attentive and respectful of each other, and to better understand each other. The class sparked their curiosity to learn more about philosophy and every student wanted more classes. (Which was the point of the program, since the more people are educated, the less likely they are to return to prison.[40])

They inspired me, too. One of the Theatre of the Oppressed activities we ran was for students to read a section of philosophy and recreate it in their own words. The most impressive moment was when two students transformed part of Diotima's speech into a rap that they spontaneously created and performed while standing on chairs in the classroom. While I cannot remember their exact words, I was entranced by their insightfulness, creativity, and intelligence.

At the end of the course, I overheard a student ask a teaching assistant, "Aren't you afraid of us? Most people out there think we're monsters," nodding toward the windows. She said no. Certainly I had been nervous—mostly because it was such an uncertain situation—but in our teacher training, we had been taught by formerly incarcerated students and knew that we were there to teach and not to judge. We learned how prison reduces people to objects in brutal ways, defining them by their past, and robbing them of a future, which is a moral violation according to Beauvoir.

We tried to create a mood that acknowledged that although the students were caught in a heavily immanent situation stripped of almost all choice, they had the opportunity to relate to one another as incomplete, ambiguous subjects with a future beyond the prison.

I don't know that I'll ever see any of them again, but for those few classes, for those few hours, they related to one another (and I believe I related with them) not only as philosophers in the original sense of the term—as lovers of wisdom—but also in the spirit of authentic friendship: evanescently opening their minds and hearts to each other, inspiring and relating to each other intersubjectively, supporting each other's flourishing, and becoming wiser in the process. Some of them may have been relating to one another in these ways already, but philosophizing about friendship in the class gave them a new framework to reflect more explicitly on their connections.

* * *

While teaching incarcerated students isn't a common experience, it highlights the fact that unequal situations, ages, and experiences don't preclude friendship. Meeting in perfect equality is rarely possible. The key is to create a relationship based on intersubjectivity. And there are possibilities for intersubjectivity even when people are not equal, or for that matter, entirely free.

Another implication of this story about friends is that it is the quality of the intersubjective bond that matters, not the length of the bond. A long friendship is not necessarily correlated with depth. Beauvoir posited that while time can create greater opportunities to intensify bonds, often long-term friendships are based on habits. People can mistake history or shared experiences—going to the same school or being part of the same sports team, for example—for authentic attachments. Within every human connection lies a possibility for friendship and collaboration, for being attentive to and challenging one another. Don't we all want to be genuinely heard, respected, and understood? It doesn't rely only on us, but extending the hand of generosity is a good first step.

Inspired by Michel Foucault, artist and activist Nadya Tolokonnikova wrote, "Prisons mirror the society around them. Unless we change both, we will all be trapped in a kind of prison."[41] This is the sort of sentiment that Beauvoir was working toward, expressed more concretely. We need to recognize one another as free subjectivities in order to ground our existences and to understand ourselves.[42] While the incarcerated students weren't practically free and it was not within my power to change that, in the classroom, there were openings for intellectual and moral freedom and, hence, for relating reciprocally to one other.

Othering frustrates reciprocity. Othering is what Beauvoir calls an "imperialism of human consciousness," a framing that people use to feel superior over others, and it happens in ways that we are not always fully cognizant of.[43] We (the instructors) attempted to neutralize superiority by flattening the standard classroom hierarchy and creating a space for intellectual freedom to flourish. My experience teaching in prison taught me that what separated my situation from the students', more than anything else, was privilege and luck. I worked hard to avoid othering the students and the idea of being incarcerated, a prerequisite that allowed us (to some degree), to form connections with one another.

Beauvoir shows that authentic friendships can inspire us to be better, making them not only pleasurable and useful, but making the world a much better place too. Things go awry when people view one another negatively in order to make themselves feel superior, or instrumentally, as resources, as the means to expand and enrich their world at the expense of others instead of treating those people as ends in themselves.

While we have to let go of the fact that we never fully know what other people think about us, and let go of the desire to recover the lost fragment of our being that the other holds, relating to friends authentically calls for a conversion: renouncing self-centeredness to nurture intersubjectivity. All human connections are fragile and precarious, but within every one of them lies a possibility for friendship. Françoise treats Xavière as an inconvenience in her life who needs to be annihilated so Françoise can feel more comfortable, but Emma, Zaza, and the incarcerated students I met reveal possibilities beyond hostility and toward reciprocity, toward authentic friendship, and toward becoming united on a grander scale.

ROMANTIC LOVE

The ideal thing would be to be able to love a woman just as well as a man, a human being pure and simple, without fear, without pressure, without obligations.
　　　　　　　　　　　　　—After The Second Sex

In a letter to the American novelist Nelson Algren, with whom Beauvoir had an intense romance, she said: "If I were proud of anything in my life, it would be of our love. I feel we have to tell to each other as many things as we can, so we are not only lovers, but the closest friends at the same time."[1] They did not, however, stay friends or lovers. Algren wanted to marry Beauvoir. She loved him but was interested neither in marriage, nor leaving Sartre, nor moving to Chicago. Was it this tension between sex and friendship that led Beauvoir to observe that being in love, for a woman, always risked tipping into a state of fear, pressure, and obligation?

In a classic line from the 1989 movie *When Harry Met Sally*, Harry tells Sally, "Men and women can't be friends because the sex part always gets in the way." Harry's point is that the man will want to have sex with the woman and the woman will fall in love with the man, which dooms the friendship. Often there is an element of truth to this argument, if in an overgeneralized and heteronormative sense. (This tension seems to be part of the tumult between Beauvoir, Sartre, Olga Kosakiewicz, and Wanda Kosakiewicz discussed in the previous chapter.)

Nevertheless, it is simplistic and cynical to reduce interpersonal relationships to animalistic impulses. From an existential perspective, while we are animals, we are also our intentions and projects. To reduce our relationships to instinct deteriorates our humanity. It renders conscious choices and higher-order decisions obsolete.

Beauvoir's writing—and an examination of her life—shows that romantic love is best when it is authentic, that is, based on the intersubjectivity of friendship. Although Beauvoir doesn't clearly differentiate between romantic lovers and friends, she did suggest that lovers imagine themselves together in the future in ways that friends do not. In a letter to Sartre she contemplated: "The strength of a relation with somebody comes from the fact that you indicate yourselves together in the future . . . The connecting link: transcendence, future, activity of consciousness, reveals itself as profoundly true in the sentimental domain."[2]

However, there are mystifications that lead us astray on our quest for authentic relationships with lovers. Freeing ourselves from these snares—such as being beholden to our passions or having misplaced expectations of what love should be—is essential. Only then will we be free to love in authentically meaningful ways.

In *The Second Sex*, Beauvoir wrote, "Authentic love must be founded on reciprocal recognition of two freedoms."[3] Authentic loving is about recognizing one another's freedom, that is, acknowledging and respecting each other as individuals, and supporting one another's flourishing. Authentic lovers are generous toward each other and the universe. And they transcend together toward shared values and goals.

This is a unique picture of love, one quite different from the traditional understanding of romantic love that views it as finding a soulmate. Authentic loving has little to do with "finding" and much more to do with choosing. The ideal of love as a oneness or merging of two people who together would make up for one another's excesses and deficiencies can be traced back at least a couple of thousand years to Plato's *Symposium*.

One of Plato's characters, Aristophanes, is a tipsy comic and playwright who tells a wild story: humans used to be different sorts of creatures. We originally had two faces, four arms, and four legs. One day, some of them climbed Mount Olympus to challenge the gods. Zeus was deeply unimpressed and as punishment, he sliced every human into two. Since then, all humans are incomplete, unfulfilled—which explains the feeling of wholeness when we find "the one" and fall in love with our "soulmate" or "other half." This is why it sometimes feels like we can't live without our lover: because their absence cleaves our very being.

The soulmate idea is one of the most damning features of our culture's understanding of romantic love. It suggests we need another person to fulfill us, that there is one particular person who can do that, and that love is destined if we just keep our eyes and apps open. For Beauvoir, looking for love to complete us is bad faith. It's an escape from taking responsibility for pursuing our own fulfillment. Beauvoir realized she had been falling into this trap in her relationship with Sartre. The realization that she was becoming dependent on him to provide meaning in her life motivated her to write and she started with her novel *She Came to Stay*.[4]

Every person is a knotty synthesis of being and nothingness, meaning that we are made up of the past we drag behind us, our present actions and intentions, and our future possibilities. The future is a not-yet, a lack at the heart of our being, until death. Death, not love, completes us.

Our future possibilities mean that we will never *be* complete while alive, let alone complete another person. Any feeling of fulfillment is illusory and fleeting. We are not empty vessels that can be filled up with coins like slot machines in a casino, waiting for the winning love token to hit our jackpot. Nor are we static beings looking for a matching jigsaw puzzle piece.

A consequence of the existential idea that "existence precedes essence" is that there is no part of our being that's fixed and can match perfectly with another being. Even if people do click, there is no guarantee that their future selves would click. The human condition is an overcoming and stretching beyond ourselves, meaning that we are forever changing—including, sometimes, preferences and passions.

Another mystification about love is that it all boils down to biology. For example, in *The World As Will and Idea,* Schopenhauer proposed that love was a "voluptuous illusion" that tricks people into procreating. But such ideas don't explain why some people want to have sex without love, why some people who love each other don't want to have sex, or why some people are attracted to those with whom they cannot or do not want to procreate.

Some dating mixers are based on the idea that love is a matter of biology. For example, some dating sites give love-seekers sweaty T-shirts to sniff with the hope that pheromones will do the hard work of finding a mate.[5] New relationships are often euphoric and while pheromones may play a part in that—as can the initial spark of attraction based on looking at someone's profile picture online— neuroscientists have found that love molecules and hormones such as neurotrophins and cortisol skyrocket during the initial phase of a relationship, but they expire within around twenty-four months of starting a relationship.[6]

Dating apps thrive on the hope that a soulmate, a true love, is just a swipe away. Certainly, apps can be terrific for creating a new way of meeting people, especially those with specific tastes and preferences, but they are not a love hack. They don't make relationships easier to be in, and they cannot and should not make choices on our behalf.

In one of its more optimistic episodes called "Hang the DJ," the dystopian television series *Black Mirror* envisaged a dating world in which an app would be able to simulate years of dating heartache and come up with an "Ultimate Compatible Other." The love app runs relationship simulations until a love match conquers all obstacles in 998 out of 1,000 situations, giving participants a 99.8 percent probability of relationship "success" in real life. Still, in real life, the relationship is not guaranteed. The existential rub is that if people are free to be in a relationship, they are also free to leave.

Even if apps, pheromone sniffing, or asking thirty-six questions on a first date do help potential lovers find someone interesting, that's only the beginning of the challenge. Relationships are not just about finding and having a partner, relationships are a mode of being-*with*-others. Our companionships, the different ways of our being with others, shapes who we become.

Beauvoir learned this lesson, at least in part, from her reading of American transcendental author Louisa May Alcott's *Little Women*. The women in the novel knew, Beauvoir wrote, that the mind and morality matter more than money.[7] Beauvoir was especially taken with Jo March, whom Alcott marked as superior to her more beautiful and virtuous sisters. Beauvoir respected Jo for her vigorous, daring intelligence, and she identified avidly with Jo's bookishness. Jo inspired Beauvoir to write short stories.

In *Little Women*, which was based on Alcott's own life, the daughters have some choice in whom they can marry, but there is still huge pressure for them to marry, and for at least one of them to marry a wealthy man who will support the rest of the family. Women were rarely allowed to be independent, so love (as a path to marriage) was a key strategy to save themselves and their family from destitution.

Meg March's choice to marry a poor teacher for love is tolerated but frowned upon, as is Jo March's resistance to marriage. Amy March's impetuous marriage to Laurie, a wealthy man who is probably not in love with her, and whom Jo has already rejected, is deemed much more socially acceptable. Beauvoir initially hated Alcott for Amy's marriage but respected that Jo eventually marries a kind and smart man who understands her. Beauvoir thought it to be a travesty that anything but love should tie people together in matrimony. Beauvoir also wanted a superior individual for herself, which she believed she found in Sartre.

Passionate love has always been a feature of human relationships in western society, but up until a couple of hundred years ago, it usually was found outside of marriage. Most marriages prior to the Middle Ages were arranged. Courtly love started to change these dynamics. Troubadours wrote love songs and poems about their crushes' charms and knights jousted for air kisses and the handkerchiefs of ladies out of their league. The relationship was rarely consummated, but the fantasy fueled the idolization of love as a virtue.

Around the late eighteenth century, Romanticism with a capital "R" arrived. The Romantics were a group of artists, musicians, architects, poets, and philosophers who rebelled against the Enlightenment's obsession with rationality and science. The Romantics thought the Enlightenment's focus on reason and strict rules was boring. Instead, they celebrated passion, emotion, and sexual desire. Thus, the term *romantic* love was popularized and went mainstream.

The Romantics transformed the fantasy of courtly love into a reality. Love culminating in marriage recognized two lovers becoming one with each other, with nature, and with God. The ideal was that lovers' bodies and souls would merge into a spiritual unity in harmony with the divine order of the universe, creating an eternal bond. The fact that God was integrally involved bestowed religious legitimacy on love marriages.

Romanticism had already revived respect for individual allure and feelings, but capitalism (at least in theory) emphasized respect for individual rights and private decisions—such as choices about whom one can date and marry—and feminism fought against women being treated as property. The result is that many people are now freer than ever to choose and refuse relationships.

*   *   *

I grew up wanting to find the one, fall in love, and live happily ever after. One of my ex-boyfriends and I love-bombed each other with gifts, honeyed poems, and declarations of desire. But we often argued about "together time." He would say love meant prioritizing one another, which he understood as spending as much time together as possible. I disagreed if it meant always choosing him at the expense of friends, family, and work. I wanted more balance. I resented the pressure. He would say I didn't love him enough and that I was heartless, cruel, and afraid of commitment. Tensions would skyrocket. We would both get angry. At times, I felt in danger.

Once, I considered jumping out the window. It wasn't far to the garden below, so it would not have killed me. But I might have risked a broken ankle, and I didn't want to be dependent on him to take me to a hospital. A knight in shining armor was a role he would have relished and expected gratitude for in return.

We hovered, as if Hegel's master-slave dialectic were happening in real time, in a combat where each consciousness sees the other as a threat. I felt terrified and was desperate to escape. He said if I left, he would break up with me. He had threatened it so many times I had lost count and wished he meant it. I ran as if I had just freed myself from quicksand. He didn't chase me. I did not return.

At the time, I was just discovering Beauvoir's philosophy and was starting to learn about the dangers of passion when it spirals out of control. Passion tends to be viewed as a good thing, especially in love. Glossy magazines bombard their readers with articles about how to keep the passion alive. Passionate love can be romantic, especially in the early stages. Love can make you feel like you were made for each other and that your lover is the only one who can make you feel this way, like in Aristophanes's myth. But the problem with being overwhelmed by passion is that it reduces us to animalistic impulses. Beauvoir believed that humans are much more than systems of mechanical or chemical forces.

Initially I felt flattered by my boyfriend's attentions, but it became horrifying when our relationship choked on seriousness, possessiveness, and jealousy. Beauvoir suggested that passionate love can be tormenting because it sucks people away from the world, isolating them: "Any conversation, any relationship with the passionate man is impossible. In the eyes of those who desire a communion of freedom, he therefore appears as a stranger, an obstacle."[8]

Beauvoir argued that a person who is singularly and stubbornly focused on their passion—whether erotic, political, or other passion—risks partial nihilism. (If it were full nihilism, even their passion would not matter.) Passionate people easily slide into tyranny when they are frustrated with not being able to unite with their obsession. Passionate people become unbearable when they fail to recognize other people as ends in themselves, viewing them as means or obstacles to fulfill their obsession.

I was merely a conduit for my boyfriend's passion, strangled by his demands wanting to know exactly where I was whenever I wasn't with him, and sick of him trying to alienate me from my friends. I consider myself one of the lucky ones who was able to get out before tensions escalated further.

While the passionate person strives to control their world by possessing the object of their obsession, in reality they end up dependent on it. My boyfriend had become dependent on me for his happiness, which he thought would be sealed with our romantic union. The problem was that he defined the terms of our unity, which demanded my submissiveness, and he blamed me for not being able to achieve the romantic ideal, which is not an authentic version of love.

One can never truly possess another, and it's a violation to try. To do so treats the Other as an object instead of a freedom in themselves. Even if you possess someone physically, their consciousness always escapes you. This partially explains jealousy. In the metaphysical dream of unity, there is no room for a third person because it goes against everything that the classic ideal of love represents: that there are two people who, together in fulfilling each other's lack, make a whole.

This perspective is one of the foundations of monogamous marriage, and why affairs, at least in the United States, are considered among the worst kind of transgression. If being "cheated on" hurts so much, it is in part because it is a personal attack that implies, often mistakenly, that someone is at fault. A person who is cheated on may feel they are a failure because they are not able to fulfill the other's needs, or that they are unable to make good decisions in choosing who to love. Psychotherapist Esther Perel argued that while adultery for men has generally been tolerated, if not normalized, throughout history, it has become much more of an issue in the modern western zeitgeist because people are calling out the sexist double standards that have always excused adultery for men but not for women.[9]

By Beauvoir's definition of authentic love, my boyfriend and I failed astoundingly on many levels: He didn't recognize my freedom. His view of love as oneness demanded my submissiveness. I could not see how to be generous without feeling like I was being annexed into his life and compromising myself. We were unable to move beyond our power dynamics. There was a gulf between us in what we expected from love and from each other. We were unable to come to an agreement about how to construct values and goals in the world together. Demanding more than a lover is prepared to give, and giving more than a lover is prepared to receive, are both toxic for relationships.

In Beauvoir's view, passionate people are both admirable and horrifying. One can admire the pride with which the passionate person chases after the object of their obsession. And being the object of desire can feel special, prioritized before and against anyone or anything else. But my boyfriend was in love with loving. He idolized love, not me. (There was plenty in me to criticize, which he very often made abundantly clear to me.) Idolizing either love or a lover is bound to disappoint.

Beauvoir discussed the tendency for women to idolize men, and the desire to be rescued by a Prince Charming–style savior. She also noted the dangers of men idolizing women: instead of reducing women to objects, idolizing women exalts them as tools that might get men closer to an ideal, such as divinity. While devotion is held up as a virtue for both sexes, equated with being selfless and generous, devotion is most often embodied in the feminine ideal of submissiveness. The problem with loving devotion, as Beauvoir sees it, is that it can turn a relationship into a religion and turn the beloved into a god or goddess to which one voluntarily becomes a vassal.

At its extreme, the vassal of love gives up her own world and adopts her lover's friends, interests, and opinions in order to create a merged life. When the god transcends, so does she. It does not matter that the devotee is not a sovereign subject, because she feels necessary to someone who is, and that can make her feel fulfilled. The problem is that it's not really a shared life, but the life of the one who is worshipped.

In Beauvoir's novel *The Mandarins*, Paula is a glamorous singer who gives up her career for her boyfriend because she thinks her sacrifice is the highest expression of love. Henri is flattered and mildly objects. Later, Paula is infuriated when he ignores her advice and makes his own choices. Paula's view is that since she gave up her career, it is *their* life, not his. Paula also claims his successes: "It was I who made Henri. I created him as he creates characters in his books, and I know him as he knows them."[10] What began as a deeply passionate romance blazes with tyranny and resentment. Henri tires of it and leaves her for a younger woman.

Henri is certainly a jerk, and Paula might seem like an extreme case, but Beauvoir's warning is not to fall into the traps that Paula did. Paula was wrong to assume that sacrificing her career for him would mean that Henri would let her control his. Paula's behavior is a classic move in Hegel's master–slave dialectic: Paula enslaves herself to a reluctant master. With her demands that he accept her submission, she becomes a tyrant.[11] Paula tries to psychologically manipulate Henri, using her generosity as a weapon. She seeks to control him by making him feel guilty, like he owes her something in return for her devotion.

Fervent devotion such as Paula's fails Beauvoir's definition of authentic loving because subordinating oneself to another mutilates one's own freedom and is a cloaked violation of the other's freedom. On the flip side, passionate obsession subordinates the other's transcendence to one's own. While there's nothing wrong with loving generosity, these examples—my ex-boyfriend and me, Paula and Henri—show that overinvestment in relationships can be harmful. These strategies fail to recognize the other's freedom because they aim to have or own the Other instead of be with them. Authentic loving involves each person defining themselves and being responsible for themselves, relinquishing power games, being and treating each other as free and equal. "Love is then renunciation of all possession, of all confusion," Beauvoir wrote.[12]

And so, how can we relieve confusion? As a teenager, Beauvoir pondered in her diary that although it is instinctive for lovers to reach toward soulmateship, the realization that perfect unity is absurd enflames feelings of solitude. Later, she emphasized being better friends more than reaching toward oneness. Friendship means creating a relationship based on intersubjectivity, mutuality, equality, tenderness, affection, and a structure that the individuals in the relationship freely agree to. This means not treating each other as property. When lovers overcome power games, they open up the possibility of connecting more poignantly.

In Beauvoir's only play, *The Useless Mouths*, a medieval village in Belgium is under siege. Food supplies are running short. The village issues an order banishing all the women, children, old, and sick people from the town, so that the (male) soldiers have more food and water and can defend the village for longer. Exiling the so-called "useless mouths"—by the patriarchal, sexist military definition of it—would condemn the outcasts to torture, rape, slavery, or murder at the hands of the enemies blockading the village. Louis, the alderman, leads the charge. His wife, Catherine, is outraged:

LOUIS, *speaking in a low voice*: Catherine, my wife.
CATHERINE: No, not your wife. An instrument that one breaks and throws on the scrap-heap when one has finished with it . . . To die is nothing, but you have erased me from the world . . . you have disposed of me as just one more stone; and you are no more than this blind force that is crushing me.[13]

When Catherine tries to stab Louis, he realizes what an idiot he has been in treating people, including his wife, as disposable objects. It's disappointing that it took a near-death experience for him to see that, but still, Catherine's defiance equalizes and humanizes the relationship and establishes it as authentic. Louis changes the plan because he realizes that without people, there is no town worth defending. For Beauvoir, love's challenge is to hold oneself between being-for-oneself and being-for-lovers, to strive for a harmony between discordant extremes—a delicate harmony that is never a given but that we must constantly revivify.

Beauvoir did not want to be a role model. She said that it's ridiculous to use her relationship with Sartre as an ideal because people have to figure out their own arrangements and styles. Yet Beauvoir and Sartre did attempt to live their relationship in authentic ways. They prioritized each other within a diversified life of projects and friends. They respected each other's freedom, they supported each other; together they worked toward ends and values they believed would enrich the universe. They decided using their arrangement for sex would be a cheap use of their freedom, so they "gave" each other the freedom to love others.

However, their open relationship created chaos and heartbreak—mostly for other lovers who wanted more than Beauvoir and Sartre were willing to give. In the aftermath of their relationships with Beauvoir and Sartre, Evelyne Rey died of suicide at age thirty-six; Bianca Bienenfeld had a nervous breakdown; and many others were heartbroken. After Nelson Algren and Beauvoir broke up, he wrote about it in *Harper's Magazine*, pointing out the callousness of Beauvoir and Sartre's pact: "Anybody who can experience love contingently has a mind that has recently snapped. How can love be *contingent*? Contingent upon *what*?"[14]

Sometimes Beauvoir and Sartre's lovers were also their students. As far as we know, the students were over the age of consent in France at the time. But some critics argue, and rightly so, that Beauvoir and Sartre's behavior was an abuse of power, a pedagogical failure, and ethically problematic.[15] Beauvoir and Sartre's habits were also authentically problematic. Although they recognized their secondary lovers' freedoms, it didn't seem to occur to them that they weren't creating values and ends together with their contingent lovers. Beauvoir and Sartre's values were already established and they imposed those values on others who could take them or leave them. The secondary lovers never had the power to evolve or adapt values with Beauvoir and Sartre. This means that Beauvoir and Sartre's fixed pact to love one another precluded authentic relationships with their contingent lovers. A more flexible pact that accommodated change and growth could have created possibilities for multiple authentic relationships.

Later Beauvoir acknowledged wrongdoing and that she and Sartre hurt others: "So our relationship is not above criticism, any more than anyone else's, because it has sometimes meant that we didn't behave very well toward other people."[16] She felt remorseful for Bianca Bienenfeld's suffering and in a letter to Sartre wrote, "It's our fault I think . . . we have harmed her."[17] In a memoir, Beauvoir admitted that her pact with Sartre—to be primary lovers to one another but also to have contingent lovers—was a defect in their system because their secondary lovers suffered.[18] Sartre seemed to be void of any sense of responsibility or remorse.

With one another, however, Beauvoir and Sartre were generally tender, happy, trusting, and (mostly) transparent. Although they disagreed on some points—like radical freedom—they agreed on important matters and profoundly encouraged and influenced each other. They never lived together so, for the most part, they were free from traditional gender roles and domestic sterility. They read and critiqued each other's work, developed thoughts together, and made decisions together.

While freedom was central to their relationship and they exercised it, authentic relationships need not insist on absolute freedom for the sake of it. Beauvoir was advocating for neither libertinism nor hedonism. Yet there are principles in their approach that are worth considering: agreeing to the terms of relationships jointly, reflecting on traditions and customs such as monogamy and the meaning of togetherness, and asking what's important for the people who are living the relationship. Yet Beauvoir and Sartre were more careful with asking this latter question of one another than those in their wider orbit of love.

At first glance, Beauvoir's approach to love might seem callous and cold because it doesn't account for what happens when one of the people in the relationship isn't capable of absolute freedom—such as when one's partner gets sick—and can't reciprocate. This is a misunderstanding because it focuses on *what* lovers do instead of *how* they love.

For example, at the end of Sartre's life, he was unable to care for himself, so Beauvoir and her closest friends rallied to support him. This was not a violation of Beauvoir's philosophy because she does not demand reciprocity of the exact same actions. The problem arises when people disrespect each other, take advantage of one another's generosity or disability, or infringe upon the capacity that the other does have to make free choices. Beauvoir didn't turn herself into a submissive woman to try to manipulate Sartre.

Nevertheless, there were moments in their relationship that might have violated her philosophy. During World War II, Beauvoir took on more domestic chores like grocery shopping and cooking for both of them because the only thing Sartre would cook was fried eggs. (Apparently, Sartre did not care to learn more.) When the doctors told Sartre to stop drinking because of his deteriorating health, he refused. Beauvoir watered down his whiskey and prevented friends from sneaking bottles to him, overriding his freedom to drink as he pleased.

Yet, care and generosity are implicit in Beauvoir's notion of authentic loving. The question is: What would you do for a dear friend in need? If you are sick with a potentially lethal condition and your partner cares for you and brings you soup, that doesn't mean either of you are violating the other's freedom. Reciprocity doesn't demand that you drag yourself out of bed to make your partner soup in return, although it does mean that you would do something similar for them if the situations were reversed. If not, that's a red flag.

Beauvoir and Sartre spent time apart, met with friends separately as well as together, and had their own activities. Beauvoir, for example, loved to hike but Sartre couldn't stand the outdoors. Beauvoir was, for a time, financially dependent on Sartre while she wrote one of her books, but she could have found a job if she needed to, and it was part and parcel of their agreement to share everything. She did the same for Sartre when he needed it. Both Beauvoir and Sartre financially supported many of their friends.

Much is said about Beauvoir's relationship with Sartre that it tends to overshadow all of Beauvoir's other romances. It shouldn't. Beauvoir found inspiration for authentic loving in her relationships with other men including author Nelson Algren, journalist Jacques-Laurent Bost, and filmmaker Claude Lanzmann. She also found inspiration in her relationships with women. Although Beauvoir denied she had sexual relationships with women, she also said she had closely physical relationships with them that were not erotic *for her*—although that clarification suggests that they might have been erotic for the other women involved.

Beauvoir also said that she could not give a frank and sincere account of her sexuality because her "confession" would involve other people close to her who would be hurt. Beauvoir's novels include accounts of sexual relationships between female characters, and in an interview she suggested that women have homosexual tendencies because women are more desirable, nicer, less egoistic, and have softer, nicer skin, than men.[19]

Another advantage of same-sex relationships that Beauvoir found was that although the participants are still often discriminated against (in 2019, homosexuality was illegal in more than seventy countries), the fact that such relationships have always been taboo has, in some ways, freed people from predefined relationship rules, customs, and conventions such as marriage, and freed them to create relationships on their own terms—although, of course, many would have preferred the same rights as heterosexual people.[20]

The lack of structure of same-sex relationships, Beauvoir believed, provides an opportunity for more sincerity, closeness, intimacy, with fewer secrets and power struggles. The absence of a social script can also open up opportunities for more collaborative, thoughtful, reciprocal relationships—and yet she also acknowledged that same-sex relationships can entail power struggles, dishonesty, and conformity.

* * *

Being-with-others is an essential part of living authentically, but it is not always the case that we have to fall in love or partner up to do it. Romantic love is not necessary to live authentically. Some people identify as aromantic, asexual, or opt out of sensual relationships entirely, finding more meaningful connections with friends, family, and pets.

In 2019 actor Emma Watson announced that she's "self-partnered" and very happy. The rapper Lizzo, too, is empowering single-positivity when she sings about loving herself, the value of friendship, not tolerating bad relationships, and not relying on anyone but herself for her sense of self-worth and validation. My friend Lucy is very happily alone with her rescue animals and the mere thought of anyone touching her with more than a friendly hug makes her shudder.

But the dominant narrative in the western world still perpetuates the Hollywood cliché that love will complete us, that love is everything, and that there's a soulmate out there if only we're lucky enough to find them. Even if you don't buy into "The One" or the "perfect match" or the "happily ever after" Disney model of love, the idea of finding a unity with another so as never to be lonely again, or at least someone to grow old with, can sound alluring. It is easy to get clogged up with commodified mystifications—or as Emma Watson puts it, the "bloody influx of subliminal messaging"—about how love should be.[21]

Still, there is no reason to write off sexual loving altogether. Beauvoir pointed to the emotional intoxication of sexual love that can liberate lovers from themselves and allow them to become more aware of the other, dissolving the boundaries between each other, creating a type of understanding that paradoxically gives the feeling *as if* they are one. Elevated above the battlefield of power games, lovers can surpass themselves instead of abdicating freedom, generously offering up their bodies to one another as they explore the limits of their being, freely exchanging without losing themselves.

Sex can be great, but so are a bunch of other ways to meaningfully and deeply collaborate, which can be just as great or greater. My friend Sabina says that one of the most meaningful connections she has is when she and her partner read a book together in the evenings while sipping wine and whiskey. In their book club *à deux*, they talk about each other's impressions, being respectful of one another's opinions—and they laugh a lot. The intellectual intoxication—of becoming aware of their sameness and differences in thinking and attitudes—helps them to understand more about each other, themselves, and their world. Their book club discussions create a sort of intersubjective communication, based on reciprocity and collaboration, without the need for one of them to be right, to be smarter, or to "win" or dominate their discussion.

Authentic relationships channel power in healthy ways, such as into cooperating, motivating, and exploring.[22] These relationships involve being generous—by which Beauvoir means that each person gives their all but feels like it costs them nothing. Each person trusts, appreciates, and respects one another as autonomous individuals who freely choose to be together, and together they constantly reassess that choice. They share lives but do not make the relationship all-consuming.

Romantic love is complicated, to be sure—it can be hard to know how to start a relationship and with whom. And once a potential partner is found, we can't know, beyond all doubt, what they are really thinking, what they want out of the relationship, what their intentions are, or how long the relationship might last. It's understandable that people want to secure it, to create a oneness, to merge into an organic whole like in Aristophanes's tale.

The challenge is to consider: If we shed the sediment of history and social expectations that cling to us, how would we love? What if we all developed a healthy skepticism of the dogma of traditional relationship scripts and freed ourselves from the impulse to cling to certainty? Some might argue that chaos would ensue, but Beauvoir shows us that the benefit of creating relationships on our own terms would be more authentic relationships and enrichment of the universe. There would be less disappointment about not achieving clichéd ideals, less violence, and less wanting to jump out of windows. The focus would turn away from power struggles and toward constructing the world together.

Beauvoir shows us that authentic loving calls lovers to accept uncertainty and separation as the very condition of a relationship. And even better than acceptance is to look for joy in the distance, to welcome and to love the ambiguity, the otherness, and the freedom. The quest for authenticity calls for realizing that a romantic union with an other half is absurd: it calls for loving the ways that the other is different from and separate to us. Authentic loving is not about leaving relationships to fate. Authentic loving is an active engagement, a choice to create a relationship together.

*   *   *

My now-partner plays a team sport, and early in our relationship I would be jealous of the time he would spend with his team instead of me. Some girlfriends gave their partners ultimatums: them or the sport. Sport often won. I was torn because I did not want to give ultimatums and wanted to be supportive of his passions, but also I found waiting on the sidelines to be boring.

It was not until I read Beauvoir's philosophy that I figured out how to cope: while he played sport, I embarked on my own quests. I caught up with friends, went on yoga retreats, read books, and worked on my PhD. Sometimes I backpacked and got lost in new places. Coming to terms with the fact that my partner had other priorities was emotionally taxing; I had to stop myself falling into the trap that one of my ex-boyfriends did. I strove to tame my desire to be his top priority and resisted thinking that if I was not, he did not love me. Giving him the freedom to pursue his goals challenged me to exercise my freedom. While there are many temptations to imprison each other in love, an authentic relationship embraces the tension between being-for-oneself and being-with a lover. The ideal is to have relationships within a balanced life of activities that you do together and apart.

Beauvoir did not give many examples of authentic relationships— partly because it is up to lovers to work it out themselves. Relationships will be different for everyone at different times in their lives. Still, she shared a few clues in her analysis of Stendhal, a romantic humanist who wrote about authentic heroines.

Stendhal has his flaws, since his heroines forget themselves in love, and he admires and desires feminine devotion. Yet what

Beauvoir takes from Stendhal for her view of authentic loving is the notion that individuals who respect one another's freedom will be able to live and love fully and adventurously.[23] The women Stendhal loves and exalts in his novels are intelligent, cultivated, and equal to men. They are subjects in and of themselves with their own futures and interests, and do not depend entirely on men. In *The Red and the Black*, Mathilde de la Mole scorns society; Madame de Rênal is generous, genuine, and critical of her milieu. Stendhal's authentic characters reciprocally recognize one another in love and their lives are better and more exciting for it.

Beauvoir also pointed to the actress Brigitte Bardot (Beauvoir refers to her by her nickname "BB") as a transcending sovereign subject free from oppression. Bardot was famous for her beauty and unabashed sexuality and was a noted sex symbol in the 1950s and 60s. In Beauvoir's portrait, BB is an über-authentic passionate being. She is financially independent. Loving is one interest among many. She affirms sexual equality because she is autonomous, emancipated, rejects social conventions, and defies myths of femininity. Almost anything seems possible for her. BB shows that you can be authentic and have fun, and that there can be playful possibilities in power struggles. Beauvoir wrote of BB: "In the game of love, she is as much a hunter as she is a prey. The male is an object to her, just as she is to him."[24]

Authentic loving involves recognizing each other as free and acting that way. Being too serious and hijacking a lover's freedom is antithetical to authentic love. But as Beauvoir's analysis of BB showed, authenticity doesn't mean you can't be playful in sexual relationships—as long as consenting people behave in constructive ways. Even BDSM relationships can be authentic as long as the people in the relationship engage on terms that they freely agree to, without exploitation, and can walk away from it or change their mind without penalty.

Authentic lovers pursue their personal projects, and also respect and support each other in their individual quests. Being supportive in this sense means tackling the world together and opening up possibilities for each other. Supportiveness is about standing side-by-side instead of head-to-head. Authentic loving is not easy and it is up to each person in a relationship to work it out together—or walk away if need be. But authentic loving is possible and it's worth it. And, Beauvoir wrote, "Our lot is to take the risk and the anguish. But why should we hope to be at peace?"[25]

Love is neither destined nor found, but created. The trouble is that people often want to turn this free creation into marriage, which is neither free nor particularly creative. Marriage comes with a whole new set of pitfalls, especially when people join together in weakness and greed instead of strength and generosity.[26] There are possibilities for authenticity within marriage, but it requires an upheaval in the way that people approach an institution that has deep and prolific roots across time and cultures.

MARRIAGE

It is said marriage diminishes man: it is often true;
but it almost always destroys woman.
                                          —The Second Sex

One drink was not enough for the predicament I had found myself in. A bar in Brooklyn. A brightly lit back room overlooking the beer garden. I was teaching "The Philosophy of Marriage," a two-hour continuing education salon-style class. Barely had I finished by asking, "What questions . . ." when a hand in the front row shot up like it wanted to skewer the moon.

"Everything you've said is meaningless. Marriage works. It has worked for a very long time," the student insisted. He was tall and his electric white hair was as luminescent as the lights overhead. Even though I was standing and he was sitting, it felt as if it were the other way around. I was afraid of public speaking and of being put on the spot. Having watched my parents' marriage end in a bitter divorce just a few years beforehand, I found marriage tough to talk about.

"Marriage is not working for a lot of people," I replied. In the United States, around half of adults are marrying, and barely half of those make it to their thirty-year pearl anniversary.[1] And that says nothing about how many people are tolerating unhappy marriages, or marriages that continue out of habit, apathy, fear of being alone, fear of being poorer, or simply fear of the uncertainty about what lies on the other side of separation.

The traditional "till death do us part" model that defines marriage in terms of submission, obedience, housework, and dutiful sex is a killer for authentic relationships. Yet traditional marriage remains such a closely cherished tradition that challenging it provokes people's ire, as with the student in my class.

"Why marry?" I asked the class, which was made up of men and women, from millennials to boomers, relationship status unknown. The most overwhelming response was commitment, which is surprising seeing as people can still commit to a relationship without getting married. What is it exactly about marriage that makes commitment seem more tangible?

Commitment in existential thought is complex. On the one hand, freedom is central to living authentically. Marriage, Beauvoir wrote in her teens, is immoral because it locks one's future being into a definitive course of action.[2] Commitment is a problem, not only because one may be mistaken, but also promising is a voluntary restriction on your freedom. To make a choice that commits your being for the rest of your life is absurd, because how can you commit a future self that will grow and change and may want something or someone else in the future? How can you know when you marry someone if you are still going to be able to tolerate them next week, let alone in thirty years?

Nevertheless, being completely free from commitments is problematic too. Our commitments define who we become. In Beauvoir's play *The Useless Mouths*, Jean-Pierre, an adopted son in love with his sister Clarice, declares that "All commitment is a prison."[3] He uses this mantra as a pretext to disengage from living, as an excuse for political and romantic apathy. He shies away from a relationship with Clarice, lest his love for her stifle his freedom. Disgusted with his village's oppressive government and in an effort to keep his hands clean, he refuses a prestigious role with the council.

Later, Jean-Pierre discovers that the council has branded Clarice a "useless mouth"—along with all women, children, sick, and old people—and is going to exile them from the village, where they will surely be raped, enslaved, or murdered. This situation is a consequence of his apathy. If he had taken the council job he could have stopped the decree. He realizes his mistake:

> JEAN-PIERRE: . . . I can't bear to live if you are dead. I love you, Clarice.
> CLARICE: Yesterday you said that that word had no meaning.
> JEAN-PIERRE: Was it yesterday? It seems so far away to me now!
> CLARICE: It *was* yesterday, and you didn't love me.
> JEAN-PIERRE: I didn't dare to love you because I didn't dare to live. This earth seemed impure to me and I didn't want to sully myself. What stupid pride.
> CLARICE: Does it seem purer to you today?[4]

Jean-Pierre realizes that in failing to commit himself to action and to love, he is being a coward, and that his silence makes him complicit in the pending carnage of Clarice and other citizens. Together Jean-Pierre and Clarice campaign to change the council's strategy. They succeed, and instead of expelling the so-called "useless mouths," the council arms everyone. Everyone fights to protect their village together.

The message of Beauvoir's play is that although we don't know who we will be, what we will want in the future, or how our commitments will work out, we must commit to action anyway. In an early diary, Beauvoir conjectured, "One must create a sort of abstract self and say to oneself: this is the state in which I find myself the most often; this is what I want the most often; thus, this is what suits me."[5]

But all too often, marriage ends up being more of a struggle against one another, and less of a collaboration. Beauvoir saw marriage as being like a lottery, and although this might seem overly bleak at first, the sentiment is true: marriage "success"—given that divorce statistics trend not far from fifty percent—comes down to the flip of a coin. Part of the reason for Beauvoir's pessimism is that she believed marriage to be one of the starkest manifestations of Hegel's dialectic (a situation where two consciousnesses meet, they struggle for dominance, and if one overpowers the Other, they enter into a master–slave relationship). For Hegel, the way out is a mature loving unity consisting of a synthesis in which "each separate lover is one organ in a living whole."[6] For Beauvoir, the way out is authentic loving.

*   *   *

Women have, historically, agreed to their subjugation to husbands because it solves some problems of how to survive financially and socially. Until recently, for most women the choice not to marry meant poverty, being cast as a social pariah, and taking on low-paid and dead-ends jobs that were not nearly as lucrative as those available to men. Technically, we always have choices, but the context in which we make choices matters. Yes, many women have been complicit in their own subjugation, but when the alternative puts your very survival at risk, it is not a fair choice.

While commitment was the most popular theme in my philosophy of marriage class, love, stability, health insurance, acceptance, visas, and taxes followed close behind. Sex, family, friendship, and children also featured. Indeed, there are lots of benefits to marriage: economic, social, moral, and psychological.

Government incentives—such as spousal access to health insurance and social security, and lower taxes—lure people into marriage. Over one thousand federal laws in the United States benefit married couples.[7] Singles miss out on those economic benefits and are also lumped with social stigmas: bachelors and spinsters are sometimes viewed with suspicion—although sometimes it is envy. While some people are rewarded for conforming into marriage, others are discouraged or banned from it if their relationship does not fit into the traditional cisgender heterosexual model.

One of the key principles underpinning traditional marriage is to regulate who has sex with whom, although in practice it has mostly meant controlling with whom women have sex. Aristotle, sexist philosopher extraordinaire, purported that because humans come from one man and one woman, it is only natural to build human society around a heterosexual nuclear family. Aristotle was also a fan of arranged marriages because, he thought, the primary goal of a human is to procreate, and you do not need to like—let alone love—the person you are doing that with.

Aristotle was right that it is crazy to want to build a lifelong commitment based on sex and sentimentality, but his appeal to nature is deeply flawed. He claims that males are "by nature fitter for command than the female," and "the courage of a man is shown in commanding, of a woman in obeying," and that women's silence is glorious, but a man's isn't.[8] Beauvoir rightly noted that this is garbage: there is no such thing as feminine or masculine nature; this is a lie perpetuated to keep women in their place.[9] It says more about women's situation, and about who claims and concedes power in certain circumstances, than it does about which sex has an allegedly natural tendency for bossiness.

The traditional concept of marriage is that husbands provide guidance, protection, and financial resources to wives, and wives provide homemaking, childrearing, and sexual services to their husbands. In the western world, and increasingly elsewhere, marriage has become the pinnacle of the romantic ideal. In one of Beauvoir's novels, Jean proposes to Hélène and it means everything to her: "She no longer had a feeling of emptiness inside her, or of uncertainty. She no longer wondered where she should go or what good it was staying there. It was as if there were a special place assigned to her on earth, and that she exactly fitted into it."[10]

Marriage can make people feel fulfilled because it is a concrete realization of two individuals intertwining their lives into one. Love marriages—as opposed to pragmatic ones—are supposed to cultivate tenderness, respect, and intimacy, although it is not the only relationship that can provide these. The institution is supposed to provide insurance against the failure of love because, theoretically, it is a sacred permanent bond in which lovers promise that the relationship will endure even if feelings change. This is why Beauvoir said that conjugal love is not really love, since if it was love, you wouldn't need the qualification. What's left, at best, is companionship and cohabitation.[11]

One of the stories in Beauvoir's *The Woman Destroyed* chronicles the slow and excruciating marital and emotional breakdown of the character Monique after she discovers her husband is having an affair. Her daughter Lucienne tells her: "But, Mama, after fifteen years of marriage it is perfectly natural to stop loving one's wife. It's the other thing that would be astonishing!"[12] Monique protests that lots of spouses love one another their whole lives. Lucienne says that they only pretend to.

This portrait is overgeneralized, since many married couples do love each other. Moreover, the fact that feelings change is why marriage can foster a sense of stability amid the tsunamis of romantic passion and uncertainty about the future. Marriage can be a strong panacea for loneliness, giving people a sense of dignity and validation. To be supported by someone who resolves to do so every single day for the rest of their lives can be deeply gratifying. Beauvoir contends that marriage often represents the concrete manifestation of happiness. It can provide a home to which people retreat, where they find sanctuary from the outside world—somewhere to belong, to settle and be settled.

The foundation of inequality in marriage persists because there is still on average an imbalance of power when it comes to careers, childcare, and chores. Laws in the western world have moved further toward achieving equal rights, but more women than men take off-ramps from their career path to look after children, hindering their career progression, potential salary earnings, and wiping out great chunks of their retirement savings—over \$1 million per woman by some estimates.[13] All this makes it easy for spouses to slip into traditional gender roles, whereby it is assumed that when babies are born the woman will put her career on hold, if not give it up entirely, to care for offspring at home. This domestic work is often seen as less important or not in the same category as paid work.

While many women of working-class families have worked tirelessly in the labor force, the narrative of traditional middle- and upper-class heterosexual marriage is that if wives devote themselves to the chaste virtuous role of domestic goddess then happiness and fulfillment will follow. But the fairytale merely serves to encourage women's passive absorption into the home and bedroom, so that they are better able to service their husband's wishes.

Beauvoir recognized that this exchange traps everyone, and has formed people's identities for millennia.[14] Women are subjugated to men and men are subjugated to society because men are channeled into the role of financial provider and pushed to succeed economically. Because women's work was so rarely paid or appreciated, women's success in life depended on their husband's success, and so women were encouraged to catch the best prospect they could, making marriage a relationship founded on manipulation, seduction, and flattery.

Marriage has, of course, evolved. Legal, medical, and social developments such as no-fault divorce, *Obergefell v. Hodges*—the United States Supreme Court case that legalized same-sex marriages—women's participation in the labor force, and the availability of contraception and abortion mean that people are no longer compelled to stay in unfulfilling marriages.

A woman's social validation and financial well-being no longer rest entirely on whether and to whom she is married. Living alone is less stigmatized. Women have better access to careers—although there are still structural issues—and some married couples are sharing financial and caregiving roles.

However, in many heterosexual marriages, women assume all of the roles, as both a full-time income earner and full-time homemaker. The roles of women as givers and men as the takers is sticking firm.[15] Same-sex marriages are also at risk of falling into the same dominant and subservient roles, along with issues such as navigating hostile political climates, from bakeries refusing to make same-sex wedding cakes to health insurance policies that don't cover same-sex partners.

The central issue with any kind of marriage is when the commitment pressures people to sacrifice their transcendence. This is the most dangerous aspect of marriage: it can put not only a person's independence at risk, but also their personhood. Marriage's monotony and vacuity can be metaphysically mutilating, cramping people's freedom. Marriage tends to be a good deal for husbands because when wives take care of the lion's share of boring, generic chores, it frees husbands up to pursue their own goals, through work or leisure activities. While many women do work and are financially independent, the amount of housework on top of paid work is unrelenting.

* * *

Women still plan, manage, and do the majority of routine housework, especially after marriage.[16] When many people worked from home during the COVID-19 pandemic, women's invisible labor—such as housework and childcare—did not become more visible and encourage more equal allocation of tasks.[17] Of course, single people do housework too, but in partnerships with mixed-sex couples, on average, women spend almost twice as many hours per week as men on housework.[18]

For Beauvoir, housework is futile because it is endless: as soon as you are done with the laundry, there's inevitably more to wash just moments later. There's no reward, there is little (if any) thanks, and it is exhausting. Beauvoir argued that housework is a negative activity because there is no victory and it does not create anything of value. Housework is like showering and going to the bathroom: it's a generic, immanent function of life. One might counter that there are many creations that do not last—a chef's meal, a theatre act, or a literary offering to the Temple at Burning Man. But housework is different because it is what Beauvoir in *The Second Sex* calls a Manichean undertaking, a constant battle between cleanliness and filth, where purity can only be created by exorcising every last bit of dirt.

Dirt devils and dust bunnies are pervasive demons that can never be truly conquered. They are temporarily overcome, but are inescapably reincarnated. Every day the battle begins anew with dirty dishes, smelly clothes, and meals to be planned and prepared. Every living moment brings with it a new ambush of decay and as long as there's life, there's no way to stop it.

There's little glory in housework. There is no calling to a greater good. Anyone who takes joy in this battle day in, day out, Beauvoir suggests, must be a sad, perhaps even angry, sadomasochist (although more masochist I suspect) because their will to power is over an enemy that cannot be dominated.[19] The fact that many women work outside the home just exacerbates the injustice.

When I tweeted an article about how much more housework women are doing than men, men flocked to tell me that women should just stop doing so much. There may be a modicum of truth to this irksome response, as long as everyone does their fair share and stops holding men and women to different standards. Beauvoir proposed that because it has always been a woman's job to do the housework, some women are reluctant to let it slide and are plagued with guilt if their home ends up in a state that they would be ashamed for others to see. Indeed, empirical evidence suggests that women are held more accountable for cleanliness than men.[20]

Beauvoir posited that one of the consequences of such harsh gazes is that women are widely expected to take on more responsibility for the domestic grind and internalize these expectations of what it means to be a "real woman."[21] By "real" woman, Beauvoir means the traditional male-constructed concept of the ideal woman who does as men tell her and doesn't complain about it. Many men are happy to let women do the bulk of housework because few people enjoy doing monotonous chores day after day after day. Tradition clings tightly to everyone. The reality is that someone has to do the basic maintenance of life, and all too often women pay the price to keep the harmony and judgmental gazes at bay.

One might argue that living in a more or less filth-free state and with sustenance is essential to life and there is great value in a clean and pleasant home. This is true, but it can be hard to know where obsessiveness and negligence start and stop. Patricia Hill Collins highlighted advantages that Beauvoir did not: while unpaid family labor is onerous, it can also be empowering for some Black women—even a form of rebellion—when they are in a position to strengthen family bonds, to nurture children, and to teach them how to survive in a hostile world.[22]

While Beauvoir was right that housework is often a bore, she underappreciated that the attitude with which we approach it is critical: chores have the potential to be transformed into a shared positive endeavor, such as when people who make the mess together clean it up while striving to improve their efficiency and free up time for other fun. My friend, the philosopher Gary Cox, told me that he treats housework as a possibility for growth: "I do most of the cleaning and tidying and treat it as a workout. I can sort my head out by tidying my immediate environment. I'm always trying to improve efficiency. Work out a quicker method, arrangement, and so on, all to save time for writing and cycling."

* * *

In traditional marriages, in addition to housework there is another routine expectation: regular sex. Beauvoir was one of a long line of women philosophers to suggest that marriage is equivalent to state-sanctioned prostitution. Mary Wollstonecraft was an advocate of marriage but argued that women need to be educated and allowed to work so they do not have to sell their bodies to marriage or on the streets.[23]

Others have proposed that prostitution is a more dignified pursuit than marriage since it is more honest and fair about the nature of the exchange. The medieval French philosopher Héloïse thought so. There are different versions of her story, but what we do know is that Héloïse and her tutor, Peter Abelard, fell in love. She became pregnant and married him despite her deep reluctance. At some point, Héloïse's uncle castrated Abelard. Reasons for the emasculation are unclear, but it's not hard to imagine how salty Héloïse's family would have been upon discovering that the teacher impregnated her and secretly married her.

Abelard's gelding mortified him. He withdrew to a monastery. Héloïse accused Abelard of breaking their friendship, but they stayed in touch through letters. Héloïse said she would much prefer to be his concubine than his wife because she resented the idea that marriage binds people together regardless of whether they love one another.[24] They had envisaged an equal partnership based on an intellectual and sexual friendship and appreciation of one other's virtues. Héloïse's vision is a good example of authentic relationships: Héloïse and Abelard were loving and sensual but not bound by a contract.

There are many contradictory tropes about women's sexual appetites, such as that women are naturally or biologically less interested in sex or that marriage is the only way to discipline female eroticism. Beauvoir rightly argued that we would do better to look at the ways marriage strips away sensuality. Sex is built deep into the foundations of marriage. Sex was the original justification for marriage. Marriage turns sex into an obligation. The perception that anyone has a duty to provide sex, or a right to take sex, is obscene because it turns bodies into machines.[25] Instead of upsurges of passion, spouses are left with another chore on the never-ending mudslide of duties.

Conjugal sex ends up being a form of "mutual masturbation," Beauvoir postulated, because spouses use one another's bodies as tools.[26] While I would suggest that mutual masturbation can be extremely nice, Beauvoir's point is that conjugal sex easily slides into the opposite of sexy. Some accept the instrumental relationship or the dry spells out of politeness, awkwardness, or embarrassment. Some put it down to sexual dysfunction and run to doctors for Viagra and flibanserin, or to orgasm workshops to learn new techniques, or to marriage counselors hoping to respark the fire or to learn to adapt to the disappointment. Others turn to porn or affairs. But there is no secret climaxing technique or magic number of orgasms per week that is going to guarantee healthy sex in marriage. Sexual desire is a much broader and more complex phenomenon than that. Desire is both physical and psychological. Beauvoir proposed that situation matters with marriage too, and traditional marriage is not conducive to women's erotic flourishing.[27]

Even when women are independent and the relationship is based on mutual respect, there still can be a gap between marriage and eroticism because the other person is always there, whether you like it or not. There is little space for missing and yearning. It can be lovely to see someone every day and to foster deep familiarity and practical intimacy. But familiarity can just as easily kill emotional and psychological intimacy.

* * *

Since the institution of marriage is so saturated with injustice, dependencies, and disempowerment, why don't we do away with it altogether?[28] As a teenager, Beauvoir hoped to get married some day and expected it to be the pinnacle of happiness.[29] But she soon changed her mind. She never married, despite both Sartre and the Chicago writer Nelson Algren proposing to her, and despite often referring to each of them as her husband and herself as their wife. She turned Sartre down because, although it would have been convenient and they would have been posted to the same area of France for teaching, she worried he would end up resenting her. In a letter to Algren in 1947, she wrote, "I really think marriage is a rotten institution and when you love a man, don't spoil everything by marrying him."[30] But she would not leave Sartre or Paris, so it was spoiled anyway.

Even though Beauvoir rejected marriage, she still came to a marriage-like agreement with Sartre. They jokingly asserted their relationship as a "morganatic marriage," and would caricature traditional couples. They would dress up and go out, masquerading as American millionaires named "Mr. and Mrs. Morgan Hattick," or sometimes as an impoverished couple named "Monsieur and Madame M. Organatique, unambitious, easily satisfied, not very well off."[31]

In their parodies, they asserted the reality of their commitment and underscored their freedom from the conformity of most marriages. The difference between traditional marriages and theirs was that Beauvoir and Sartre never cohabitated, but were always essential to one another, no matter who else they loved.[32] Children might have swayed Beauvoir's decision about marriage, but ultimately she decided that procreating would distract her from writing, and could find no good reason to bring another person into the world.[33]

Even if spouses are financially independent, marriage invites participants to take one another for granted. If spouses do love one another it is usually in spite of marriage and not because of it. The problem, as Beauvoir saw it, is that we confuse assuming with loving. To assume a marriage is to live it in its immediacy, that is, unreflectively. Unreflective relationships have little value. You can't love someone authentically if you don't have a choice in being with them. The bedrock of most marriages is their consistency, their constancy—which is an anathema to what Beauvoir thought was critical to living an authentic life. Authentic living calls for holding ourselves and the world around us in question, including institutions of marriage as well as governments, policies, laws, and injustices, for example.

In Beauvoir's novel *Les Belles Images*, meaning "beautiful pictures," Laurence is an immaculately brought up young woman who marries a husband who seems ideal. She becomes an impeccably successful advertising executive, has two beautiful daughters, and after ten years of marriage with good sex, safety, peace, and a fiery eighteen-month affair, she's perfectly bored with her perfect middle-class life set carefully in an aspic of habits. She wonders,

> Why one man rather than another? It was odd. You find yourself involved with a fellow for life just because he was the one you met when you were nineteen . . . she was amazed that something so important should depend upon mere chance. No particular reason about it. (But everything was like that.) These stories of twin souls—were they ever to be found outside books?[34]

Growing up, Laurence thought she was freely choosing her life, but she comes to realize that most of her existence was already laid out for her. Living feels like sliding along rails because her life trajectory is so similar to everyone else's. Spouses ask the same questions, they have the same problems, the same arguments, the same conversations, and even when arguments seem new, they are usually just a different iteration of the same issue. "People are so very interchangeable, you know," Laurence says to her lover Lucien, who is so appalled that he wants to hit her.[35]

Nevertheless, there can be value in marriage. It has been ubiquitous amongst human societies in some form or another, although the rules and norms have varied drastically. Marriage has not always been between a man and a woman, nor has it always been a lifelong arrangement. Marriage has not always involved love, sex, cohabitation, financial cooperation, property, or the state. Nor has marriage always been between whole, living beings either.

In Chinese and Sudanese ghost marriages, one of the partners is dead, but the wedding tradition brings living people together. In Pacific Northwest societies, such as the Bella Coola and the Kwakiutl, if families wanted to trade but there was not anyone to marry, they would wed a dog or another person's foot.[36] Now, people are marrying the Statue of Liberty, Eiffel Tower, train stations, roller-coasters, and anime holograms. A woman who married her truck says the sex life is great. (Marriages to inanimate objects do not appear to be legally binding at the time of writing this.)

One alternative to traditional marriage is a temporary commitment. By this I mean intentionally temporary, not temporary by virtue of divorce. Early in their relationship, Beauvoir and Sartre agreed to a two-year commitment, on a stone bench by the Louvre. While it was neither state-sanctioned nor enforceable, the psychological contract was strong. They wanted intimacy and freedom without the risk of decay into duties and inertia.

Beauvoir had qualms but trusted Sartre and convinced herself not to worry. Beauvoir does not say specifically what those qualms were, although she knew that she could trust Sartre and he would not harm her. She reflected, "With him a proposed scheme was not mere vague talk, but a moment of actuality. If he told me one day to meet him exactly twenty-two months later on the Acropolis, at five o'clock in the afternoon, I could be sure of finding him there then, punctual to the minute."[37] It mostly worked out for them and, after the two years, they made their commitment permanent, and theirs remained a deeply intimate relationship until the end of their lives.

There are advantages to temporary marriages: it gives people a chance to reassess their relationship regularly, encourages people not to take each other for granted, and creates an opportunity to exit more gracefully than a messy divorce. What about children? Caring, separated parents can be drastically better for children than dysfunctional or toxic married households. Beauvoir pointed out that there are lots of well-cared-for children outside marriage, and lots of poorly cared-for children within marriages.

Many marriages are temporary, so is it not better that we are honest about it up front? Yes, but it takes strength because the idea of temporary marriages foils the sense of security and reassurance that traditional marriage provides. Deadlines for love whittle away security and romance. Relationships are not like gym memberships. People have to wake up and affirm their membership in the relationship every day.

While the choice to live and love together is ideally a free and ongoing one, there are a number of structural factors and agreements that can be made to ensure the longevity of these choices. Eighteenth-century French feminist, playwright, and abolitionist Olympe de Gouges—whom Beauvoir held up as one of the few feminist icons in history—claimed "Marriage is the tomb of trust and love."[38] In an attempt to save trust and love from marriage, Gouges advocated for voluntary unions in which each partner has equal responsibility and rights in property, inheritance, and children.

Gouges thought that this type of equality would help people create more fulfilling relationships and happier families. She drafted her ideas about marriage on a pamphlet in 1789 with a two-hundred-word ready-to-use partnership template. Her "Frame for a Social Contract between Man and Woman" is as follows:

> We, *name* and *name*, unite with one another of our own free will, for the length of our lives and for the duration of our mutual inclinations, on the following conditions: We understand that we willingly put our fortunes into communal ownership, reserving for ourselves, however, the right to separate them in favor of our children and those persons for whom we may have a particular inclination, mutually recognizing that our assets belong directly to our children, from whatever bed they come, and that all without exception have the right to bear the name of the fathers and mothers who have acknowledged them. We commit ourselves to respect

the law that punishes the denial of one's own blood. In case [our union ends in] a separation, we also obligate ourselves to divide our wealth and to set aside for our children the portion that is specified by the law. In the case of a lasting union, the one who dies first will divest himself of half his property in favor of his children; if he dies childless, the survivor will inherit by right, unless the decedent has disposed of half the common property in favour of whomever he thinks proper.[39]

Gouges foresaw that the haters were going to hate. She expected that "the tartuffes, the prudes, the priests, and the whole damned lot of them" would dismiss her suggestion as bizarre, but hoped that it would lay the moral groundwork for wise people to establish more fulfilling marriages.

Four years later, Gouges was beheaded for sedition. Her views on marriage were not the reason for her execution, although they probably contributed. Her reputation for publishing radical ideas upset many people. She was disappointed in the Revolution and had called for a referendum on the form of the new government. Her referendum included the option of a constitutional monarchy. Simply including this option was deemed to be supportive of it. Supporting the monarchy was a capital offense.[40]

While Beauvoir didn't consider civil unions, and although she was deeply skeptical of marriage, there is an opening for authentic marriages in her philosophy, which is similar to formal civil unions. Beauvoir's focus was on making sure we have options about how we want to structure our relationships. Whether you marry or not, what's vitally important is the attitude with which consenting adults approach the relationship, and that you do it thoughtfully and intentionally. An authentic marriage, in Beauvoir's view, is a union in which partners are equal, earnest, generous, and bravely accept the inherent risks and ambiguities.

All relationships are uncertain, but attempting to escape the ambiguity through a marriage certificate is unreliable. Marriage can't save anyone. Marriage is a situation that necessarily creates a tension between being-for-others and being-for-oneself, but becoming authentic calls for a balance between them both. An authentic marriage must be freely chosen. An authentic marriage must be one in which people marry neither out of necessity nor because they are pushed into it, but because they want to be together. Feelings can only be authentic when they are freely given.[41]

An example in popular culture of a marriage that becomes authentic is in the 2005 film *Mr. & Mrs. Smith*. John and Jane Smith, played by Brad Pitt and Angelina Jolie respectively, have been married a few years. They are both independent, work full-time jobs, and do not have children. Jane puts dinner on the table every evening for when John gets home. He is led to believe her meals are homemade but they are not. And they have banal disagreements about curtains. In a couples therapy session, when asked how often they have sex, Jane responds, "I don't understand the question." Her answer reveals the staleness of the marriage in which they both fulfill their spousal roles as if it were another job. They're both bored senseless with their domestic life.

The twist is that they are both secret assassins and only find out when they're assigned to kill each other. As each tries to eliminate the other, they learn about one another's past and skills, recognize each other's strengths, come to respect each other, and treat each other as equals. As their bond strengthens, they unite and fight together as a team against their absurd missions, instead of against one another. In existential terms, it is only when their relationship is based on friendship, sincerity, and mutual understanding that they can relate authentically. "We're going to have to redo every conversation we've ever had," John says after realizing that everything they had said to one another since meeting is based on a lie.

*   *   *

I sometimes wonder: Was my marriage freely chosen, or was it a sign of my resignation to external forces? I cannot be sure that I was not railroaded into it. When I moved in with my long-term boyfriend, my father said, "Cohabitation leaves a bad taste in my mouth." The comment cut deep and I still feel that metaphorical knife dripping with judgment. Did I marry because of a deep-seated wish to be accepted in society? That is probably part of it. However, what is valuable existentially is to be able to see what clings to us, to recognize it for what it is, to consider alternatives, and to make definitive choices in light, and in spite, of influences.

My partner and I did not need a marriage contract to state that we wanted to be together. We worried that a contract would be unromantic and make our lives messier. And yet. There were arguments for it: a joint mortgage, less hassle and confusion when we came to having children and moving abroad, and I liked my husband's surname better than my own. But these were all convenient and trivial rationalizations. I married because I wanted something more dynamic than an essential relationship. I wanted a definitive, life-affirming, leap into the future, a bold "I choose you," and I'm going to let everyone know about it. Like Jean-Pierre and Clarice in Beauvoir's *The Useless Mouths*, I wanted a collaboration with someone to struggle together on Earth.

Had I not discovered Beauvoir, the outcome of my choice might still look similar, outwardly: it may have been the same pink dress, the same suit on my partner, and the same marzipan-covered chocolate cake in the same summer garden. But inwardly, it feels fulfilling, albeit possibly more anxiety-ridden. My marriage, in light of Beauvoir, calls for wrestling with big choices and to-gether making decisions about our relationship that support the values and ends that we create together.

My partner and I strive to acknowledge one another's freedom within our agreement. I hope that when our boundaries are tested in significant ways, we will be able to discuss and agree on what works for each of us. And if we cannot agree, then it is important to us to know that while we are free to choose to be together, we are also free to leave.

People are always going to have pressures on them pushing them one way or the other. Parents nagging. Friends bursting with blissful fulfillment on their wedding days. It can be exceedingly difficult to tease apart what is influenced by outside forces and what one authentically wants—what we can and can't control—so what's important is for us to raise our awareness to those pressures and to create a society where people can choose differently without penalty, so that they can live in sincerity, with or without marriage.

* * *

Let me return to the beginning of this chapter: after my class in the beer hall, one of the students came up to me and said that his wife had announced to him that she'd like an open relationship. He seemed confused, angry, and disappointed that I hadn't defended traditional marriage. His feelings were understandable given that it's not what his wife and he agreed to.

I didn't know what to say that I hadn't already said in the class. In retrospect, what I should have said—assuming his wife was being sincere and it was not a provocation to break up—was that her de-cision to have that conversation with him reveals not only that she needs something else in her life, but also that she is courageous and trusts him enough to talk about it. He could ask about her situation:

What does she find lacking or challenging in their marriage? Is there an issue with the allocation of housework? Would she like more time for herself, or with her friends? Would she like him to dress up like a fireman? (For example.)

In authentic relationships, partners acknowledge each other's freedom: She is free to want something else and it is entirely normal that she's changing, that her desires are changing. Traditional marriage does not easily accommodate change, but it could. She's venturing on a quest to reevaluate their relationship. Hopefully he can get past his bruised ego to explore possibilities with her. He is free to embark on this quest with her, or to end the relationship. Beauvoir wrote, "In order to discover their own possibilities, divorce is often a necessary condition."[42] Yet, his wife's invitation is as much an opportunity for divorce as it is an opportunity for poignant connectivity and honesty.

Adrienne Rich wrote, "An honorable human relationship—that is, one in which two people have the right to use the word 'love'—is a process, delicate, violent, often terrifying to both persons involved, a process of refining the truths they can tell each other."[43] It's hard and it can be terrifying, but telling the truth can disclose the complexities and possibilities for relationships. To lie is to lose sight of this, to sacrifice the riveting drama of truth for the dreary drama of untruth. Marriage, then, becomes a promise to support each other's subjectivity as best you can. And to be honest.

Yet standard wedding vows are mostly lip service or wishful thinking. It is absurd to expect two people to satisfy one another for their entire lives. That is a huge amount of pressure to put on one person. If we were to sashay down the aisles with the understanding that marriage is not designed to live up to that lofty romantic ideal of oneness, and that marriage tends to—but doesn't need to—ossify a relationship, then spouses might have a better chance of creating authentic marriages that are dynamic and lively.

In an authentic marriage, lives are shared in a way that does not try to close the other person in on the relationship. Spouses might worry that too much freedom is an invitation to drift away from one another. It is possible, but holding the other too close can be suffocating and just as risky.

People ask about my marriage and how my study of philosophy has influenced it. "A married existentialist? That's unusual!" they joke. We laugh and respond, "So far, so good." It sounds flippant but it is a serious statement too: The existential influence is to recognize that relationships are contingent, no matter how we try to secure them. What is working now is not guaranteed to work forever. In philosopher Judith Butler's words, "We can always fall apart, which is why we struggle to stay together."[44]

Adopting an authentic attitude helps my partner and I not take one another for granted. Every day I appreciate his free choice to be with me and I appreciate my free choice to be with him. This perspective shifts the focus from the fixed status of being married toward a more flexible attitude that recognizes the tenuousness of life and love, and challenges us to be creative, to actively accept the responsibility of navigating agreements, and to look for ways constantly to rejuvenate ourselves and our relationship. My marriage is far from perfect, but it's a work in progress—a quest for fulfillment. In existential terms, we are *becoming*, together.

So it was with Beauvoir and Sartre's relationship. They said they felt a oneness, and Beauvoir often referred to him as her life, her happiness, her absolute. In a letter to Sartre, she wrote, "The novelty and romance and happiness of my life are with you, my dear companion of 20 years."[45] For their whole lives, they encouraged each other and discussed all their ideas together. They found it splendid to be able to find and inspire each other, even without marriage. They did not, however, have to contend with children, who, clutching at caregivers' breasts and ankles, make authenticity more difficult to scout.

MOTHERHOOD

It is the woman who has the richest personal life who will give the most to her child and who will ask for the least, she who acquires real human values through effort and struggle will be the most fit to bring up children.

—The Second Sex

Women's capacity for choice—in motherhood as in the other areas—has been, and continues to be, a choice that is easily blurred with mystifications, limited by social, economic, and legal factors outside her control. This means that for women, some choices are made on false pretenses, throwing us into a world that we are not prepared for and compromising our struggle to become authentic.

It might seem odd to look to Beauvoir for guidance on motherhood, since she didn't have firsthand experience of raising a child. (Although Beauvoir adopted a close adult friend, Sylvie Le Bon, for the purpose of managing her estate.) It infuriated Beauvoir that there were double standards: she was criticized relentlessly for not being a mother and she was often asked if she felt unfulfilled. She responded, "One doesn't need to be a crow to write about crows," and no one ever judges men for not being fathers.[1] No one ever asked Sartre if he felt unfulfilled for not being a father.

Beauvoir was highly attuned to the ambiguities of maternal choices and the crucial struggle between a mother's sense of self as an individual—with her own desires and needs—and her new-found role as caretaker to a largely helpless dependent who will require care for the next eighteen years (give or take a few or more). A mother is very often torn between being-for-herself and being for the child. Moreover, there is inherent friction between what society expects and demands from a woman as a mother and how she sees her own role and place in society. For example, economic policies and incentives can push women into being mothers even when they would love to do something else, like philosophizing, for example.

For Beauvoir, having a child can be an authentic choice when a parent actively wills parenthood. To freely choose to parent requires freedom from mystifications about parenting, but also the freedom to make informed choices. Beauvoir didn't consider artificial insemination, IVF, or adoption in her writing, but as long as they are actively chosen, they are authentic options within Beauvoir's philosophy. Pregnancies and births resulting from coercion are inauthentic. The freedom to choose for or against becoming a parent is vital.

The act of choosing motherhood is what makes one a mother. As philosopher Sara Ruddick defines it, "Anyone who commits her or himself to responding to children's demands, and makes the work of response a considerable part of her or his life, is a mother."[2] Beauvoir's sentiment was similar. Because we create our essence through our choices, being a parent is not defined by the biological process of providing an egg or sperm or giving birth. A mother and father are defined by the act of choosing to care for a child.

New parenthood can be both exciting and terrifying because every new person creates new worlds of possibilities and disruptions.

Feminist and cultural critic Jacqueline Rose, drawing on Hannah Arendt and Adrienne Rich, wrote that "every new birth is the supreme anti-totalitarian moment," because every new human represents a new beginning pregnant with the capacity for creativity.[3]

But precisely because babies embody great possibilities, they pose great dangers to existing conditions. Arendt wrote that totalitarianism swells in response to disruptions: "Terror is needed lest with the birth of each new human being a new beginning arise and raise its voice in the world."[4] Some caregivers do respond to new births in totalitarian ways, and indeed huge amounts of effort are put into the world to make sure that children conform and grow into compliant cogs. For others, babies are the pre-reflective totalitarian terrors carving out new worlds, and caregivers are the minions.

For new parents, having to deal with pre-reflective totalitarian babies can feel alienating. Alienation hits when the quotidian is torn and we find ourselves in new situations or discover new perspectives in familiar situations. The tumultuousness is disorienting because we don't always know how we will react to a new situation, what consequences our actions will bring about, what the situation will be after an upheaval, and what conventions and duties we will find upon arriving in a new paradigm. It's one of the reasons people rely on routines and traditions: because repetition provides some comfort amidst uncertainty, even if illusory.

Newborns are thrown into a world that they had no say in creating, into the arms of caregivers they did not choose, and into absurd existences with no inherent meaning. Parents—whether they're biological, surrogate, or adoptive—are also thrown into a realm for which little can prepare them. Adrienne Rich recalled how she would read parenting books and find the archetypal mother so far from the drama of her own lived experience that she might as well have been reading about an astronaut:

No one mentions the psychic crisis of bearing a first child, the excitation of long-buried feelings about one's own mother, the sense of confused power and powerlessness, of being taken over on the one hand and of touching new physical and psychic potentialities on the other, a heightened sensibility which can be exhilarating, bewildering, and exhausting.[5]

Some psychic crises of new parenthood are instances of clinical depression requiring medical intervention and treatment. Others are cases of extended sleep deprivation. However, most mothering experiences are a complex and ambivalent mixture of bliss and misery, elation and enervation, success and failure, choice and thrownness. The problem is that society tends to group mothers into binary categories of good and bad.

At one extreme, the ideal mother delights in her role and finds it easy and even sensual (or so I hear). At the other extreme, the bad mother is inadequate and incapable: Beauvoir cites the ancient Greek myth of Medea who kills her children and herself. Or, Beauvoir noted, the bad mother is cruel, as in the trope of the evil stepmother.[6] Consider Cinderella's stepmother and the queen in Snow White.

Many crises lurk between the extremes—the despair, the flailing in uncertainty, the overwhelming feeling of guilt because one is failing at what is supposed to be an entirely natural activity. These experiences reflect a sense of alienation because a mother ceases to exist for herself and turns into someone who is supposed to be completely for others.

Beauvoir suggested that morning sickness is part of the alienation because it is an existential, not a physiological, response.[7] Beauvoir wasn't joking, and she is clearly mistaken. Hormones have a lot more to answer for than fear when it comes to morning sickness. Nevertheless, it is true that having children throws some parents into a bog of existential dread. I was one of them.

*   *   *

It's hard for me to pinpoint the lowest moment of motherhood, but one of the many was the morning after a largely sleepless night, just one of many sleepless nights that had come before it. My son cried and cried. My mother came over to bring moussaka and take my son out in the stroller, but they were back within minutes because he was still crying. I fed him, changed him, checked his temperature. All clear. He cried so much that he vomited all over my shoulder and onto the couch.

I carried him with me to the kitchen to fetch cleaning supplies. On the way back to the couch, screaming baby in one arm, paper towels and spray hanging precariously from my clenched fingers, I felt something warm and damp under foot. I looked down. His diaper had quietly exploded. Like lava seeping out of a volcano, creamy feces oozed down his leg, leaving a trail of brown drizzle on me and the carpet.

"Well, that explains it," my mother said. We laughed. She picked up her bag and said, "I should go. You have your hands full. I don't want to get in your way," and she left me to it. My laughter was, as Søren Kierkegaard once wrote, really tears. I don't blame my mother: my child was my and my partner's responsibility, not hers.

I gave my son a birdbath, dressed him in fresh clothes, and lay him down on his jungle playmat where he was mesmerized by a stuffed monkey that played music as it swung from the arc above him. I stripped off my own clothes and wiped down my sullied skin. The monkey stopped its swinging. He cried again. I cried again. Naked, I knelt down on all fours and scrubbed the carpet with detergent and despair, disgusted with my failure to overcome feelings of self-pity and abandonment. The image of the ideal mother that I so desperately wanted to be smeared into the carpet.

The existential condition has never been more apparent to me than at that moment: my son didn't choose to be born and certainly didn't seem to *want* to be born, and I felt alienated, alone, guilty for making this choice for him. My partner worked long hours and slept solidly all through the night while I was awake with the slightest noises, even with earplugs and different rooms, albeit in a small apartment. I was part of a mothers' group but they all seemed to be handling everything exponentially better than me—or at least they said they were. I wondered: How could I have got it so wrong? My cousin Claudia told me that when she had a child, she realized why she was put on this earth. Why didn't I feel that way? Where was the beautiful, happy, and fulfilling experience that I had been expecting?

Existential therapist Naomi Stadlen wrote that she knew procreation was a completely normal process and, "I thought my difficulties meant that there must be something radically wrong with me."[8] She pointed out that so much has been left unsaid about mothering because it's so hard to describe, and describe precisely. Mothers tend to be not only physically isolated but also isolated from meaning about their experience and it's difficult to cobble together the words to communicate it.

Perhaps the so-called "baby brain" isn't because hormones stifle intelligent capacity, but the opposite: the experience stretches mothers into realms beyond anything they've ever learned. One of Stadlen's clients, a mother of a six-month-old, said of her experience at a dinner party, "I couldn't talk about the only things that mattered to me. And even if I had, no one would have understood me."[9]

I felt the same way, and was confused by the fact that I had chosen to be a mother but reality sucker-punched me. Child-rearing is so all-consuming that mothers—and some fathers—are called to sacrifice much of their own lives. It's one of the reasons Beauvoir never had a child. When she was in her sixties, she felt lucky to have dodged it. "I am genuinely glad to have escaped that," Beauvoir said, "I congratulate myself every day on it."[10]

* * *

Motherhood is dangerous, Beauvoir wrote, because the responsibility falls heavily on mothers, making it a form of enslavement.[11] Beauvoir's analogy is insensitive because she blurs the line between slavery and sexism and she overlooks that the situation of women of color has been much more dire than for white women.[12] With this caveat in mind—that Beauvoir doesn't go far enough to acknowledge how much worse it is for women of color—it is still the case that motherhood locks many women into a set destiny, annihilating their freedom. It's not that the notions concerning freedom are gendered, but the hindrances to personal liberty cut along the lines of gender.

Beauvoir argued that one of the most dangerous mystifications is maternal instinct. Having babies might seem like a perfectly natural activity—after all, humans are animals and procreation ensures survival of the species. Beauvoir pointed out that convincing women that their natural vocation and highest destiny is to be a mother and homemaker is like a covert advertising campaign—one that has worked for thousands of years.

One of the ruses of oppression, Beauvoir argued, is to propose that the situation of the oppressed person is natural, as if we can't deny nature. Under the guise of nature, women have been lured—if not actively pushed—into a state of being-for-others at the expense of being-for-themselves, that is, to stay home, have children early and often. Restrictions on birth control forcefully usher girls into feminine roles where onslaughts of decisions are made for them.

Forcing women into motherhood—and caring for others in general—is a scam and very little has changed since Beauvoir wrote about this. Now it's called the "second shift," "mental load," or "time bind," which are all the family tasks and project managing that's done when a caregiver gets home from a paid job. These responsibilities tend to overwhelmingly fall on the mother.[13]

Recall our earlier discussion of existence and essence: while biology is an undeniable fact of existence, it does not define a human. What does define people are actions, how we transcend our situations, and the way we engage in our relationships. The implication of Beauvoir's ideas about motherhood is this: appeals to maternal instincts are red herrings. So too are appeals to unconditional maternal love.

When I was pregnant, friends told me that I would love my child more than anyone or anything in the world, including my partner. I found that hard to believe at the time, but after my son was born I soon discovered that there was much truth to it. It wasn't love at first sight, or at any sight during the first six months. I didn't know how to love someone that siphoned so much energy and attention from me. When he fell asleep, I felt released.

Mostly I was clueless about who he was, but even so, I took the responsibility of choosing a child very seriously, and he quickly became the most important person in the world to me. He was so small and fragile, yet his wrinkles made him look so old and wise that I nicknamed him Benjamin Button. His gummy giggles and his occasional moments of recognition when he looked at me were validating. For those fleeting moments, I felt less thrown.

The problem is that society exploits these feelings—rare or not, since there are some mothers who do appear to exist in a near perpetual state of bliss and connection with their newborns—by imposing the ideals of unconditional love and quietism upon mothers. As Jaqueline Rose wrote,

What is being asked of mothers when they are expected to pour undiluted love and devotion into their child? . . . After all, whenever love is expected or demanded of anybody, we can be pretty sure that love is the last thing being talked about. Like the injunction to be spontaneous, a state that can only arise unbidden, the demand to love crushes its object and obliterates itself.[14]

The obligation—that women should love and devote all of themselves to their children (and others)—is the crux of living as a woman. To be a woman is to give and love unconditionally, to be self*less*, implying that an ideal woman is not a full person because she is defined by how much of her being she gives away to others.

Virginia Woolf called such obligations "the Angel in the House," referring to a Victorian-era poem in which the male author, Coventry Patmore, idealizes femininity as domestic service, deference and obedience to husbands, and usefulness in bringing men closer to God.[15]

Woolf found that this villainous angel—"*the woman that men wished women to be* . . . the ideal of womanhood"—was always shadowing her and whispering to her to be sympathetic and charming. Woolf had to exorcise the angel to be able to write freely, truthfully, openly, and without feeling the need to flatter. The murder was self-defense: if she hadn't killed the angel, the angel would have killed her by wrenching the heart from her writing.[16]

Killing the Angel in the House still is a challenge for women. Beauvoir's philosophy calls our attention to similar phantoms: We have been led to believe selfless love is angelic but the requirement to love until we are completely drained is, in fact, demonic because it tugs us away from becoming authentic. A feeling cannot be demanded and the performance of love is an inauthentic farce.

* * *

Sisyphean torture is built implicitly into the mother's job description but it can be hard to grasp what one is signing up for. Labor can be excruciating. Breastfeeding can be difficult—cracked, bleeding nipples and painfully swollen, clogged ducts, not to mention the challenges of nursing in public. At times I felt like I had been reduced to a life-sustaining mechanism by a tiny fragile tyrant.

I spent long dark hours slouched in an armchair, nursing and cuddling until my arms ached and my shoulders cramped. Like a cow, I produced milk. I could have stopped the flow, but in the Australian culture in which I lived at the time, there was a strong theme of "breast is best." Good mothers breastfeed, so they say. The influence of attachment parenting has been stifling in the United States, too. One friend told me, "[Attachment parenting] made me feel so inadequate as a first-time mom."

The Sisyphean rock that mothers push up the mountain daily consists of piles of dirty diapers, explosions of milky vomit, and what can feel like never-ending rivers of tiny tears. After the baby phase, the rock turns into torrents of organizing: applying to schools; booking after-school activities; transporting to sports, playdates, and birthday parties; shopping for presents and food; planning and cooking meals; managing babysitters, the Easter Bunny, and the Tooth Fairy; tidying and cleaning the home; managing clothes shortages because the laundry schedule was out of synch or there was a growth spurt which rendered clothes too small en masse; scheduling doctors' and dentists' appointments; planning vaccinations on Fridays so as to minimize missed school and work in the likely case of feverish bedridden days; negotiating screen time; creating bribes for leafy greens consumption and tidying up. Am I coming in to read a book to the class on my son's birthday? Have I volunteered for the school carnival? Sending something for the bake sale? No pressure, but that's what some parents do. All this often while working a paid job too.[17]

A friend once said, "The first forty years of parenting are the hardest," and certainly, the entire span of motherhood—but the first eighteen years most acutely—is a slog trying to live up to impossible standards. Motherhood is still very much a long-term condition of constant sacrifice and bouts of unhappiness and dismay. Beauvoir acknowledged that professional work can support a woman's independence but inevitably brings with it acute fatigue.[18]

It's no wonder that many mothers pause their career or give it up entirely to manage anxiety, guilt, and stress, or because they are unable to juggle work without parental leave, or their job doesn't pay enough to cover childcare. To say that the demands of having a child can be overwhelming is a gross understatement. It takes years of generosity and self-sacrifice.

In a viral 2014 campaign, American Greetings advertised for a "Director of Operations," which demanded full-time, 24-7 on-call unpaid work without breaks, insurance, or holidays. The job description included a long list of requirements such as managing at least ten projects simultaneously with unlimited patience and a positive disposition. They interviewed a handful of candidates who, when the details were explained over video call, said things like "That's inhumane," and "That's insane."

When applicants were finally told that the "World's Toughest Job" described a mother's role, they all nodded, tearily waxing lyrical about their amazing mothers. The advertisement encouraged people to send mothers a card for Mother's Day. Sounds good, right? The problem is that despite more than eight million views, it received backlash for exactly the problem that Beauvoir highlighted: it reinforces the mystification of the ideal mother, stereotyping what mothers—but not fathers—are expected to do.

Recognition between a parent and child is lopsided, and finding an equilibrium is exceedingly difficult and—even if achieved—short-lived. But mothers shouldn't complain—ever. It is a sure sign that they are bad mothers if they do. Where does this painfully misguided idea come from? Some philosophers assert that complaining is soft, weak, and feminine, and burdening others with one's pains is a sure way to lose self-respect as well as the respect of one's peers.

Aristotle said, "People of a manly nature guard against making their friends grieve with them . . . but women and womanly men enjoy sympathizers in their grief."[19] The better type of person is, apparently, the one who suppresses and hides their grief (which sounds *so* healthy). Immanuel Kant agreed with Aristotle's sentiment when he wrote that, "No true man will importune a friend with his troubles . . . If, therefore, the friendship is noble on both sides, neither friend will impose his worries upon the other."[20] Aristotle and Kant both sound like terrible friends.

Friedrich Nietzsche exhorted women to shut up because he worried that knowing too much about them would spoil the mystery and allure of the ideal woman: "He is a true friend of women who calls out to women today: *mulier taceat de muliere!*" which means, "Women be silent about women."[21] Nevertheless, to Nietzsche's credit, he also recognized the dangers of cover-ups and wrote, "Let us speak of this, you who are wisest, even if it be bad. Silence is worse; all truths that are kept silent become poisonous."[22]

This gendered stereotyping, which has defined much of the western philosophical canon, has put women in a double bind. Beauvoir argued that many faults that women are accused of are a direct result of their quests being blocked by men. Women are criticized for not investing enough in their career when they're squashed up against glass ceilings that men build and enforce. They are accused of being lazy while being chained to the home. After having a baby, they are criticized for going back to work too soon or not soon enough. Stay-at-home mothers are perceived as doing nothing when in reality they barely have a moment to themselves. Women everywhere are criticized for complaining, and admired when they stoically resign to their suffering, their patience lauded for being a virtue.

The consequence of this silencing is not only unjust but can be lethal. People of color and women are, in general, undertreated for pain because of racial and gender bias in pain perception and treatment, and that includes mothers.[23] Every year in the United States hundreds of mothers die in childbirth and over 50,000 come close to death—and it's worsening over time.[24]

When my friend Jamie was pregnant, she could not stop vomiting. "I lost twenty percent of my body weight before I was out of the first trimester. The first emergency room doctor said I should seek treatment for an eating disorder," she said. Doctors dismissed her pain as though she were overreacting or lying. It wasn't an eating disorder. It was hyperemesis gravidarum and she was on the precipice of kidney damage from acute dehydration.

Black women are up to four times more likely to die of birth-related complications than white women, and Black babies are twice as likely to die as white babies—primarily because of the plethora of discriminations that Black women face.[25] Cultural critic Mikki Kendall contends that this is because there is a "paucity of care for those communities where motherhood is perceived as a sin instead of a sacrament."[26] In America, Black mothers are often denied the hallowed treatment that white mothers receive. Their image and legacy are still tied to awful stereotypes of welfare mothers or irresponsible parents, a negative inversion of the mystification of the ideal mother.

Dismissing pain and distress is a way to prevent mothers from talking honestly about their troubles, understanding them, and exploring ways to resolve them.[27] Franz Kafka wrote that, "The inner world can only be experienced, not described," but that's lazy and potentially deadly. The ideal mother is still elevated on a pedestal, peering down on the myriad grittier experiences that real mothers face.

While complaining isn't always a virtue, it can be, especially when it discloses and acknowledges shared experiences amongst vulnerable people and helps them to flourish. Bringing attention to shared suffering, and in circumstances that are difficult to change or can't be changed, is a skill we can cultivate.[28] We ought to be able to speak our truths and listen to one another without condemning others for their experiences—and doing so will help change the narratives around motherhood and shift the way society views and treats it. People can't make authentic choices when they're afraid of being punished or dismissed for being sincere.

*　　*　　*

Before our son's birth, my partner would say that our lives wouldn't need to change post-baby. I was skeptical and wondered what, then, is the point in having a child? He did his best to uphold his promise to himself: foregoing the paid parental leave that he was entitled to, working normal long hours, doubling up on sport most weekends and many weekday evenings, and sleeping through the night every night.

His reasoning was that he couldn't breastfeed, therefore he couldn't help. I knew he wasn't being malicious; but I didn't know that he was defaulting to the traditional gender norms just as I was, and clinging to a life that was more familiar and secure. "I felt pressure to be the Ideal Father," he told me later. "Being an uber-provider and working harder seemed to be the easiest option because I knew how to do that and I knew that was useful for our family." I'm still not sure how sport fit into that equation, but as long as the burden of child-rearing falls to women, there will be inequality between the sexes, which thwarts authentic relationships because it calls for women to subordinate themselves to the family.

Our child was a joint decision and a shared responsibility that my partner was resisting, while increasing his leisure time and re-asserting his transcendence at the expense of mine. I was heading for a breakdown. I broke my silence and admitted I was not able to be the ideal mother I was expecting and expected to be. "But I have a whole team counting on me," he protested. The statement had barely escaped his lips when he realized that his home team was counting on him too.

Sure, men can't breastfeed, but they can do every other activity related to children. There's a reason we only had one child: because I didn't want to risk the abandonment and alienation all over again. I didn't want my being reduced to my generic reproductive functions at the expense of the rest of my life. It's bad faith to blame anyone else for one's choices, but I had found it exceptionally difficult to reconcile my choice with the reality of parenthood. If the grueling parts were going to fall to me and only me, I didn't want it, and I had learned there was no one to join me in the endeavor in a way that didn't make me feel like I had to give up being-for-myself. Some mothers told me I'd soon forget how hard it was and want more children. Despite how delightful my son is, my brain couldn't erase the nightmare of the early phase. Thankfully I had access to birth control and could make definitive choices about the future, but many women do not have this basic right.

For parenting to be an authentic choice, it must be a free choice, free from mystifications such as the ideal mother and father, and free from manipulation about the diversity of mothering experiences. Parenthood is a commitment that, once chosen, calls for responsibility and accountability to the child.[29] This means that people also must be free to opt out of childbearing. Unless abortion and contraception are freely available and there is social and personal support for women's choices, a woman will face undue restrictions on her choices.

At the age of seventeen, Beauvoir was horrified that abortion was illegal. She wrote, "What went on in one's body should be one's own concern."[30] Her life's work only further cemented Beauvoir's opinions on a woman's right to choose. Beauvoir thought abortion to be so important that in *The Second Sex*, the first ten pages of her chapter "The Mother" argues for it. Banning abortion and contraception does not stop women from using them. Prohibition relegates abortion and contraception to class and race crimes, accessible to those with money and who can travel as needed to access it. But it renders the most vulnerable women in society even more vulnerable to the danger, pain, and suffering of risky back-alley operations. After *The Second Sex* was published, Beauvoir's office was overwhelmed with letters and visitors asking for recommendations for abortion services.[31]

In 1971, Beauvoir signed a manifesto, as one of 343 women claiming to have had an abortion, that petitioned for abortion and contraception to be legally and freely available to all women. Beauvoir's protest was personal. But the personal is also political. Her actions signaled solidarity and indignation. In a statement about why she signed the manifesto, she said it was important to change the attitude and culpability of women before the law.[32]

Women's legal right to their own bodies is still threatened around the world. Around 700 million women of reproductive age live in countries where abortion is banned or highly restricted.[33] In 2018, a United States politician said of women wanting the right to abortion: "I understand that they feel like that is their body. I feel like it is a separate—what I call them is, is you're a 'host.'"[34] He wanted to require women to have permission from the male sexual partner before getting an abortion, meaning that women's bodies belong to the embryo, and both women and embryos should be under male control. More broadly he implied that women's bodies are meant to service men's desires.

Contraception removes roadblocks from women's freedom, but simply making it legal is not enough. Even with adequate contraception, women's right to choose abortion as an option must also be respected. In post-Soviet Russia in the second half of the twentieth century, abortions were legal and widely accessible. However, the government was pro-birth and women who sought the procedure were treated horrifically.

Anthropologist Michele Rivkin-Fish described the clinics as "meat grinders," in which women endured abortions without privacy or anesthesia. The reason, she explained, is that some doctors believed that women deserved to suffer and be punished for having an abortion.[35] While men can be shunned and shamed in some communities for not bearing children, there is little pain and punishment when a man refuses fatherhood. This is striking considering a woman is capable of one pregnancy a year, while a man is capable of contributing to hundreds of pregnancies a year.

* * *

As long as women are punished for their maternal choices, authenticity will be compromised. All too often societies that ban abortion also leave mothers without support and with children, in a world that no longer cares for those children's rights and interests once they've left the mother's uterus. Beauvoir pointed out that the choice to accept or refuse motherhood throws a woman's body into question, too: she was brought up to believe the ability to give birth is sacred but it becomes a curse. In many jurisdictions, if she chooses to abort, she finds herself a criminal, held responsible for a pregnancy that wasn't entirely her choice, which is a perverse kind of morality.[36]

Forced birth is not based on morality, but on sadism and bad faith. It's sadism to force motherhood and unwanted children into the world, often in poverty and misery, and in Beauvoir's view, this policy is a direct result of men's fear of women's freedom. Bad faith lurks within the hypocritical claims that a fetus is autonomous and does not belong to the mother, but then exalts motherhood and the sacred symbiosis between mother and child, when one publicly denounces abortion but privately encourages it, and when a man demands that a woman sacrifice her body for his desire and then punishes her for his moral and prophylactic failures. Birth control is vital to authenticity because it allows a woman to transcend her natural functions and turns parenthood from surrender and resignation into a vivacious venture.

If one does choose parenthood, authentic parent–child relationships would be possible, Beauvoir envisaged, when parents do not abandon their transcendence. When a parent doesn't lose herself in the role, but continues to exist for herself *as well as* the child. When she can choose both a child and other interests, having a child can be a freely chosen responsibility and an authentic engagement. A parent will not need to worry that by having other interests they are neglecting their child because, Beauvoir wrote, "It is the woman who has the richest personal life who will give the most to her child and who will ask for the least, she who acquires real human values through effort and struggle will be the most fit to bring up children."[37]

But women still cannot have it all. As Michelle Obama said: "That whole 'so you can have it all.' Nope, not at the same time . . . That's a lie. And it's not always enough to lean in, because that shit doesn't work all the time."[38] Such indicators would suggest that perhaps one step toward changing perceptions is not having children. Yet Beauvoir conceded that if a woman wants a child, then she should be free to do so.

Beauvoir also warned that it's important to detach the decision to procreate from the decision to marry because the nuclear family is the patriarchal mechanism that exploits free labor from women.[39] Beauvoir rightly acknowledged how incredibly difficult it is to care for children without support, but she didn't address how single mothers often come to rely on the labor of other mothers, their own mothers, or underpaid childcare workers. And so the vicious cycle is perpetuated.

A few years after she published *Lean In,* Sheryl Sandberg's husband died, leaving her a single working mother of two. In a Facebook post, she acknowledged how hard it is for single parents and widows to lean in: "Before, I did not quite get it. I did not really get how hard it is to succeed at work when you are overwhelmed at home."[40]

My friend Jamie, now a widowed mother of two young boys, sometimes says she feels like she is going to be physically devoured by despair: "Being widowed is a horror show. Raising children who must navigate a grief they barely have words to express is a constant heartbreak." A successful day, she says, is when the three of them are still alive. Indeed, for most single and low-income mothers who survive with little to no support, health and life can never be taken for granted and it's a travesty that society abandons them.

For all of us to authentically choose our futures with or without spouses and children, we need a transformation in society. What if we reversed the trend in western society toward individualization and isolation of families? Beauvoir envisaged a society that supports mothers and shares children's care with a larger group, which would help overcome the social neglect that oppresses and harms everyone but the most privileged.[41]

A shared caregiving structure would enable parents to continue their quests for fulfillment both within and beyond their caretaking role. Maternity leave policies merely reinforce gender stereotypes, encouraging mothers to stay at home and fathers to stay at work. Parental leave policies such as those you find in Scandinavian countries are vital to opening up choices for both parents. The policies include paid carers' leave, flexible employment laws and policies, and good options for childcare that do not create a new cycle of oppression by exploiting carers.

*　*　*

As my son edges toward independence, I think he has forgiven me for throwing him into the world—at least as much as an eleven-year-old can forgive. From Beauvoir, I learned to challenge my assumptions about motherhood, which gave me a footing amidst my thrownness. For many people, parenting a tween is much harder than a newborn because the fulfillment of being able to care for a baby outweighs the depression, overload, and sleep deprivation.[42]

Having not found fulfillment in having a baby, but having found immense joy in our relationship after the baby stage, I find it hard to believe that teenage years are going to be harder. But armed with what I've learned from Beauvoir, I hope that I am better equipped to deal with the onset of puberty. At the very least, I can say, "So far, so good." I hope that my son and I can navigate life in a way where we can continue to develop a reciprocal relationship and to pursue our individual quests for fulfillment together.

The possibility of authentic parenting requires greater widespread awareness, acknowledgment, and understanding of the Herculean effort that children call for, the context in which people are choosing and not choosing children, and what's said and not said about the experience of parenting. We must, as individuals and as a society, become brave enough to talk candidly about the truth of motherhood, lest we slip into bad faith, lying to ourselves or one another, hiding the truth, or ignoring it and hoping for the best.

When partners engage more deeply in family activities, and

when mothers reaffirm their sisterhood, then together, we will be able to lift the veil from the mystifications of the ideal parent and reshape our collective understanding—not only of motherhood, but of *parent*hood. Until then, we can't expect any change in western society's bait-and-switch program that promotes and idealizes motherhood without supporting mothers in any meaningful way. There are not enough social, economic, or health policies to make the so-called crucial nature of mothering accurately reflected in a woman's daily experience.

Understanding how people are thrown is helpful because such insights counter the idea that mothers have to have it all together, and that motherhood follows a set trajectory dominated by the characters of the ideal and the bad mother. Awareness of the challenges of caregiving can help us make sense of the ambiguity of being a mother, in a way that enables mothers to own their lived experience rather than be owned by it.

Awareness can help us to understand parenting as a state of becoming that's indefinite and that can't be embodied in a fixed role. Instead of striving to be ideal mothers—a project that sets women up for failure—it would be better for parents to look at their task as a commitment to a loving relationship between oneself and the child. Just as there is no right way to be an ideal mother, so too is there no single right prescription for being in a parent–child relationship.

Instead of thinking about motherhood as a static ideal, we should prioritize connection. We should treat motherhood as a constantly shifting dynamic that acknowledges the parent–child relationship must be constantly created, recreated, developed, and nurtured—often in unexpected ways.

Beauvoir suggested that friendship is at the core of the relationship between parents and maturing children. In *The Mandarins*, the main character Anne struggles with her relationship with her teenage daughter, only to have it harmonize into friendship when they feel themselves equal. To become an authentic parent is to support a child in becoming self-sufficient and growing up to pursue their own quests for fulfillment. You don't need to be best friends with a child, and there are dangers in forcing friendship to make yourself feel younger, but becoming an authentic parent means acknowledging the inequality of age and experience but also recognizing the child's subjectivity and helping them to flourish.

Parenthood is a lesson in a planned obsolescence—that eventually the day will come when you aren't central to your children's well-being and it's a good thing when that happens. We may not be able to fully relieve the inherent ambiguity of the experience of parenthood, but we can help one another to find more clarity amid the turmoil. For everyone's benefit, we must acknowledge and help one another understand the existential thrownness of the human condition, and to see possibilities beyond despair. "Let us beware," Beauvoir wrote, "lest our lack of imagination impoverish the future."[43] While imagination is vitally important at all stages of life, it is often neglected in elderhood and yet that's the very stage of life when authenticity is, for many people, most within reach.

AGING

Nothing should be more expected than old age: nothing is more unforeseen.

—Old Age

As we grow older, well-being is not only about biological survival, but existential thriving. We must continue our quests for fulfillment. Everyone needs a reason for living, even, and perhaps especially, older people. Without a purpose, existence is simply passing the time like a moving corpse. Beauvoir reimagined elderhood as a stage of life, different from adulthood, but filled with possibilities.[1]

For Beauvoir, the question lurking underneath the crisis of old age is, "Can I have become a different being while I still remain myself?"[2] In other words, who is this being that I am becoming—a being that is aging before my eyes while I still feel young? Beauvoir observed the many ways elderhood takes self-determination out of our control, through our deteriorating bodies and in the ways society defines aging on our behalf.

Experiences of elderhood vary drastically, but Beauvoir's pessimism about her experience inspired her to write about aging intensively. She discussed aging in her memoirs, *The Second Sex*, and a six-hundred-page book titled *Old Age* (*La Vieillesse*). She wrote

Old Age when she was in her early sixties, to help her cope with her dread of aging and to give a voice to older adults who she saw as being silenced, ignored, and misrepresented. What concerned her most of all were the many clichés and lies about aging, and how it is often treated as a shameful, taboo subject. One of Beauvoir's overall goals in life was to cut through veils of mystifications, and *Old Age* was part of her attempt to reveal the truth of aging.[3]

In *Old Age*, Beauvoir described elderhood somewhat cruelly as a stage of life in which a person becomes decrepit, dried, and diminished, shrunken and shriveled, mutilated, and at risk of being overwhelmed with nervousness, anxiety, and memory loss. In her view, growing old drains people of strength, siphons off passion and enthusiasm, and replaces them with a mix of fatigue, boredom, inertia, idleness, sadness, emptiness, loneliness, and depression. These are all factors that at any other age—at least all together and unremittingly—would be unusual, but as we age, they are entirely normal, making elderhood what Beauvoir calls a disconcerting "normal abnormality."[4]

When she was in her fifties, Beauvoir felt "attacked by the pox of time for which there is no cure," and saw nothing but misfortune in her future.[5] She dreaded waiting for death so much that she often thought about ending her life. Not everyone feels this way, but many people do try to avoid growing older. Unless we die early—through choice, accident, or illness—elderhood is humankind's universal destiny.

Beauvoir catalogued a number of inescapable factors of elderhood in an attempt to understand what was in her control and what wasn't. One factor is that aging is something "unrealizable." Beauvoir, crediting Sartre, defines an unrealizable as "my being seen from without which bounds all my choices."[6] Aging bounds our choices because ageist gazes close down possibilities for older people—such as work opportunities. Aging forces us to live a reality that we can't fully comprehend. There is often a great disconnect between how we feel inwardly and the ungraspable gazes of others.

Beauvoir reflects: "A Frenchwoman, a writer, a person of sixty: this is my situation as I *live* it. But in the surrounding world this situation exists as an objective form, one that escapes me."[7] Our aging is a situation that exists outside of us; we are old *for* others. A common cliché is that you are only as old as you feel, but that is oversimplifying. Other people also define us.

Sometimes people adapt to life so well that they don't pay attention to their age. Beauvoir pointed out that Lou Andreas-Salomé— the Russian philosopher, psychoanalyst, and onetime friend of Nietzsche—did not notice that she was old until she was sixty and her hair fell out after an illness. If not for blatant incidents such as hair loss, we might continue feeling ageless.[8]

But if we are not ready for growing old, the aging process can throw our whole identity into crisis. Death can haunt us at any age because it is a perennial possibility, but for most of us, elderhood hovers as a distant possibility so far into the future that it can appear as something not quite real. Our hair does not thin and gray overnight; it starts with a lone silver strand that appears (or disappears) mysteriously, slyly, then another, and another. By the time Beauvoir came to terms with the fact that she was forty, she was already fifty. And at age fifty, people would refer to her as an old woman. She was unimpressed when people told her that she reminded them of their mother.[9]

As we age, othering intensifies exponentially. A whole new set of social expectations arrives as a host of unwelcome guests (who will never leave). Sometimes older adults are othered to such a degree that they are effectively cast as a different species. Beauvoir argued that while elderly people are promised dignity, the reality of aging looks more like oppression: their personhood is diminished, their subjectivity is stripped away.

Beauvoir offers us an explanation of ageism. She analyzes it in terms of "exis" and "praxis." Adults are mostly praxis, that is, doing, transcending, stretching deliberately toward particular goals. Older adults are perceived and treated as exis, meaning that they are mostly caught in immanence, without power, without projects, being pulled toward death.

Although children are also seen as exis—being, not doing—they are treated differently than older adults. People see a child as holding future potential but, Beauvoir said, "the aged person is no more than a corpse under suspended sentence."[10] Older adults are treated as inhuman—that is, exis—by default, and they often come to see themselves as exis, internalizing torpor. They are still wholly capable of praxis, even if in different ways than younger people, but older people's abilities tend to be overlooked.

In societies that reduce people to their profitability, as many capitalist societies do, age dehumanizes people. The more unproductive people are assumed to be, the more burdensome they appear to society. The older people are, the more they are exiled and the more they are cast as "useless mouths" (also the name of Beauvoir's play).

Knowledge and wisdom were once the bargaining chips for older adults, but now, the rapid pace of technology means that their knowledge is generally considered obsolete, making age increasingly disadvantageous. This is still common in political rhetoric. The focus on fast profits, stock prices, and quick wins, over long-term sustainable and responsible operations, dominates concerns for caring for elderly people. Many people assume that older adults do not contribute to society anymore, when the truth is that often they are heavily involved in childcare, volunteering, and other work.[11]

Beauvoir thought that it is strange that older people should be so overlooked. After all, those who are building the structures to treat older adults are laying the groundwork for how they will be treated themselves in the future. But in modern capitalist societies, those with power and wealth aren't afraid of this destiny.[12] They know they have the resources to avoid much of aging's unpleasantness, and so they make human sacrifices of the less privileged on stock market altars. Young people sometimes fall into a similar trap of bad faith: they mock and demean older people, an exercise in othering that ignores that we are all on the same continuum of life—that either we will all be old one day or will die beforehand. Both options can be terrifying to come to terms with.

* * *

The barriers that older people face, such as employment discrimination, are part of what Beauvoir called the "practico-inert," a second inescapable factor of elderhood.[13] "Practico-inert" is a Sartrean term Beauvoir used to describe situations in which human choices harden into a type of facticity. The practico-inert is the outcome of past human activities that shape the ways we are able to exercise our freedom in the present. The practico-inert is *praxis* (practical activities) that creates *inertia* in our lives.

There are internal and external dimensions to the practico-inert. Externally, the practico-inert is the legal, political, cultural, environmental, and social systems in which we live. These systems are necessary for human flourishing and expand freedoms for many, but they also operate in discriminatory ways that frustrate many people's well-being.

Climate change is an example of the external practico-inert. The greenhouse effect is the result of human choices to burn fossil fuels and is now melting icecaps, increasing the average temperature of our environment, and creating volatile weather patterns such as severe storms, heatwaves, and wildfires. Climate change creates inertia in many people's lives because it impedes our movements, our plans, and our access to power, food, and water.

Internally, the practico-inert is the sum of our past choices, such as skills, knowledge, relationships, duties, tastes, interests, and activities. These features, or facticities, define a person's situation and provide a basis from which they project themselves into the world. The practico-inert represents the existential notion that a person is the sum of their actions, the culmination of their past, the image of what they have become, and how they appear to others.

If we consider the metaphor that our lives are like a poem, the paper and the table underneath the sheet are the political, legal, and other systems of our lives. Our activities are like scribing inky words on paper. As our ink dries on the page, the words leave imprints which form the ever-evolving foundation of our lives. If we are struck with inertia, if we stop sketching words (designing our essence), the poetry of our lives stops too.

The practico-inert weighs particularly heavily on elderly people because the older they grow, the vaster their past, the narrower their future, the more solidly defined they appear to others, and the more limited their possibilities. All of this hems older people in, slowing down their becoming, often to a grinding halt. There is a stigma attached to older people as being unwilling and incapable of change, as in the familiar saying, "An old dog can't learn new tricks." The practico-inert is that aspect of our being that hardens behind us, like inky words on a page.

This phenomenon is one of the reasons, Beauvoir suggested, that older people tend toward conservatism: having less time to live means they are less interested in new and uncertain situations.[14] Old habits become one of the internal dimensions of the practico-inert. Routines can be reassuring, providing a kind of security. Patterns in life give people a sense of who they are. Habits can protect people from anxiety about the future because routines promise that tomorrow will be just like today. This repetition becomes comforting as the days toward death draw ever nearer.

Habits are also like reflexes: they help jog people's memories before they have to think hard or to ask what they should do. Routines can give people a sense of control over their lives, lifting them from the bog of stagnation. Habits can take on a kind of poetry that revives the past. Consider Japanese tea ceremonies that become a ritualistic artform, or the practice of raking sand in a Zen garden as meditation. Everyday habits can bring a similar sense of peace and reassurance.

Nevertheless, there are dangers in venerating habits. An obsession with them fosters curmudgeonly and sclerotic behavior, and these actions tyrannize others who feel obliged to conform to the older person's wishes. An overreliance on habits can also turn a person into a warm corpse, merely going through the motions of life but not living in any meaningful way.

Beauvoir described the existential challenge for older people: "To move forward he must perpetually be tearing himself free from a past that holds him with an ever-tighter grasp: his advance is slow."[15] This is not to say that advance is impossible. Julia Child wrote her first cookbook at fifty. *Little House on the Prairie* author Laura Ingalls Wilder published her first book at age sixty-five. Anna Mary Robertson "Grandma" Moses started painting at age seventy-eight and became a celebrated artist in the last decades of her life. At age ninety-eight, the artist Luchita Hurtado held her first solo exhibition and appeared in *Time* magazine's list of the one hundred most influential people in 2019. The practico-inert does not completely determine a person's future. Habits can be changed, global warming can be slowed, but these are complex and challenging tasks.

A third inescapable factor of growing old, Beauvoir noted, is that aging shifts our relationship to time. When we are young, everything is new and exciting and novel. We busy ourselves in the present, hurrying toward a future that stretches wide before us. As we grow older, there are fewer new things, fewer major events, and fewer discoveries that blow our mind and stick in our memories.[16]

It would not be too much of a stretch to accuse Beauvoir of ageism. When she was thirty, she promised herself she would give up sex by the time she turned forty. She thought it was improper for older women to flirt, to make exhibitions of themselves, and to have sex lives. In a cringingly ageist statement, Beauvoir wrote: "I loathed what I called 'harridans' and promised myself that when I reached that stage, I would dutifully retire to the shelf."[17]

When she was thirty-nine, Claude Lanzmann upset her plan to "shelve" herself. Lanzmann was an editor at Beauvoir and Sartre's journal *Les temps modernes.* He was seventeen years her junior when he called and invited her to go to the movies. Beauvoir agreed, hung up the phone, and promptly burst into tears. Her body said no. Her imagination said yes. Her imagination won. As she embarked upon her liaison with Lanzmann, she fast discovered that her body was not as washed up as she thought it was. She wrote, "I leapt back enthralled into happiness."[18]

Yet as she grew older, aging horrified Beauvoir more than death. In her memoir *Force of Circumstance,* published when she was fifty-five, she said she found herself cutting her own plans short. She felt her bonds to the world loosening. She still traveled and gave lectures and made plans, but she was no longer as eager, no longer as ambitiously extending herself into infinity. She wrote, "The full impulse that urged me on has been broken . . . And this brief future is a blind alley. I am aware of my own finity."[19]

Had Beauvoir been given another hundred years of healthy and hearty life with loved ones—and it is entirely possible that in the not-too-distant future the average human health span will increase that far—she thought she might have been excited to explore new realms and leap into fresh endeavors, despite her fear of aging. What Beauvoir lamented most about aging was losing clear memories of her friends, including Albert Camus, Alberto Giacometti, and Maurice Merleau-Ponty. All she could recover was a "frigid imitation" of them which she knew bore no relation to the reality of the fullness of her time spent with them.[20] Beauvoir speculated this might be one of the reasons that older people love telling stories about their past: they are keeping alive the legend of themselves, and trying to cement themselves as the person they once were in relationships they once had.

* * *

I do not see myself as old, but having passed forty, every time there is the slightest change in my body, I am shocked. When I met up with a male friend who I had not seen since college, and he told me, "You look the same but with crow's feet!" I wanted to tell him to get lost, but instead replied, "Ha! You too!"

Recently I asked my optometrist what was wrong with my eyes. "How old are you?" he asked. "Eyesight is one of the first things to go," he chuckled. I gasped. His remark pierced me like the first nail in my coffin. A friend gifting me a book called *The Menopause Manifesto*: another nail. Getting a hangover from one alcoholic drink: nail. Suffering yoga butt from overstretching: nail. Putting on ten pounds since my last medical checkup: nail. Not all of these are exclusively age related, but with each one I feel attacked by time.

In *Old Age*, Beauvoir pointed out that some societies revered elderly people, mostly male. These societies see older people as closer to the divine, rising to the crown of life, or at the very least, they treat the elders' accumulation of knowledge and experience like treasure. In Confucianism, elderhood and wisdom are synonymous. For the ancient Chinese philosopher Lao Tzu, elderhood is a virtue and men over sixty are esteemed to almost holy status. Roman politician and historian Cato the Elder, who lived until eighty-five, felt that the older the man, the wiser and more authoritative he becomes. Aristotle thought that old age brings *phrenosis*, meaning prudent wisdom, which guides us to behave in a morally correct fashion.[21]

But veneration of elders has not always been the norm—especially if the older person was a woman. In 2500 BC the Egyptian philosopher-poet Ptah-hotep complained that old age is miserable and evil.[22] Aphrodite tells Homer that the gods loathe aging. Horace sees old age as a bitter pill; he bids farewell to happiness and hello to frigid winter. Even Epicurus, who supposedly achieved ataraxia (equanimity), was sad about old age.[23] Some ancient societies banished elderly people; some elders killed themselves in rituals, others were voluntarily buried alive. The Roman Empire drowned some of their elders. Beauvoir contended that in many societies, life traps older bodies in indecent, cruel suffering.[24]

Modern society still fears and shames aging and atrophy. Given that older people are discriminated against at work, pushed into retirement, mocked for being forgetful and redundant, and assumed not to be able to learn new things or operate technology, it's no wonder that people go to no small length to avoid it. In 2019, the global longevity market was estimated to be worth around $110 billion, and it's growing rapidly.[25] Some companies are editing DNA in the hope of reversing aging, and others are looking to the digital realm for "virternity" (virtual eternity). Philosophers such as David Chalmers say that one day we will be able to upload our consciousness to a virtual cloud, leaving the dead weight of our physical bodies behind.

We are living longer, and perhaps one day technology will enable us to transcend the facticity of aging and death. But at the time of writing this book, elderhood is still our common fate. The elixir of youth has not yet been found, and I am not holding my breath. We are still being churned through the machine of life, what Beauvoir calls the "crusher" of humankind.[26]

Many people, even before they grow older, attempt to sidestep the biological process. In her fifties, Beauvoir said, "I go to the hairdresser about twice a month and have it washed, set and dyed. I'm going grey, you see, and it's just at the pepper-and-salt stage when it looks grubby. The chignon is a postiche, as I have very little hair of my own."[27] While I disagree that salt-and-pepper hair looks "grubby," many people do color their hair, get manicures and facials, and tweeze stray stubble. There's little harm in these rituals. However, more drastic procedures, such as injecting toxins into one's face, call for more serious consideration. The plastic surgery market—including botulinum toxin type A (Botox) injections, fillers, facelifts, liposuction, and tummy tucks—is prolific and worth billions. Women spend around seven times as much as men.[28]

* * *

The feminist mantra is that women should be happy with our bodies just the way they are, or that at least women should respect and support one another enough to each make our own choices. A liberated woman, according to this popular wisdom, is not beholden to the gazes of others and not worried about sex appeal. She is not concerned about whether her breasts are too big, too small, too on-show, whether she wears too much or not enough makeup, whether she grooms her body in ways acceptable to whoever's gaze is currently objectifying her. Beauvoir recognizes that we are all beholden to the gaze of others, and more so as we age.

"Have you had work done?" Like plastic surgery. "No. I'm all natural." Many do not want to admit that they have had work done. Some are ashamed of their age or worry they are betraying feminism. They feel guilty for caring about looking young when they are not supposed to. Others do not want to admit to themselves or each other that time has affected them. They do not want to be judged as being old, and they do not want to be othered, so they try to cover it up as much as possible. Aging often causes an inner turmoil: a vicious cycle of guilt and self-loathing about getting older. People worry that they have peaked and the future is all downhill. Every wrinkle indicates life lost, moments lost, time lost, and with these changes our optimism can atrophy.[29]

Beauvoir loathed it too. In her early fifties Beauvoir would look in the mirror and see "the eyebrows slipping down toward the eyes, the bags underneath, the excessive fullness of the cheeks, and that air of sadness around the mouth that wrinkles always bring."[30] Beauvoir wanted to smash her mirrors like the Countess of Castiglione, a nineteenth-century Italian aristocrat and model for imperial court photographers. The countess banished mirrors from her home so that she could not see herself aging. Catching her reflection, Beauvoir would remember, more and more vaguely, the person she once was, and she deplored the atrophy—not only of her face but of her heart, and her will to revolt against death and enjoy life.

In 2016, Debora Spar, the then president of Barnard College—the women's college in New York City where I teach—published an op-ed in *The New York Times* confessing that she was torn between wanting to be a good feminist and role model for younger women on the one hand, and avoiding ageism through plastic surgery on the other.[31] The problem, Spar rightly pointed out, is that older women are caught in the collective action dilemma: everyone is better off if no one does it.

There's nothing inherently wrong with altering the facts of one's body, an example of transcending existentially toward a different future. But the particular issue with cosmetic surgery is that ageism, sexism, and classism infect the practices. And when some people augment their bodies toward youth, it hurts everyone who doesn't, since discrimination and loss of agency muffle aging bodies.

I tried Botox a couple of times, but ultimately I stopped. I didn't recognize my own face, and it felt like a betrayal to myself and others. It was also absurdly expensive. The older I grow, the more challenging it becomes to avoid the temptation of more, especially when I see how many people my age are looking ever younger. Yet, I find it disconcerting to talk with people whose poker faces, like Stepford spouses, lack the micro-movements and nuances of intimate and authentic conversation. I find it strange to see the void, or the absence of complexity, in faces that seem to deny existence. I feel like a dimension of reciprocity is lacking.[32]

Lying about cosmetic procedures is even more problematic than getting them in the first place. The lies project bogus body standards on everyone else. It's like insider trading that hides information from some for the exclusive benefit of privileged others. This practice is harmful for those who can't afford to participate. And many people do lie, both by omission and commission.

The travesty of the otherwise excellent film *Legally Blonde* is that the fitness instructor Brooke Windham—whom the protagonist and law student Elle Woods defends in court—would prefer to go to prison for a murder she didn't commit than confess she had liposuction. It's true that people who have work done and are honest about it are shamed and judged—as Spar was.[33]

When Spar's op-ed came out, the discussion on campus was heated. Some students were disappointed. If a woman in a position of power like Spar succumbs to the pressure of society telling us that aging is undesirable—if even she does not have the confidence to take a stand against the pressure to conform—then is all hope lost? Others found her honesty refreshing.

Philosopher Martha Nussbaum has no such qualms. Nussbaum argued in her book *Aging Thoughtfully* that, "It's stupid to veto all cosmetic procedures simply by saying 'unnatural.'" Nussbaum refuses to succumb to self-loathing in a society that views aging as ugly, declaring, "I'll take cosmetic procedures any day." Botox, fillers, and photofacials are, Nussbaum claimed, totally fine because they are about looking better, not younger, and they "don't cost much money."[34] But a couple of hundred dollars every month or so doesn't count as "not much" for very many people. And it is worth noting, that looking better, in Nussbaum's view, means fewer wrinkles—which does happen to equate with looking younger.

Nussbaum dismissed Beauvoir's *Old Age* wholesale as deceitful and outrageous. Nussbaum claimed that Beauvoir perpetuates social stigma, injustice, and fatalism, because Beauvoir assumed that age just happens to you and there is nothing you can do about it. Nussbaum wrote that she exercises, she's active, and she does not feel negative effects of aging or that she's going through a metamorphosis. It's great that Nussbaum has the means to delay the effects of her aging, but her analysis underestimates her privilege. While it is true that Beauvoir emphasized the negative aspects of elderhood, she worked hard to challenge ageist stereotypes, and strongly encouraged people to stay active and engaged.

Beauvoir's view seems to be sympathetic to both Spar and Nussbaum because, Beauvoir wrote, "Whether we like it or not, in the end we submit to the outsider's point of view."[35] Beauvoir respected that each of us exists in unique contexts with unique pressures. I don't know what my future self will look like or what challenges she will face. But I expect she will continue to hear Beauvoir whispering to her in a raspy French accent that although she's free, she also has a responsibility to consider the impact of her choices on other people.

Anti-aging procedures can be inauthentic when they are a form of disguise, another mask we put on, a flickering shadow that we project to others from our personal caves, creating illusions that are exponentially harder and more expensive to keep up. These procedures usually only accentuate our decaying youth, and we can be tempted to use them as a shortcut to save ourselves while we ignore the real work of challenging ageism.

In discussions of aging, we must ask, whose aging are we talking about? Masking aging is only a question for those who have enough privilege to afford it, financially and in terms of leisure time. Class has a huge impact on aging and not everyone can afford to spend many thousands of dollars every year on anti-aging treatments. Being old and poor, Beauvoir wrote, is often tautological. For women in more conservative and sexist societies, or poor and marginalized people everywhere, aging is even grimmer. For older women, their "lack" of beauty and youth makes them invisible; they are not seen as wise, but wizened; not curious, but a curiosity. But the more prestige, power, and property people accumulate, the more protected they are from the costs of aging, and the more easily they are able to slide comfortably into and through elderhood.

*   *   *

Not until we all gracefully accept that aging is normal—that it is not ugly or shameful—will the situation of elderhood change. Beauvoir wrote, "In order to resolve the 'identification crisis' we must unreservedly accept a new image of ourselves."[36] Over the years I have come to believe that this is both brutally hard but also absolutely necessary. Lives become different in old age, and that is okay. It really is.

We should not reject medicines that extend health spans and cure illnesses. What we need to work on is the attitude that continues to treat old age as abnormal and debilitating. And we should not simply distract ourselves from the inevitable by keeping busy—although keeping busy is important. We must embrace the facticity of our aging body, to acknowledge that aging is another stage in our quests toward fulfillment, one that presents new situations but does not define how we should behave.

In *The Second Sex*, published when Beauvoir was in her forties, she proposed that menopause creates a brutal rupture in women's lives. The biological tumult is fierce but the psychological experience can be eviscerating. Menopause abruptly marks a new life, but it's all too easy to be caught lurching between the excitement of entering a new phase of life and the doleful despair about time's passing.

Beauvoir wrote that menopause strips women of their fertility as well as their femininity and sexual attractiveness. While this sounds like an ageist statement, Beauvoir was talking about how women are often perceived to be. The reality is that we live in an ageist society that still judges women as sexual beings. Until we can overcome the injustice where sexism meets ageism, menopause will continue to tie women in existential binds. And menopause will continue to be a stage in which, in Beauvoir's words, "anxiety grabs the throat of the one whose life is already finished, even though death is not imminent."[37]

There can be lots of benefits to aging if we are willing to look for them—wisdom, experience, and deeper self-understanding, to name just a few. Some find old age to be a release. Once women get past the hormonal hell it creates, aging brings relief from menstruation.[38] (When Beauvoir wrote this, it's unlikely she had experienced the symptoms of menopause herself.) It can be an advantage not to be so deeply embedded in society. Some distance allows you more easily to excuse yourself from social obligations and expectations. And older people do not have to worry so much about pleasing others.[39]

The ancient Greek poet Sappho lamented that age withered her skin, grayed her hair, and took its toll on her heart and knees. However, she also suggested that maturity delivers gifts that younger generations don't appreciate—not only wisdom, but also a more nuanced perspective of life. She wrote, "And Eros has given me beauty not found in the light of the sun: the passion and patience for life that so often is lost on the young."[40]

Elderhood also opens up an opportunity for deeper authenticity. Elderhood enables people to have a better relationship with themselves. Older people can choose to be more responsive to their own needs and less obliged to everyone else. The existential key to growing older is to keep pursuing fresh projects, to continue engaging in the world, to persist in the quest for fulfillment. It is no use being on Earth if you choose to hang on as a living corpse. But we cannot transform the experience of aging solely through our attitudes. We must alter the world that makes it hard for older people to seriously engage in it.

"To grow old is a gift," my mother told me. "Look at the tragedies of people dying too young. What's important is how you live it, and how you deal with what you have to live with that's beyond your control." The practico-inert can be tough to shift. Ageist gazes cleave tightly, and time pushes all of us toward the grave. Being active and creative become particularly critical in elderhood, and it takes a lot more effort. In Beauvoir's words: "There is only one solution if old age is not to be an absurd parody of our former life, and that is to go on pursuing ends that give our existence a meaning—devotion to individuals, to groups or to causes, social, political, intellectual or creative work."[41]

Discovering new paths of progress toward a better world is the best way to engage people in society. These efforts are good for everyone. Compulsory retirement can be a release from the hamster wheel of drudgery, but it can also be devastating for those who find work fulfilling, and often society doesn't support people in retirement. Beauvoir rightly suggested that forced retirement is morally atrocious because it is tantamount to banishing elderly people to the scrap heap.

It is vital that older people have the option to participate in activities—work, hobbies, art, associations, or volunteering. These endeavors make space for older people to be engaged members of the community and can relieve loneliness, depression, and sickness. Martha Nussbaum argued that societies interested in justice for older adults should remove mandatory retirement age so that those who want to continue to work, can. Moreover, we should be building better infrastructure such as health care, good support systems for retirees, and adequate public transport. Public transport allows those who can no longer safely drive to be mobile and engaged in activities that are important to them.[42]

It is hard to find new goals in life as one ages. It takes strength and effort to stay engaged and to maintain a vibrant raison d'être. Beauvoir was not thrilled about growing older, but she (mostly) came to terms with it. She wrote books and published essays well into her senior years, although by the time she was seventy she said of writing a new work, "I don't have enough time ahead of me."[43] Still, she took on greater activism roles than she had ever done before, worked on shaping her ideas for new audiences such as a screen adaptation of *The Woman Destroyed*, and embraced the "feminist" label that she had downplayed for much of her life.

Beauvoir recommends adopting the attitude: "I haven't very much longer to live. I must say the last things I have to say, and say them quickly."[44] I say, let's not wait until elderhood to remind ourselves of this. Wisdom in elderhood can bring people closer to authenticity than at any other stage of life. In elderhood, people tend to be less susceptible to the illusions of earlier ages. Because in elderhood we are closer to death, closer to the end of our becoming, elderhood has the potential to bring us to a point at which we are closer to fulfillment. "It is harder to adopt than falsehood, but," Beauvoir wrote, "once reached, it cannot but bring happiness. This sweeping away of fetishes and illusions is the truest, most worthwhile of all the contributions brought by age."[45] Nevertheless, bearing wrinkles is different than bearing death. The thought of nothingness, of an inky void, of the unforeseen, can be both alluring and horrifying.

DEATH

*What else were they to do, if not drink, laugh, tickle
each other? As long as they were alive, they had to go
on living.*

—The Mandarins

Beauvoir was brought up as a devout Catholic which gave her
young self a rosy outlook on life and death. Her life with God was
happy. She would lie on the floor, cross her arms, and dream of a
celestial heaven of snowy angels, where she would have shimmering
wings and fly amongst resplendent sunshine and flowers.

At age fifteen, Beauvoir read the story of *The Little Mermaid*.
The mermaid renounces her immortal soul for love, and then turns
into seafoam, silently washing up on a deserted beach. The story
destroyed Beauvoir's ecstatic illusions. The idea of nothingness, of
extinction, reduced her to violent chills and tears of terror. Upon
realizing that God was irrelevant, that he was dead for her, and that
she too was going to die, she broke down in despair, screaming and
writhing on the red carpet. "How do other people manage? How
shall *I* manage too?" she wondered.[1]

The thought of annihilation haunted Beauvoir throughout
her whole life. When she was in her twenties and thirties, death

seemed outrageous to her. Later, she wished that her death would come without pain. She hoped that the ties that held her to the earth would slowly erode with time so that she could face her disappearance with indifference. Sometimes she contemplated suicide because waiting for death filled her with dread. At other times she despaired that the hours passed too quickly as she tobogganed toward her grave.[2] In a documentary filmed in her sixties, she reflected on her wild ambivalence about death: "Perhaps because when you are young . . . you believe yourself to be more or less immortal, and so the idea of being annihilated runs counter to everything that you feel in your consciousness, everything that you live and believe."[3]

Although Beauvoir did not fully come to terms with her mortality, she pointed to a few ways to approach death authentically. We can be drawn to the escape of death and deny death's reality, but an authentic attitude to our mortality beckons us to face death bravely, to be stubborn in our choice to live, and to be optimistic in our quest to choose and pursue fulfillment.

* * *

Beauvoir rejects Heidegger's claim that the authentic project is being-toward-death. Being-toward-death is the realization that we can only live authentically if we confront the inevitability of our mortality. Certainly the temporal limitation of death gives our lives structure, shape, and urgency, but Beauvoir's view is that "every movement toward death is life."[4] Our lives are not *for* death. We are *for* life. For Beauvoir, the authentic project is being-for-life.

Being-for-life neither denies death's finality nor its draw. People do try to deny death's finality: obsessions with anti-aging procedures, refusals to draft wills or advance directives, which creates heartache for those left behind, unhealthy habits and reckless choices to try to prove that they are beyond death. But an authentic attitude is one in which we salute death as life's destiny and assert our existence in spite of it.

Death is not only a natural fact and limit of the human condition, but it is also an invitation, one that is always open, to love our mortality—and others' too. Beauvoir described this tension between existence and mortality: "Existence must not deny this death which it carries in its heart; it must assert itself as an absolute in its very finiteness; man fulfills himself within the transitory or not at all. He must regard his undertakings as finite and will them absolutely."[5]

Beauvoir comes to the conclusion, rightly I think, that immortality would be fun for a while but would quickly become boring. Yet more than this, mortality is the condition for creating meaning in our lives because it gives weight to our actions. In her novel *All Men Are Mortal*, the main character Raimon Fosca drinks a potion that makes him immortal. Fosca longs for eternal life because he is afraid that his self-chosen humanist project—of organizing the world into a cohesive and peaceful society so that people can live better lives—will die with him. High on a God complex, he believes that he is the person to achieve this project. But he fails time and time again. Fosca comes to realize that immortality doesn't make him omnipotent, and world peace is as eternally elusory as he is.

Suspended between life and death, and steeped in apathy and inertia, Fosca's existence becomes a terrible curse. He bemoans: "I'm alive and yet I'm not living. I'll never die and yet I have no future. I'm no one. I'm without a past, faceless."[6] He is like the walking dead. While mortals are engaged and passionate, Fosca wallows abstractly in eternal repetition and languor. He is free from risks and free from failure because he will always have another chance, another friend, another love. There are no meaningful consequences to his actions. Fosca soars above the law because he kills but cannot be killed.

He tries to forget that he is immortal, but everyone Fosca meets and loves dies. He is forever alone. On occasion, he hopes that love will revive him, by giving him something to defend and to suffer for. Yet he has met so many women that his lovers' efforts, failures, and stories all sound the same to him. He has seen too many women, smelled too many roses, and survived too many springs.

As Fosca tells his story to Regina, she hopes that his immortal gaze will make her immortal because he will remember her forever. But she quickly realizes that in the context of eternity, she is just one of billions. Like a blade of grass that looks the same as all the others, she is reduced to an abstraction, indistinguishable from all Fosca's other loves.

The story ends with Regina's scream of anguish when she realizes that mortality is a curse: a curse because it means her existence is fleeting and precarious. She hasn't written books or had children to leave her memory behind. Fosca will forget her. "There would be no one to remember that singular taste of life on her lips, the passion burning in her heart, the beauty of the red flames and their phantasmagorial secrets."[7] Only death can end her anguish.

* * *

Despite the tragic ending of *All Men Are Mortal*, Beauvoir's challenge to us is to recognize that the risks of action inject life with danger and desire. Action brings with it the possibility of death, making life infinitely precious. Our limited time creates anguish but also urgency—the urgency to engage in life.

Immortality would be like an insurance policy: it wouldn't matter how badly you screw up, you'll always be able to do it all over again. A safety net would whisk away the risk of actions, but also whisk away the potential rewards of our choices—irrevocable, precious, inviolable. This is why it is better to learn to love our mortality.

Religion provides some people with comfort: there should be no need to fear death if one has faith in a happy afterlife. Beauvoir's mother, Françoise, was terrified of death and fought hard against it. Since she was devoutly Catholic, people wondered why. She wasn't afraid of the moment of death or what lies beyond it, but she feared this life being no more.

There are various views about immortality, from passing through the pearly gates to, as Diotima in Plato's *Symposium* describes it, hereditary immortality through one's children to creative immortality through works of art and literature that live on posthumously (as in Beauvoir's case). Whatever view of immortality one endorses, Beauvoir cautioned, "If you love life immortality is no consolation for death."[8] It's like not wanting a beloved book or film to end, even if you've heard the sequel is good. From an existential point of view, it doesn't matter whether you're atheist or pious; death makes each moment priceless because, as far as we know, there's only one iteration of this timeline with these particular relationships we have now. It's a gamble what happens thereafter.

Even if corporeal immortality is undesirable, is there a problem with believing in spiritual immortality? What if Beauvoir hadn't lost her religion? Another philosopher of Beauvoir's acquaintance, the activist and mystic Simone Weil, argued that belief in the immortality of the soul is a distraction.

Beauvoir and Weil met at college, where Beauvoir learned that Weil cried when hearing about people starving during a famine in China. Beauvoir wrote, "I envied her for having a heart that could beat right across the world." When Beauvoir found the opportunity to speak with her, Weil told her that the world needed a revolution so no one would go hungry. Beauvoir responded that people needed reasons to live. "It's easy to see you've never gone hungry," Weil retorted, implying that Beauvoir was arrogant and bourgeois.[9] They never spoke again. Weil died of cardiac arrest in 1943 at age thirty-four, possibly while on a hunger strike in solidarity with war victims.

Although Weil's perspective was religious, she comes to a similar conclusion to Beauvoir about death: the notions of immortality and life after death are harmful because they rob death of its precious purpose. It doesn't matter if the soul is *actually* immortal. For practical reasons, Weil wrote, "We must completely accept death as an annihilation."[10] Otherwise, as long as we're not in front of a firing squad, it's too easy to become complacent.

Instead of twisting ourselves in knots about how much or how little time we have left, we should get on with living. Take Socrates who, while in prison awaiting his death sentence, learned to play the lyre. Weil proposed that every one of us is like Socrates, waiting for death, and we should take his lead—not necessarily learning the lyre, but living and learning right up until our last breath.[11]

Socrates doesn't care that he won't have the opportunity to show off his musical dexterity to his friends or ever play in a concert. He hasn't given up living because death is looming. We should all starkly and fully acknowledge our mortality and make the most out of our earthly moments. Death reminds us not to take life for granted and to love the universe we have in the here and now.

* * *

After a night out drinking with Camus and Sartre in 1946, Beauvoir staggered home at daybreak. Sartre was giggling over the fact he was about to deliver a lecture on writers' responsibilities that very day. Beauvoir was despairing over the human condition. She leaned out over one of Paris's bridges and cried into the Seine at dawn, "I don't see why we don't throw ourselves into the river!" Sartre, also crying, exclaimed, "All right, then, let's throw ourselves in!"[12] They didn't jump. They went home for a couple of hours to sleep and nurse their hangovers with amphetamines. And yet a final leap remained in the realm of the possible.

The question Beauvoir asked while dangling over the Seine is a fundamental one: If there's no inherent meaning of life, why should we bother to live? If we have to resign ourselves to our mortality, why not get it over and done with sooner rather than later?

Nihilism is the tempting conclusion that, since we're all destined to become worm food, nothing really matters. All our efforts are ultimately futile, and therefore it's senseless to get worked up about anything. Although this mindset reflects the ambiguity of the human condition, it's only part of the story.

No one asks to be born. And at times it might feel like every heartbeat brings us closer to death. True enough. Nihilists—those who believe that the meaning of life amounts to nihil (nothing)—are right that we are here on Earth without an absolute reason. Nonetheless, Beauvoir suggested, "the nihilist knows that he is alive."[13] We transcend ourselves toward our own goals and in doing so we assert our existence and create reasons for being here.

In Beauvoir's novel *The Mandarins*, the brilliant psychoanalyst named Anne tells her husband, Robert, "Things are never as important as they seem; they change, they end, and above all, when all is said and done, everyone dies." Anne expresses the flippant, nihilistic view that we're all going to die so nothing really matters.

Robert criticizes Anne for using the meaninglessness of life as a convenient excuse to escape her problems. He accuses her of effectively dying before she's dead. His counterargument to Anne is that, "The fact of living proves you've chosen to believe in life . . . You like certain things, you hate others, you become indignant, you admire—all of which implies that you recognize the values of life."[14]

Still, Anne finds herself in a Sisyphean cycle of pushing her rock up a hill and despairing in her lucidity. Unlike Sisyphus, she cannot imagine being happy. She agonizingly trudges through the emptiness of her life. "Death nibbles at everything," she says. "How even and mild the light of death is!" Once she saw her life and the world around her as exciting and boundless, but now she marinates in ennui. She muses, "The earth is frozen over; nothingness has reclaimed it."[15]

Ties no longer bind Anne to the earth or other people. Her fervent love affair has ruptured. Her daughter has grown up and no longer needs her. She is bored with her work. When once Anne felt a unique bond with her husband, she now believes he would be just as happy with any other woman. Severed from others and growing older, Anne laments, "Each of us is alone, imprisoned in his body, with his arteries hardening under his withering skin, with his liver, his kidneys, wearing out and his blood turning pale, with his death which ripens noiselessly inside him and which separates him from everyone else."[16] Suicide seems like an escape from the languor.

*   *   *

For those who feel despondent, broken, or bored, death can seem vastly preferable to the pointless misadventure of life. Many people do actively choose death: in the United States, suicide is the tenth most common way to die. In 2017, there were almost 1.4 million attempts, and around 50,000 succeeded, if that is the right word. It's increasing too: the suicide rate in the United States has risen 33 percent over the last twenty years and, worldwide, 60 percent over the last fifty years. More people die of suicide than homicide.[17]

As I started writing this book, I learned that one of my best friends died by suicide after a long struggle with post-traumatic stress disorder after working as a peacekeeper in conflict zones in the Middle East. He was seeing doctors, although he had limited access to help. Psychiatrists would not see him because he didn't have the money to pay out of pocket. Besides, they told him, suicide patients are too much of a litigation risk.

My friend tried all the treatments available to him: yoga and meditation (he became an instructor), revolving doors of psychotherapists and psychiatrists, Adderall, Ritalin, diazepam, transcranial magnetic stimulation, electroconvulsive therapy, hospitalization, marijuana, psilocybin, LSD, and ketamine drips. "I'm essentially a lab rat," he said.

I tried to help—talking with him, going out for tea and dancing, sending him readings, encouraging him to write or create a film, and calling psychiatrists on his behalf at his request to appeal to them to take him on as a patient. They said no and told me if I really believed he was going to attempt suicide, to call emergency services. My friend told me he wasn't going to do anything soon and pleaded with me not to commit him to a psychiatric ward because it would be a certain kind of hell with no privacy or humanity. This setting would be the worst thing for him, he said, and it would only intensify his misery and craving for death.

"I'm a ticking time bomb," "I have nothing to lose," and, "I'm a recipe for disaster," he would say. He was staring directly into the abyss, telling whomever would listen that he was ready to jump but no one knew how to pull him back from the precipice. He held out some hope for ayahuasca—he asked his life partner if, as a Christmas present, he could attend a ceremony. He never made it that far. Tired and worn down at age forty-two, two days before Christmas, life ultimately broke him.

My friend once asked me if the existentialists would have

thought him pathetic because he was miserable and hadn't killed himself yet. I said no because often it takes more strength to stay than to leave. Yet, since we are free, we are always free to choose death. Suicide can be a tempting—or at least an understandable— response to the absurdity of human existence.

Compared to Beauvoir's time, we now have a greater understanding about mental illnesses. If conditions such as depression and post-traumatic stress disorder are part of our facticity then, as in the case of death from cancer, despair and the will to oblivion can overtake us without our choosing it. But Beauvoir's concern was with the *choice* of death and she judged suicide in terms of freedom.

*   *   *

For Beauvoir, suicide is not an authentic choice when it's a response to nihilism. Beauvoir advised against suicide because the act robs us of freedom. In choosing death, you could be being unfair to your future being who might have other possibilities, and would be grateful to you for pulling through tough times so you can go on to a better life.[18] In *The Ethics of Ambiguity*, Beauvoir describes a brokenhearted young girl who overdoses on phenobarbital. Her friends find her, get medical help, and save her life. If she goes on to lead a happy life, then in Beauvoir's view, her friends did the right thing because she had made a hasty decision.

However, if this young woman were to attempt suicide again, Beauvoir proposed that friends and doctors who prevent her from exercising her freedom become tyrants because they are perpetuating her anguish. Even if we find this a bitter pill to swallow, the pivotal existential point is that other people cannot be responsible for the young woman's choices—they are hers and hers alone.

If you're feeling queasy about this case, consider another: An elderly, sick, and paralyzed woman wrote to Beauvoir despondent that doctors insisted on keeping the woman alive. The woman wondered why free love is allowed, but not free death? Beauvoir echoed, "And indeed, why? Why?"[19]

Beauvoir's conclusion in both cases—the young woman and the older woman—is that we have to let people make their own choices about if and when they want to die. In such situations, it is possible that the only path is to reject extreme suffering, which may be via suicide or assisted dying.

For some people, like my friend who died of suicide, the suffering is too great to stay. The only escape for him were ketamine drips that, for a few fleeting moments, would calm him and lift him out of the drudgery of his existence into a trance. He stayed as long as he could for his life partner, but felt that he had exhausted all paths. "It feels like my brain is on fire," he said. "My quality of life is that of an invalid. This is no way to live."

Beauvoir's philosophy taught me that I was there to be a good friend, but it was not my responsibility or right to perpetuate his suffering against his will. To be an authentic friend was to acknowledge that he made an authentic choice and that his plans were not a whim but a result of years of deliberation.

Repeatedly, my friend told me that he wanted an ethical death, meaning that he wanted no one to be surprised. He would have a farewell party so we would know. He didn't have a farewell party and I'm mad and sad about that. He seemed to be happily texting me the day he died about socks with his face printed on them that he bought for his life partner for Christmas. We shared laughing emojis. But I can't say that his death was unexpected.

Despite my torment about what else I could have done to help, I keep telling myself that it was not my call to institutionalize him.

Maybe one day I'll be able to fully believe it, and to fully respect him for his choice. That's what an authentic friend would do—at least in this particular situation.

*   *   *

In Beauvoir's *The Mandarins*, just as Anne meditates upon the brown phial of hydrogen cyanide that she stole from her friend Paula, Anne hears her daughter outside her room. Her mind drifts to wondering about how her death will affect others.

Like elderhood, death is an "unrealizable," meaning that we can see others die but not ourselves. Reflecting on our own death—our corpse, our funeral, our absence—is a vague exercise in imagination. We can't know what it feels like, how it happens, or whether it comes at the right time—until it's too late. The fact that we don't know anything about what death involves in any subjective sense can make it exceptionally difficult to come to terms with. We can only envisage what our death will be like *for others*.

Anne does not choose death. She worries about the impact that her passing would have on those she loved, those whose happiness she cared most about. Anne's realization that other people matter does not suggest that other people's feelings ought to be prioritized over those who ideate about suicide. But Anne's brush with death shows how death is not an individual experience.

Authentic choices acknowledge our interconnectedness. We exist in webs of relationships, amidst calls and appeals. Even suicide, which seems like a purely individual choice, affects others so acutely that they ought to be taken into account. Anne realizes that her death belongs to other people because they will live her annihilation which is why she says, "Condemned to death; but also condemned to live; how long?"[20] Although she chooses life, the option for death forever lingers.

Although there are rare occasions where suicide can be an authentic choice, the greater challenge for most of us is how to live given that both life and death are inescapable. Paula, another character in Beauvoir's *The Mandarins*, asks Robert for advice about whether she should take prussic acid. After Robert advises her against the poison, she responds: "But then how shall I live?"

Paula's question vexed Beauvoir. There is no single answer for how to project ourselves toward being-for-life. It is up to each of us to decide for ourselves what to live for—whether it's our future selves, loved ones, or self-chosen projects, for example.

The key argument against suicide in *The Mandarins* is that Anne's attachment to her daughter and granddaughter justifies her existence. It's not enough to make her happy, but it's enough to bring her back from the dead. "Since my heart continues to beat, it will have to beat for something, for someone," she resolves.

Beauvoir said later that she wanted Anne's survival in her mundane existence to seem like a defeat. Anne returns to a quotidian that doesn't quite fulfill her and confronts a series of tomorrows that she isn't wholly convinced is worth it. Anne's choice isn't meant to be a definitive solution for everyone. Beauvoir said: "I showed some people [such as Anne], at grips with doubts and hopes, groping in the dark to find their way; I cannot think I proved anything."[21]

What Beauvoir does prove is that living isn't just about breathing; living implies that you actively recognize value in the life you carry forward. Other people don't always infuse our life with joy, but they can, and they can give our lives meaning. Let's not undervalue that we love, we make friends, we take pleasure in objects, projects, and events, and our lives are commensurate with these attachments. This is radically different to some Buddhist views, for example, in which attachments are the cause of our suffering. For

Beauvoir, attachments are the meaning and source of values. Attachments are worth our effort, even if we risk suffering.

* * *

How might it be possible for those who experience other people's deaths to cope in authentic ways? In Beauvoir's essay "My Experience as a Writer," she proposed that when we experience great pain, such as a loved one dying, suffering ambushes us from two directions: from the shattering misfortune itself, and from the grief that makes the person going through it feel as though they are unbearably alone in their unhappiness. Writing, talking, or reading about death—an experience that binds us all—can help bring people together, to feel more connected and less isolated. Beauvoir found that sharing sorrows and confessing pain sometimes helped.

In order to help her deal with her feelings about her mother's death from cancer, Beauvoir wrote. (Beauvoir often wrote about her loved ones' deaths, including Sartre in *Adieux* and Zaza in *Inseparable* and elsewhere.) Beauvoir was accused of irreverence for taking notes by her mother's deathbed and condemned for taking advantage of the situation for her own personal gain. But for Beauvoir, writing was a form of benediction.[22] Writing was comforting and therapeutic because Beauvoir found that her words could preserve her loving memories of her friends and family. Journaling helped her to reflect on her own mortality, to ponder the question of suicide, and to manage her grief. Helping readers deal with their own losses was an unintended benefit:

> If you can write, the very act of writing breaks down this separation; writers often describe painful experiences not because they create literature from just anything at all, in a sacrilegious way, as is sometimes said, but because for them

speaking of it is a way of surpassing their grief, their anguish, their sorrow. And it is the same for the people who read, since they no longer feel isolated in their sorrow or anguish, they bear it better.[23]

This kind of communication is especially important when coping with suicide because suicide diffuses socially, meaning that often those who die of suicide know people who have died of suicide.[24] Someone might think: I am not responsible for how other people handle my death; others are free to face death however they choose. But this is only partly true: Beauvoir reminds us that we are also responsible for one another because we coexist.

Staying alive in itself is precious because it deters others from suicide. And talking about death and pain can save lives—our own and others'. Although suffering makes people feel isolated and different from everyone else, sharing stories is a way of reminding each other that we matter, and that choosing life matters.

*   *   *

Every day the world beckons us to consent to tomorrow, but resigning ourselves to the quotidian isn't good enough. Beauvoir shows that death is a risk with each step we take (or don't take) into a future saturated with ambiguities and complexities. The choice to continue to live is constantly reaffirmed every time we make the effort— sometimes the excruciatingly painful effort—to create the next line of our life's poem.

Life always hangs in the balance between being and nothingness, between the possibility of death and reasons to live another day, between affirming our freedom and accepting the dismay of nihilism and apathy. Life is vulnerable and fragile. The inevitability of death perpetually looms. Looking for ways to live with the uncertain future—to fulfill it, to question it, to persevere in the quest to fulfill ourselves—is valuable in itself. This is the meaning of an authentic life carried freely toward an authentic death.

When Sartre died from edema of the lung at age seventy-four, Beauvoir said, "His death does separate us. My death will not bring us together again. That is how things are. It is in itself splendid that we were able to live our lives in harmony for so long."[25] Now, they are buried next to one another in Paris's Montparnasse Cemetery. We may die alone, but we should live together—really live with vitality—as if our lives were going to carry on beyond our oblivion.

"To survive is, after all, perpetually to begin to live again," Beauvoir wrote in *The Mandarins*.[26] As long as our hearts continue to beat, it's up to each of us to answer: How? For what? For whom? And with whom? Beauvoir encourages us to perpetually begin to live again, to face all our tomorrows. This perspective transcends her life and her philosophy.

In the next section, we'll look at a few more of Beauvoir's ideas about how to find a fulfilling project and how to evaluate which projects are worthwhile. We sabotage ourselves when we seek to justify our lives by orienting ourselves toward being-for-ourselves at the expense of being-for-others, obliterating ourselves in the pursuit of being-for-others, or pursuing happiness as an end in itself. Becoming authentic calls for us to scrutinize these distractions and to push back against them. It's not enough only to push back against them for ourselves, however. Beauvoir's ethics challenges us to clear paths for both ourselves and others through rebellion so each of us can pursue our quest for authentic fulfillment.

PART III

TOWARD
FULFILLMENT

SELF-SABOTAGE

I no longer asked myself: what shall I do? There was everything to be done . . . to combat error, to find the truth, to tell it and expound it to the world, perhaps to help to change the world . . . everything was possible.

—Memoirs of a Dutiful Daughter

Forgetting ourselves by drifting into robotic archetypes is inauthentic and there are many ways we do this. Beauvoir proposed that some people sabotage themselves by idolizing lovers or subsuming themselves unreflectively into traditional roles such as wife or husband. Others squander their freedom kneeling before an idealized image of themselves (narcissism) or a spiritual power such as religion, astrology, or other pseudoscience (mysticism).

Narcissism and mysticism are not always problematic in themselves. But they can be inauthentic ways of focusing too heavily on being-for-ourselves at the expense of being-for-others, or being-for-others at the expense of being-for-ourselves. How can we become authentic when all action involves a tension between these two modes of being-for-oneself and others? Beauvoir advises, "To do great things, today's woman needs above all forgetfulness of self: but to forget oneself one must first be solidly sure that one has already found oneself."[1] If we forget ourselves too soon, we lose ourselves.

There's a high price to pay for forgetting oneself through worship. Groping for salvation in a higher power (God, a supreme leader, a sainted guru) is, according to Beauvoir, inauthentic because it's a form of self-sabotage. Voluntary subordination in the name of faith means acquiescing to unconditional trust and unquestioned power.

This kind of submission encourages people to ignore (or manipulates people into discounting) important questions about the world. It's downright dangerous. One of the most perilous strains of self-sabotage shows itself in the veneration of spiritual healers. Many spiritual leaders would more accurately be described as cult leaders because they have a checkered history when it comes to healing people, and in many cases abuse and take advantage of people instead.

Not all forms of mysticism are self-sabotaging. Beauvoir pointed to Saint Teresa of Ávila as an example of an authentic mystic. Teresa was a sixteenth-century Roman Catholic luminary nun. Canonized forty years after her death, she is a patron saint of Spain. She was also the first of four women Doctors of the Church—a title given to thirty-six saints (as of 2020) whom the Catholic Church recognizes as having made especially deep and orthodox contributions to theology.

Saint Teresa philosophized through mystical meditations, modestly insisting that she was merely channeling the words of God and that it was an accident that He chose her. As a mystic, she philosophized in careful and self-deprecating ways, calling herself a wicked, wretched, imperfect, faulty, and base woman, so that men in power wouldn't feel threatened.

However, Saint Teresa's work was so groundbreaking that René Descartes, who most likely knew of her work, was inspired by her writing on self-knowledge. Descartes adopted the same rhetoric as her, tweaking it into the maxim that he became famous for: "I think therefore I am," and neglected to credit Teresa for her methodology.[2]

Saint Teresa was often unwell. She was prone to fainting fits and violent fevers; she was paralyzed for two years; she probably suffered from epilepsy and rheumatoid arthritis; and she was assumed dead and almost buried multiple times. Despite these challenges, she asserted herself as an agent in her own life. She was passionate about her chosen quest for fulfillment but, at least in Beauvoir's view, wasn't beholden to her passions. Beauvoir thought Teresa was an existential hero of sorts. Beauvoir wrote, "She should be admired for the intensity of a faith that penetrates to the most intimate regions of her flesh."[3]

Saint Teresa's faith did penetrate her deeply, double entendre intended. It is no accident that the famous Italian Baroque sculptor Bernini's statue of her is called the *Ecstasy of Saint Teresa*. The statue, in a chapel in Rome, shows Teresa reclining on a cloud, swooning at the feet of an angel holding a golden spear. A hidden window filters in natural light, revealing golden heavenly rays, the sensual glow of her spellbound face, and her lips gaping ardently. The sculpture is based on a passage in Saint Teresa's autobiography describing her divine encounter:

> I saw that he held a great golden spear. The end of the iron tip seemed to be on fire. Then the angel plunged the flaming spear through my heart again and again until it penetrated my innermost core. When he withdrew it, it felt like he was carrying the deepest part of me away with him. He left me utterly consumed with love of God. The pain was so intense that it made me moan. The sweetness this anguish carries with it is so bountiful that I could never wish for it to cease.[4]

Not everyone reads eroticism into this passage or Bernini's statue, but it is hard not to. Even Teresa was undecided: "I am not sure that I know when love is spiritual and when there is sensuality mingled with it, or how to begin speaking about it."[5]

What makes Teresa an existential saint, in Beauvoir's view, is that her orgasmic gestures are an expression of her freedom. She eclipses her personal sexual feelings by intellectualizing her relationship with God, giving the bond meaning beyond her individual reality and connecting it to the universal human experience of life and death. Saint Teresa's experience wasn't about her personal pleasure: she embodied the spiritual joy of a divine relationship.

Saint Teresa chose to become a nun against her father's wishes, despite how heart-wrenchingly painful it was for her to do so. She thought being a nun would help her to become fulfilled. Teresa wasn't only interested in fulfillment for herself. She rebelled against the Protestant Reformation and the Spanish Inquisition. She wrote philosophical meditations, reformed the Carmelite order, founded a religious order, and established convents based on her philosophy. People called her disobedient and stubborn because she ignored the decree that women should not teach, and she was repeatedly suspected of heresy.

While there is no doubt that Saint Teresa achieved incredible success, there's a fine line between what Beauvoir sees as the authentic mysticism of Teresa and cultish fanaticism. Abuse, manipulation, or emotional blackmail would violate the conditions for authenticity. But here's the thing: Saint Teresa encouraged her readers to think for themselves. Teresa believed that evil lurks in unreflective reasoning, impulsive behavior, and dull-wittedness, so she encouraged people to pray in ways that are authentic for the person doing the praying. In a strikingly existential passage, she also advises people never to forget their own nothingness, to vigilantly watch out for the wily devilish vipers of self-deception, and always to be open to learning, introspection, self-knowledge, and humility.[6]

What is most admirable about Saint Teresa, and women like her, was that the social respect they earned enabled them to do great things, such as founding new communities where people would come for encouragement and advice. Teresa's physical maladies became a way for her to transform herself and the structure of her world. In Beauvoir's reading, Saint Teresa's spirituality wasn't a narcissistic indulgence. Teresa freed herself from women's lot, transcended her gendered condition to live the human condition—which, at the time, was the male condition—and shaped the world for the better in profound ways.

Saint Teresa actualized her freedom, engaging concretely in the present world. She didn't glorify and abstractly contemplate the afterlife at the expense of this one. Teresa teaches us that this world matters, and regardless of whether you are religious or not, it's up to all of us to take responsibility for engaging in it. We must create concrete goals and projects and improve life for everyone in it.

Catherine of Siena, a fourteenth-century Dominican mystic and Doctor of the Church, is another existential hero, in Beauvoir's view. Catherine was a courageous leader, ambassador, and peacemaker who advocated for charity and advised popes and royalty. She integrated her spiritual and communal life.

Although Saint Catherine was not an existential philosopher, some of her teachings contain seeds of existential authenticity, such as her commitment to truth over passivity. Catherine wrote, "We must proclaim the truth openly and generously, never letting fear silence us."[7] However, she was finely attuned to the dangers of speaking out, and she emphasized that a healthy dose of congeniality can sweeten the truth. This is good advice for everyone: speak your truth, speak it with love and joy. But also speak the truth with care. Avoid using honesty as a weapon to heedlessly bludgeon foes.

Although Beauvoir thought that it's up to each of us to choose our own quests for fulfillment, not God, Saint Catherine's sentiment was similar when she suggested that with a fervency that stretches toward authenticity, one can transform the world for the better, and which may involve destruction: "If you are what you ought to be, you will set fire to all Italy"—and beyond.[8] When Saint Catherine channeled her energy toward what she felt called to do—when she launched herself into caring for the poor, teaching, and counseling the papacy—she felt fulfilled.

It was precisely Saint Catherine and Saint Teresa's mysticism that enabled them to commandeer their freedom, to have confidence in themselves, and to avoid inferiority complexes.[9] Catherine of Siena questioned equality directly in a prayer, where she said that her sex was against her because men look down upon women. Allegedly God responded that men and women are equal. Saint Catherine and Saint Teresa shared His belief in the equality of women. They also shared sheer nerve in declaring their views. They dedicated themselves to acting beyond traditional female roles, rejecting male authority, and passionately pursuing humanitarian goals. Being-for-themselves and being-for-others dovetailed into doing good in the world.

Beauvoir didn't talk about Muslim mystics, but there are some great intellectual and spiritual leaders in the Islamic tradition that also would meet her criteria for authenticity. In eighth-century Basra (Iraq), Rābiʿa al-ʿAdawiyya al-Qaysiyya ("Rabia") was a slave girl who became a Sufi leader and saint. She challenged patriarchal traditions and rituals. Rabia refused to be bound by rules, including marriage, despite many proposals. She asserted herself as equal to men in intellectual and spiritual ways.

Rabia also encouraged people to think for themselves. She advised steering clear of organized religion and, instead, developing a personal relationship with Allah based on love—not punishment and rewards—which was radical at the time.[10] She also knocked back her many suitors, scolding some for lustiness and giving others philosophical challenges that showed why she shouldn't marry them.[11] (In the television series *The Good Place*, Rabia was named as one of the few people who made it into heaven.)

Rabia lived until eighty, but other women paid a high price for their courageousness: Joan of Arc was burned at the stake. Catherine of Siena scandalized people and was a victim of attempted assassination, although probably died of anorexia. Other women failed to convince people of their connection to God and were thwarted in their attempts to pursue fulfillment. Beauvoir pointed to famous thirteenth- and seventeenth-century nuns Saint Angela of Foligno and Marie Alacoque, respectively, who did not accomplish their freedom authentically because they were not aiming for transcendence; they were looking for their own salvation through God's attention, getting off on being "chosen" by Him. They used their devotion as an excuse for quietism and passivity.

When Marie Alacoque licked up someone else's vomit and Saint Angela drank water with which she had washed lepers' feet and got a scab stuck in her throat and swallowed it like communion, they each thought they were performing acts of devotion. While I suggest these are acts of insanity, or at least ridiculous and desperate cries for attention and validation, Beauvoir judges them to be narcissistic. While Saint Teresa exalted her freedom, Saints Marie and Angela's gestures annihilated their freedom. Marie and Angela turned their bodies into sacrificial temples, hurt themselves, and helped no one with their absurd and useless offerings.

* * *

Narcissistic personality disorder is the label given to people who have a grandiose sense of self-importance, lack empathy, and crave admiration. While most people are not pathological narcissists, many people have narcissistic moments. Beauvoir's philosophy attempts to explain why some people behave narcissistically in some situations. It is not simply that they feel worthless and seek out the gaze of others to feel important. Narcissism is an existential response: an escape from facing up to the task of creating our own worth and values. Instead of being echoes of others—subordinating themselves to lovers or spouses, for example—narcissists subordinate themselves to an ideal image of themselves.

Beauvoir saw narcissism as a crisis of character, a process of escaping oneself into a state of alienation.[12] In other words, the problem arises when I set up an image of myself as the central meaning in my life and wallow in it. I fail to live authentically when I lose myself in my reflection, daydream about idealized versions of myself, and do whatever I can to become the center of attention. Some people look for the spotlight on a stage, which is why many turn to social media for followers. Others seek out the gaze of a doctor, psychoanalyst, a palm reader, or secret lover. Narcissism is a strategy to make oneself loved and desired by anyone who will look and listen, even if they have to be paid to do so.

If it's up to us to create our essence, could narcissism be an authentic choice of being-for-oneself? For Beauvoir, the answer is a hard no. Although narcissism might seem like a way of boosting our self-esteem and worth, narcissism undermines us by vacuuming meaning from our lives. Narcissism tempts us to put our real appearances behind masks. We become so comfortable wearing masks that we forget they're there and waste time curating inauthentic images. Filtered and augmented social media posts are examples of people hiding behind masks and misrepresenting themselves to others.

Narcissism can lurch up from a desperate desire to create a cohesive portrait of ourselves. The existential problem is that this goal denies the evolving and fragmentary nature of becoming. Beauvoir explained this urge as the desire to establish ourselves as a pure being like a god.[13] Feeling as if you are the center of the world can be intoxicating. The sensation can be exalting, but the truth is that the feeling of delirium results from asphyxiation. Narcissists cut themselves off from the rest of the world, but our very connection to others enables us to breathe.

Self-help books are filled with ways to love yourself, but self-love is equally as dangerous as narcissism. We are rarely encouraged to turn inwards—and when we are, it's usually in superficial, inauthentic ways. For example, capitalism encourages us to worship money and possessions over genuine bonds with others. bell hooks proposed that we've become a mass consumerist culture, defined by a debased version of Descartes's famous maxim coined in Barbara Kruger's artwork: "I shop therefore I am." I'm afraid hooks and Kruger are not wrong. We're bombarded by advertising that tells us our spiritual hunger can be filled by buying more things. We're led to believe that the path to self-love is paved with receipts. hooks laments that, "We may not have enough love but we can always shop"—or post more selfies.[14]

Ultimately, Beauvoir proposed, a narcissistic approach to life is hypocritical: narcissists want others to value them, but the only thing narcissists value is themselves. They don't have a reciprocal relationship with the world. It's unlikely that narcissists can love authentically, Beauvoir argued, as they are too superficial and arrogant and their greed far surpasses their generosity.

Regina in Beauvoir's novel *All Men Are Mortal* is an archetypal narcissist. She is a "pseudo-artist" because she's a self-centered actor whose raison d'être is to achieve fame. She attempts to become famous not through an authentic commitment to her art but by sleeping with influential men. Some people treat acting as work that pays the bills, others act because it flatters their vanity, but authentic artists strive to become genuine creators. Through their art, they transcend themselves, become conduits to artistic creation, appeal to others, and forge new possibilities and ideas.

Narcissists such as Regina play at authenticity. They seek appreciation for their mere presence instead of their actions. They can't forget themselves enough to go beyond themselves. The possibility of insta-fame—of becoming famous for doing very little or for simply generating a unique or curious online persona—appeals as a shortcut to fame without having to do all the authentic work.

Regina pursues fame, glory, and adoring fans, but she has no interest in revealing the truth of the human condition through her performances. She knows what she is doing and she hates all of it—the makeup, the forced smiles, and her fake voice. She knows better but sabotages herself anyway, dooming herself to immanence and ennui.

You might object to Beauvoir's take on Regina. After all, curating oneself can take a lot of work, time, energy, and skill. But for Beauvoir, the intention makes all the difference. There's nothing wrong with designing beautiful Instagram posts, but if what drives it is a manic craving for followers and admiration rather than the quest to create something meaningful, then that's a red flag. Choosing a quest primarily based on winning other people's approval, instead of choosing to express what one values, is inauthentic.

Getting likes on selfies is one way to feel less lonely, but chasing followers and their reactions as a means to define ourselves is a capricious strategy. When we do this, we avoid the risk and anguish of defining ourselves in authentic ways. Even if a photo or insightful tweet goes viral, eventually the engagement subsides and we're left with emptiness, again, looking for ways to chase the fickle dragon of fame.

Social media isn't inherently narcissistic, but it can feed our tendencies toward narcissism. With every tweet, story, hashtag, or post, we should be thinking about whether we are opening up possibilities and freedom for ourselves and others, and whether we are creating innovative ways of seeing the world. If not, we should keep our fingers off the share button. This should be an injunction we all agree to before signing up to a social media app.

* * *

I am guilty of filtering photos on Instagram. I'm guilty of hoping that when I post to Twitter, my "followers" will like and retweet. Beauvoir might accuse me of wasting my freedom because my actions are not contributing to the benefit society. It is no good posting about #MeToo and #BlackLivesMatter movements if I don't go out and march, donate, and volunteer. If I don't follow up my statements with action, social media is just me constructing a superficial image, filling the void in my life with meaningless noise, and distracting myself from authentic fulfillment.

While social media can be an important platform from which to organize and rebel, all too often it is filled with misinformation and distracts us from what is really important. Beauvoir's message about narcissism is a warning about being too dependent on others to define our worth and value in the world. We must struggle against letting our vision become too clouded by the mist of fecund self-regard to see beyond the black mirrors of our phones.

We sabotage ourselves when we are so self-preoccupied that we stifle our ability to create genuine relationships with others and the world around us. Beauvoir proposed that one of the reasons people, especially women like Regina, wallow in narcissism is because they are barred from direct access to real engagement in the world. They have been brought up to see themselves as passive and desirable objects of adoration, and so it is a short step for them to internalize that adoration for themselves. Beauvoir suggested that this phenomenon is why girls love dolls: many dolls represent the ideal woman. But quiet, pretty, compliant dolls covertly normalize the process of objectification.[15]

The #MeToo movement has thrown a spotlight on the high prices that women pay to avoid self-sabotage. Privileged, famous, wealthy celebrities brought high-profile visibility to an issue that affects very many people in vulnerable positions—waitstaff, cleaners, precarious workers—who endure everyday harassment at work, not to mention the harassment and abuse endured in relationships.

Many women's careers and livelihoods across many industries are beholden to powerful and narcissistic men (and some women) who act as gatekeepers to jobs. Many men have demanded sexual favors in return for access, and punish women who do not comply. Very many women are appreciated not for their talent, but for being an object to reflect men's dominance, a dominance that only exists because of women's submissiveness.[16]

Beauvoir's issue with this dynamic—people being appreciated for their bodies and sexual services instead of their talent—is that objectification perpetuates oppression. Being viewed as a sexual object to be hunted and possessed alienates people from their own bodies. Women and some men, but women more frequently, become means to sexual ends instead of being seen as ends in themselves. This puts women in a double bind. Either women sabotage their careers by walking away and into career or social suicide, or women sabotage themselves by choosing to play by men's rules. It's not a fair choice.

When women accept men's demands, they become complicit in their own and others' objectification and exploitation. In accepting their otherness they reinforce the idea that it's permissible for men to do this. Even if women escape such gatekeeping, they're still subject to industries in which harsh male gazes dominate. Women's bodies are shaped, manipulated, and used for profit and others' entertainment and gratification. To be successful, they need to play the game or be ostracized from it. Either way, their authentic quests for fulfillment are sabotaged.

In *Becoming Beauvoir*, philosopher Kate Kirkpatrick emphasizes Beauvoir's claim that sexual objectification is the reason for women's continuing oppression. Kirkpatrick identifies this concept as one of Beauvoir's most powerful and original ideas. This notion is one of the reasons Beauvoir campaigned against sexist advertising and degrading imagery. Advertisements that exploit women's bodies encourage men to see themselves as masters and women as objects to be manipulated for (mostly men's) profit or pleasure.

Beauvoir rightly objected that for most advertising, it would be pretentious to call it art. Claiming that sexual objectification in advertising is freedom of speech is foolish. People usually do not actively choose to see advertisements. Advertising violates people's freedom from having images imposed on them. Beauvoir wrote: "But it is not useless to act on images. Children also have eyes, and the images make an impression on them. Preventing these images from inspiring in them a scorn for women would already be a victory."[17]

* * *

We must move beyond weak efforts to educate women to put up with the current forms of patriarchy. We must develop what Beauvoir called an "anti-sexist reflex."[18] We must create cultural conditions that won't tolerate sexism—such as male violence against women—and will support people in standing up against injustice. We must give people legal recourse to fight injustice, so they can protect their lives and dignity.

Oppression of the male gaze encourages women toward narcissism as a survival strategy. According to Beauvoir, one of the reasons women accept men's objectification is that the feeling of being dispossessed sparks a fear of being just one person lost amongst billions of others.[19] Narcissism is a strategy to escape this fear of not being acknowledged as unique. Beauvoir noted that one way people try to feel less alienated is to create a unique character and quirks—and then to magnify them in a calculated campaign of self-promotion.

A twenty-first-century trend in this genre is the #NotLike-OtherGirls subreddit and hashtag where women highlight how they're different—read: more special, superior—to other women. Other girls shop for makeup, clothes, and high heels; a #NotLike-OtherGirls girl invests in bitcoin, plays video games, and wears sneakers. In denouncing gender stereotypes about femininity, #NotLikeOtherGirls perpetuates tropes about how "other women" allegedly are. In Beauvoir's terms, #NotLikeOtherGirls is a way of adopting the male gaze to *other* women, putting others down to pull attention toward one's own idiosyncrasies.

It is not only actors, rock stars, and social media influencers who risk constructing a platform for narcissism. Beauvoir criticizes women writers for being self-indulgent and insincere.[20] This is one of my greatest fears, especially with writing about personal experiences. I worry that readers will perceive my vulnerability to be cringeworthy or invalid, or that I've left out important philosophical arguments and examples and perspectives that others will criticize me for.

In a writers' group I shared my story about teaching in prison. One person asserted I had no right to write about incarceration because I haven't been incarcerated myself. Another disagreed on the basis that no one can take my experiences away from me. I remind myself of this tension constantly, and whether I am judged to have succeeded is not up to me. All I can do is try to move forward carefully in spite of the ambiguity, in spite of the fear of being judged and perceived as a failure, in spite of the looming demon of imposter syndrome who relentlessly dive-bombs around my head and whispers that I have no right to write about anything and that I am cosplaying as a philosopher but with cute shoes.

Saint Teresa of Ávila wrote: "Please have patience with me, dear reader, as I must cultivate patience with myself in writing of things I know almost nothing about. Because, really, sometimes I grab pen and paper like an utter fool. I have no idea whatsoever how I am going to begin and what I am going to say."[21] This didn't hold Teresa back, and she proceeded with humility and vulnerability, knowing she might be mistaken, but speaking of what she understood. I identify with Ávila's attitude, but Beauvoir's philosophy suggests that in my case there might also be a splash of narcissism—not grandiose narcissism (I hope), but vulnerable, self-involved narcissism.

My fear stems from wanting to create an image of myself as a good and thoughtful writer. I have sabotaged myself, turning down possibilities because I'm afraid of what other people think of me. For example, I dread all media appearances. I've turned down being a guest on an important podcast because I'm afraid I won't know what to say, or the words won't come to me, or I'll forget important points, or I'll just sound stupid.

This is a form of narcissism because media appearances and this book aren't about me the person. Saint Teresa knew this all too well, and she was heard precisely because she prioritized her ideas. I know I need to focus on using myself as a conduit of philosophical ideas, yet I still wrestle with letting go of myself, struggling to free myself from an image I want to create of myself. An authentic attitude would be to strive to become comfortable with such tension, such ambiguity, and leap into it anyway, because to take risks, to hazard failure, is a form of transcending.

*   *   *

Beauvoir was accused of narcissism. She wrote four autobiographies and many books with strong autobiographical elements, such as an account of her mother's death. She published her personal diaries and letters. Initially she was afraid to write about herself because she worried it would be presumptuous, but Sartre and her friends encouraged her.[22]

When she was in her seventies and looked back upon her writing career, she defended against the accusation of narcissism, countering that in writing about herself, she spoke about experiences that concern many others: "The 'I' that I use is actually very often a 'we' or a 'one' which refers to the whole of my century rather than to myself."[23] She thought that her "I" went beyond her singularity to address the universal human condition. "What I wanted was to penetrate so deeply into other people's lives that when they heard my voice they would get the impression they were talking to themselves."[24]

As already discussed, Beauvoir had variable success in this respect. Beauvoir's voice was less universal than she hoped: women of color, of less privilege, and of different abilities did not see themselves in her work.[25] Did narcissism prevent Beauvoir from seeing the limitations of her analysis? When I asked existential psychotherapist Leon Garber whether he thought Beauvoir was narcissistic, he said, "Without a doubt."

Garber cited her limited empathy for the people who loved her and her hyper-contrarian impulses in her desire to upend the system and destroy the establishment. He suggested that anyone who writes multiple volumes of autobiographies has to be somewhere on the scale of narcissism. Furthermore, Beauvoir was hyper-fixated on death and worried about the world continuing to exist without her in it. In a memoir, Beauvoir said that she hoped to achieve immortality through her writing. Instead of God's love in the afterlife, "I should have the undying love of millions of [readers'] hearts."[26]

At times, Beauvoir was myopic with respect to some women's

experiences, and she didn't always recognize the limitations of her thinking. Still, it's not wrong for a person to write about the way they see the world. When Beauvoir wrote about herself, she discovered that there were aspects of her work that spoke—and still do speak—to many people, and so she continued. Beauvoir knew her work resonated because readers wrote mountains of letters to her. She responded to many. These epistolary conversations, of reciprocal recognition, affirmed that her voice mattered. In 1972, one correspondent wrote: "Why did I write all of this to you? Because I have never felt such a human closeness as I do with you, Madame, whose writing can express the whole gamut of emotions."[27]

Labeling Beauvoir as narcissistic, however, is potentially an example of telling a woman to stay in her lane. It would have been self-sabotage for Beauvoir *not* to write about her experiences. Writing was, for Beauvoir, an authentic quest for fulfillment that helped many people.

Kate Kirkpatrick pointed out that throughout Beauvoir's entire life people threw ad feminam attacks at her, undermining her work and reducing her to a failure as a woman, a thinker, and a human. When Beauvoir was twenty-eight, her father mocked her writing and yelled: "You are a dried-up old prune . . . too old to think anymore, never mind to write a decent book. You'll never amount to more than the Worm's whore." The "Worm" was Sartre whom Beauvoir's father resented because they did not marry.[28] As Beauvoir became more well-known, journalists and others called her an "also-ran," "la grande Sartreuse," "Notre Dame de Sartre," Sartre's muse, disciple, ambassador, fangirl, nurse, biographer, jealous woman, and obsequious sycophant.[29]

Talking with Sartre also thrust a sense of self-doubt, intellectual inferiority, and mental modesty upon her. As students at the Sorbonne, Beauvoir and Sartre would discuss philosophy for hours in the Luxembourg Gardens. Sartre would punch holes in her arguments.

Beauvoir imagined that she had been lost in arrogance and confusion for years, her reasoning clouded with biases and carelessness. Sartre would tell her that she was unoriginal, that her ideas were uninspired, and he infantilized her. She came to think that the "intellectual universe was a great jumble of ideas in which I groped my way blindly."[30]

Sometimes Sartre pitted his contingent lovers against Beauvoir on the pretext of inspiring her. In her memoirs, Beauvoir wrote about "Camille" (Simone Jollivet). Camille was slightly older than Beauvoir, beautiful, glamorous, an avid reader and writer, and an actress. For a time, she was a sex worker who would stand next to the fireplace, naked, waiting for clients, while reading Michelet or Nietzsche. "[Sartre] frequently set [Camille] up as an example to me when trying to goad me out of my inactivity," Beauvoir recalled.[31]

Boorish behavior was not out of character for Sartre. In a published interview with Beauvoir in 1974, Sartre told her how he was never attracted to ugly women and, "in our relations I liked a woman to be pretty because it was a way of developing my sensibility."[32] One of Beauvoir's friends told her Sartre was oppressive. Her friend wasn't entirely out of line to say so, but Beauvoir dismissed it.[33] She insisted, "Sartre is not at all an oppressor."[34]

Beauvoir was jealous of Sartre's esteem for Camille and her independence. Yet Beauvoir knew Camille's freedom came at the price of love and the hardships of sex work. Beauvoir reassured herself that all she needed was time to write.[35] When writing petrified her, she revisited her early reminder to take her time: "Every time I start on a new book, I am a beginner again. I doubt myself, I grow discouraged, all the work accomplished in the past is as though it never was, my first drafts are so shapeless that it seems impossible to go on with the attempt at all." But moments would arrive when her words catapulted her excitedly toward completion:

"Each page, each sentence, makes a fresh demand on the powers of invention . . . Creation is adventure, it is youth and liberty."[36]

* * *

Beauvoir recovered from self-sabotage despite the barrage of others undermining her and pulling her in different directions before she'd had a chance to create herself in authentic ways. For example, Beauvoir was selective as to whom she spent time with: less family and more friends (although not less Sartre), reiterating the oft-misquoted mantra, "Blood of the covenant is thicker than the water of the womb." You cannot choose your biological family but you can choose your logical family, that is, the people you surround yourself with. That might mean distancing yourself from toxic people who put you down in destructively critical ways—especially if it is under the guise of love, duty, or being cruel to be kind.

Whether Sartre's criticisms of Beauvoir were constructive or destructive is up for debate, but Beauvoir turned what she perceived to be his critical but superior gaze into motivation. Perhaps he galvanized her because she felt he respected her or he validated her intelligence. Possibly his words provoked her to prove him wrong or inspired her not to let him down. She did not consider herself inferior in every dimension, though. She found Sartre's thinking to be impressive, but his expression was clumsy.

Beauvoir was impressed with Sartre's attitude: he was aware of his shortcomings but they did not concern him. He maintained a clear understanding of what he wanted to do. He had an unshakable belief in himself, his vitality, and his pending success.[37] Appreciating her own situation, Beauvoir knew that Sartre and her peers were more advanced in their thinking because they had had twice the time she did to study. Their other advantages included being male, meaning they had a more rigorous education; being more used to philosophical discussions; and having more solid ideas about what they wanted to do and to write.

Beauvoir gave herself a break. She also was wise to focus on learning and her potential growth. This attitude is an important shift in perspective because it takes the pressure off the present and channels our energy toward the future. Beauvoir set out to satiate her curiosity, to explore the world, and to help change it for the better:

> I saw opening out before me a clearly-marked field of activity . . . I no longer asked myself: what shall I do? There was everything to be done . . . to combat error, to find the truth, to tell it and expound it to the world, perhaps to help to change the world . . . everything was possible.[38]

Beauvoir transformed her self-doubt into writing. From the moment she began working on her first novel, *She Came to Stay*, she almost never stopped writing. She believed in her work, she had things to say, and she built the confidence to say them. The war, however, forced her to step back and look at life from a different perspective. She saw misery everywhere and realized that nothing could be taken for granted. Writing was not a panacea against despair, but it helped her to deal with the ambiguity of the human condition, to make sense of the gap in between the anguish and joy of life, and between reality and appearances.[39]

Beauvoir learned to give herself credit where credit was due. When she went to a dinner party with novelist Colette Audry and philosopher Jean Wahl, she surprised herself with how well she was able to converse with so-called serious people, and she realized that appearances are often fake.[40] Many people seem to be more serious or intelligent, but often these mannerisms are superficial.

When Beauvoir's ideas were attributed to Sartre or others, she objected. For example, people criticized her work on *Old Age* as being derivative, but she insisted that her work was original.[41] Many did not listen, but it was important for her to stick up for herself. Authenticity involves affirming our freedom by advocating for ourselves, and pushing back on false public opinion.

The antidote to an inferiority complex is reciprocity. We should surround ourselves with people who can be both supportive and challenging. And we should be kind to ourselves. It's important to recognize that different people have different doors open to them. We can strive to open doors for ourselves and others, and we can engage in collective projects to learn, to be curious, and to pursue truth.

Part of recognizing freedom as an end goal is to realize where we can seize power to create opportunities for our own happiness—or to be confident in saying no to things we think will make us unhappy. Authentic happiness isn't about what we have or what we are, it lies in creating and doing. For Beauvoir, happiness doesn't fall from heaven; we have to try to construct our own happiness.[42] Neither happiness nor unhappiness are given and so an attitude of entitlement to happiness is self-sabotaging. Yet, such entitlement is not uncommon. The United States Declaration of Independence states that the pursuit of happiness is an "unalienable right," and it is not much of a leap to jump from the pursuit of happiness being a right to happiness in itself being a right. But such a leap is a mystification.

HAPPINESS

What good is happiness if it not only does not bring me truth, but even hides it from me?
—Force of Circumstance I

Happiness used to mean something completely different than what we understand it to be now. The word came from the Old Norse word *happ*, as in happenstance, and meant being lucky. One's fate—fortune, health, and happiness—lay in the hands of God(s), and happiness was what happened *to* you. Now, happiness is more commonly understood to be as a more or less momentary feeling of joy. But the philosophical meaning of happiness is more substantial. The ancient Greeks spoke of *eudaimonia,* meaning well-being or flourishing. In the philosophical sense, happiness is not so much about feeling pleasure in the moment, but about your life going generally well. It is this understanding of happiness that Beauvoir built upon.

Beauvoir's analysis in *The Second Sex* focused on possibilities in terms of freedom, not happiness, but happiness is a recurring theme in many of her other works. Authentic happiness, Beauvoir suggested, is a particular kind of flourishing that comes from living in harmony with the world. Harmony does not mean quietism; it means embracing our freedom, taking responsibility for our lives, pursuing truth, and creating genuine connections to the world and others. The problem for most of us is that there are thick webs that block and distract us from authentic happiness, and Beauvoir sought to see beyond the haze.

At the heart of Beauvoir's idea of authentic happiness is the existential notion that we are constantly torn between being subjects for ourselves and objects for others, between mastering our world and being crushed by it. We cannot dictate the terms of the world around us, we cannot become the omnipotent center of the universe, but we can strive to embrace the ambiguity of these tensions and in-betweens, and to delight in them. This gap—between subject and object, between grasping and bending—is the space of existence. In Beauvoir's words, "I experience [the gap] as a triumph, not as a defeat. This means that man, in his vain attempt to *be* God, makes himself exist *as* man, and if he is satisfied with this existence, he coincides exactly with himself."[1]

In a 1946 essay, Beauvoir pointed to Jean-Paul Sartre as an example of a (presently) happy person. He was satisfied with his existence, he coincided with himself, and he was in harmony with his world. He didn't rely on anyone else for joy. He was imaginative and engaged in activities he was passionate about, such as writing, women, and whiskey—not necessarily in that order.

Sartre didn't worry about anything too much. Death didn't faze him, since he saw it as a necessary and important condition of his life. Sartre knew what he liked. He preferred eating canned foods instead of raw fruit and vegetables, and as Beauvoir put it, "More than the pure air of the mountain peaks or the open sea, he enjoys an atmosphere full of tobacco smoke and warmed by human breath."[2] Most important, Sartre appreciated his freedom and his control over his happiness, and he was confident about the possibility for others to be happy, too.

Beauvoir did not acknowledge that Sartre's happiness often came at the expense of others. He left a trail of unhappy people—mostly ex-girlfriends—in his wake. He did not carry the weight of racism, sexism, or classism. It was easy for him to drink his whiskey and sit in cafés without discrimination, walk down the street without being catcalled, and exist without fear of violence or hate. Sartrean happiness is not only ethically questionable, but remains out of reach for many people.

Nevertheless, what is important about Beauvoir's version of authentic happiness is that it is integrally tied to taking responsibility for our lives, seizing control of our freedom, and enabling others' freedom too. To will freedom, Beauvoir wrote in *The Ethics of Ambiguity*,

> is to will the disclosure of being in the joy of existence; in order for the idea of liberation to have a concrete meaning, the joy of existence must be asserted in each one, at every instant; the movement toward freedom assumes its real, flesh and blood figure in the world by thickening into pleasure, into happiness.[3]

If we don't love life, if living doesn't bring us happiness, why are we here? Perhaps to learn how to love it properly, but we should learn as quickly as possible. If we plod through life on autopilot, relentlessly striving toward money or appearances, devoid of passion, then our actions become meaningless and futile. It all means nothing if there is no joy in it. We might as well be dead.

* * *

Existentialism isn't known for being a happy philosophy. Its focus is more on death, anxiety, and the cold hard truth. Part of the reason that existentialism gained this gloomy reputation was that its popularity grew during the material and psychological devastation of World War II. Existentialism's fame also meant that the philosophy was often misunderstood. One of the reasons Sartre delivered his famous 1945 lecture "Existentialism is a Humanism" was to attempt to clarify the philosophy for general audiences—although he later worried he'd oversimplified it.

Around the same time, Beauvoir was also pushing back against existentialism's bleak reputation. In Beauvoir's essay "Existentialism and Popular Wisdom" (1945), she argued that cynicism and platitudes in popular culture distort our perceptions of what will make us happy. The platitudes include the sentiments: the goal of life is happiness; we all deserve to be happy; don't be too ambitious; don't aim for too much; don't try to be a hero; we are all going to end up dead so nothing really matters; and it is as futile to hope as it is to despair.

This pessimism is convenient because it calls for low effort and gives people an alibi to do nothing. In Beauvoir's view, popular wisdom is bleaker than existentialism. "It is because I reject lies and running away that I am accused of pessimism; but this rejection implies hope—the hope that truth may be of use. And this is a more optimistic attitude than the choice of indifference, ignorance or sham."[4]

Popular wisdom has changed in many ways since Beauvoir's time. Nevertheless, there is one mystification that still pervades: that happiness is a goal—if not *the* most important goal—of life. Modern-day platitudes abound on T-shirts and notebooks telling us, "Don't worry, be happy," and "EAT, SLEEP, *fabulous*, REPEAT." Advertisements tout: Buy this for happiness! Go on this trip for happiness! Get this degree or job or whatever and you will be happy!

While having a base level of material security—read: money

and the stuff that it buys—makes a huge difference to survival and well-being, one of the biggest mystifications is that more stuff will make us happy. Capitalism, Beauvoir wrote, is based on an illusion to make people forget about pursuing authentic justifications for their lives.[5] Capitalism sells endless diversions. The entire marketing industry is dedicated to coming up with ever new strategies to get us to believe that a widget will make us happy, and that we need to continually purchase widgets for maximum happiness.

This is the premise of fast fashion, which convinces many people that they need new clothes every season. Fast fashion results in colossal amounts of landfill and pollution. Clothing chemicals poison the earth. Rivers are turning black from the cocktail of dyes, carcinogenic chemicals, and heavy metals that clothing manufacturers dump into them.

Fast fashion, slot machines, social media feeds that constantly refresh, the ticks that let you know someone has read your message, and the dancing ellipses that let you know when someone is responding to you—all these are designed to get us addicted to the dopamine hits that newness sparks. These tiny moments build pre-reflective habits of gorging on stimuli while corporations constantly leech money and information from us.

Many people keep craving more possessions. Beauvoir rightly argued that goods that promise instant gratification—such as alcohol, drugs, news, films, and social media—only serve to distract us from authentic fulfillment. A lack of imagination tempts us toward mindlessness, lubricating our slide into decadence. We use these diversions to flee our lives because, Beauvoir said, we lack "inner fire."[6] When we indulge in them as an escape, it reduces us to what Beauvoir called a "vain living palpitation"—and that is a bad thing because it's bad faith to escape ourselves and bad faith to slide into passivity and inaction.[7]

Part of the problem with obsessive consumerism is the misguided desire for novelty. In her essay "An Existentialist Looks at Americans," Beauvoir criticizes people (Americans specifically, although they are certainly not the only ones) who are obsessed with incessant and feverish sensations of newness. Always chasing something new while annihilating the past is dangerous. Our present actions are important, but only in the context of our lives as a whole, as a synthesis of the present *with* our past and future. Authenticity bids us to create a genuine relationship with our past, present, and future.

Overemphasizing the pleasures of the present amounts to treating life as an unending series of little deaths of each moment. It's unclear whether Beauvoir was alluding to *la petite mort* in the postorgasmic sense of the term, or more literally. Either way, living life as a series of orgasms might be a lot of fun. A healthy dose of pleasure is important to living a good life. But when we constantly indulge our animalistic impulses, and flit from one state of unconsciousness to another, our existence becomes gratuitous.

Beauvoir said that living contingently makes life an "indefinite flight," lacking true and deep foundations, with only "dry bones." To jettison our past and future turns the present into an "honorary corpse" because we've given the moment a death sentence before we've even lived it.[8] Beauvoir's character Laurence, an advertising executive in *Les Belles Images,* explains:

> People wanted novelty, but with no risk; they wanted products to be exciting and yet of solid, sober quality; of high prestige value, but low price . . . She was always faced with the same problem: how to excite curiosity, to astonish and at the same time to reassure; behold the magic product that will completely change our lives without putting us out in the least.[9]

There is no magic product or alchemic formula for happiness. A society that hawks optimism makes many people feel lost and then sells them cures to help them temporarily lose their awareness of feeling lost. Of the "disconcerting miracle that is America," Beauvoir wrote, "To adapt here is really to resign yourself; to be happy is to be willfully blind. Many things would change among Americans if they were willing to accept that there is unhappiness on earth and that unhappiness is not a priori a crime."[10]

Yet many people do turn happiness into a false idol. Imagine you decide that happiness is your goal. The first thing you do is to think about what will make you happy. What are your unmet needs? What are your voids calling to be filled? What will bring pleasure? What will minimize pain (assuming you're not a masochist)?

Beauvoir analyzes this situation: you are turning your self into an object. Already you are focusing on superficial self-interest. Already you are treating your self as if it were a static thing. You are looking within a fixed thing—which does not exist—to determine what its wants and needs are. And there are armories of products rapaciously waiting for your credit card so you can fulfill yourself with junk that will leave you emptier than ever.

While it might seem like self-interest is the guiding explanation for a lot of behavior, the existential view is that the self is not mapped out in advance like that. The self is not a thing, it starts as *no*thing. But we are *creative* nothings. We surge forward in the world without predetermined interests or projects (although many are imposed on us).

When you look back in hindsight, it might appear as though your life was destined, but each of our life trajectories is the result of a cascade of choices. It is up to each of us to assume or deny our freedom, to recognize our capacity for choice as a fact of our existence, and assertively to choose ourselves as in charge of our own destinies. Happiness is not an existentially valid goal; it collapses in self-interest which is deterministic.

*   *   *

The obsession with mainlining happiness is now a global trait. Happiness is often pegged to economic growth. As economist Kate Raworth said, "We are addicted to endless growth and that is the existential economic question of our time."[11] Most governments focus on gross domestic product as the benchmark of collective well-being. March 20 is the International Day of Happiness, on which the United Nations releases an annual World Happiness Report that, in addition to measuring economic growth, includes factors such as healthy life expectancy, generosity, and social support.

Beauvoir was concerned about the never-ending quest for happiness because it risks feelings of inadequacy and sends people reeling into vicious downward spirals of disappointment. In Beauvoir's novel *The Mandarins* Anne complains about how a lack of definite happiness is in itself a pervasive source of unhappiness. Consider social media, which is filled with performative happiness, and influencers whose careers are focused on branding themselves as happy thanks to all the products they are paid to tout. This culture creates a collective mask of happiness and wealth, implying that if you are unhappy you are a failure. It's no wonder that antidepressants and self-help books are so popular: we are led to believe that happiness should be the default, and we yearn for quick fixes.

Some believe that happiness can be willed into existence. With some thirty million copies sold, Rhonda Byrne's *The Secret* (2006) is one of the best-selling books in the world. The premise is based on a movement called the "New Thought," which promotes the core belief of mind over matter in an extreme way. You will be happy and successful if you follow the formula: ask, believe, and receive.

Visualize what you want and it will manifest itself into your world. The vision-boarding fad is based on a similar principle: flip through glossy magazines, cut out pictures of supermodels and designer clothes, paste them on a poster-sized sheet of paper, and looking at it will help you achieve your dreams. These endeavors are efforts to manifest wishes by praying either to a god or some other surrogate force that underpins the universe.

Evidence is mixed as to whether positive thinking helps people be happy. One study found that optimistic Catholic nuns ended up living longer than pessimistic ones.[12] Another found that people who practiced loving-kindness meditation were better able to break out of the hedonic treadmill—to be less depressed and more satisfied with their lives—than those who did not meditate.[13] Still another found that pessimists had higher cortisol levels than optimists, meaning that pessimists felt more stressed out about their stress than optimists.[14] And another found that optimistic (but not grateful) patients recovering from heart failure were physically more active and had fewer cardiac readmissions.[15]

Positive thinking might boost our health, but our health might boost positive thinking. And some of it may simply come down to a placebo effect. *The Farewell*, a 2019 film directed by Lulu Wang, is based on Wang's life and toys with this idea. In the film, a young woman named Billi finds out that her grandmother Nai Nai has been diagnosed with terminal lung cancer and has only a few months to live. Nai Nai's family decides not to tell her. Billi is torn between loyalty to her family and tradition on the one hand, and on the other hand, guilt about lying and falsifying medical records. The family keeps it a secret and the credits reveal that six years later, the character that Nai Nai was based on is still alive. (I don't know if she has seen the film and knows now.) The film does not make any specific claims about positive thinking, but it certainly raises the question as to whether the grandmother would have died if she knew about her terminal diagnosis.

Beauvoir faced the same dilemma with her mother's death. Her mother, Françoise, was at a clinic dying of sarcoma. Beauvoir said that doctors' mistakes meant the disease had long gone undiagnosed. The doctors constantly told Françoise it was peritonitis—serious but curable—and that she was recovering. Beauvoir lied to her mother about her fatal condition, then reproached herself for her own complicity.

Yet Françoise had a good instinct about her situation: she knew she was getting worse by the day; she refused to see a priest and others whom she thought might disrupt her illusions that she wasn't dying; and after her death, Beauvoir found a notepad in which her mother had written, "I should like a very simple funeral. No flowers or wreaths. But a great many prayers."[16] How far can prayers take one? That is unclear, but Françoise knew all along that she was dying.

* * *

Many skeptics question whether positivity can affect reality. Optimism is necessary to move toward goals. You need to be optimistic, for example, that studying is going to help you pass an exam, or that training for a marathon will help you complete it, or that developing a skill will help you master it. But too much optimism can reduce your motivation to achieve those goals, if you start reaping the psychological benefits of achievement—relaxation, enjoyment, lower blood pressure and heart rate—before you have done anything.[17] Basking in the glory of world peace, for example, might make you feel happy, but it is not authentic happiness as Beauvoir conceived of it because the feeling is based on an illusion.

Desires not materializing can create a huge anticlimax. When we do nothing to pursue our goals, we're left with inertia and longer-term unhappiness. The expectation of magical rewards muzzles our happiness of achieving something as the accomplishment of our effort. Like a narcotic, optimism can make us feel better for a time, but too much too frequently can turn us into addicts. Toxic positivity can make us worse off long-term because we miss out on the benefits of concrete action—like transcending beyond wishful thinking.

Setting expectations low and focusing on the worst possible outcome can be a good way to prepare oneself for life's ups and downs, since if you do achieve your goal, you will be pleasantly surprised. The Stoics call this *premeditatio malorum*—the premeditation of evils—to imagine things that can be taken away from us so that we appreciate them more.

Toxic optimism can have even more pernicious effects than just inadequacy and disappointment. When I got to the part in *The Secret* where Byrne wrote, "Nothing can come into your experience unless you summon it through persistent thoughts," I wanted to throw the book into the recycling bin. Byrne posits that victims of car crashes, war, genocide, and other tragedies die because their own thoughts put them in those situations. "The frequency of their thoughts matched the frequency of the event," she wrote, asserting that what you choose to think becomes your experience.[18]

Beauvoir's analysis gives us better tools for understanding these events: oppressed people often pretend to be happy because it is what's expected of them.[19] To purport that oppressed people are to blame for their situation is massively disingenuous. It ignores the deliberate exploitation that prevents people from choosing freely and takes responsibility away from the people who have made choices that impact others in negative ways.

Feminist Sara Ahmed argued that there are profound "unhappy effects of happiness."[20] Narratives around happy house-wives, happy slaves, and domestic bliss are used to justify oppression of people in these groups. These storylines seem to pre-scribe the steps toward happiness but in reality, for most people, they corrode happiness. And too many people resign themselves to elusive fantasies, mistaking passivity—quietude, stagnation, rest, or routines—for authentic happiness, in the name of care, protection, or avoiding tension.[21]

Audre Lorde also came across this kind of victim-blaming when she was recovering from a mastectomy. In a medical magazine she read about a doctor who said that happy people don't get cancer. Initially, she felt guilty, wondering if her disease was her fault, but realized that victim-blaming obscures the truth of life. It is easier to convince people to be happy and optimistic about monstrous situations than to improve those situations.

Given the realities of racism, sexism, pollution, abuse, inequal-ity, injustice, homelessness, suicide, and greed, Lorde asks, "What depraved monster could possibly be always happy?" Lorde's solu-tion is to be vigilant against lies—"false happiness and false breasts, and . . . false values"—that taint our lives. Authentic happiness can be found in the fight to reveal the truth of our situations. In Lorde's words: "The only really happy people I have ever met are those of us who work against these deaths with all the energy of our living, recognizing the deep and fundamental unhappiness with which we are surrounded, at the same time as we fight to keep from being submerged by it."[22]

* * *

In Beauvoir's fictional work *The Woman Destroyed*, Monique asks her friend Isabelle whether she is happy. Isabelle responds, "I never ask myself, so I suppose the answer is yes," and defines happiness as liking the moment she awakes.[23] But not hating life and not thinking about whether one is happy are superficial notions of happiness. Being too busy to reflect doesn't mean you're happy in an authentic way.

Women have long been assigned the role to be providers of happiness, while men and children benefit from women's efforts. But it has been unimportant whether women have been happy to fulfill these roles. There is no model for women about what it means to be happy that's about her own happiness and is not, ultimately, an evaluation of how well she contributes to others' happiness.

Making other people happy can be an absorbing vocation. In *The Woman Destroyed*, Monique follows her social script and dedicates her life to creating happiness for her husband and children. Yet, just as it is deviously inauthentic for oppressors to force people to be happy through domination, so too is it inauthentic to force people to be happy through submission. Caretaking can become toxic when you sacrifice yourself to make others happy.

Monique's husband and children all end up miserable. When her husband leaves her and her daughters grow up, leave home, and have no real interest in a relationship with her, the foundation of Monique's happiness crumbles. She was so heavily defined as a mother and wife that she didn't know who she could be without them. She wonders, "The world is an amorphous mass, and I no longer have any clear outlines. How is it possible to live without believing in anything or in myself?"[24] Monique's (and many others') mistake is believing that their happiness depends on others.

As a teenager, Beauvoir made the same mistake when she became obsessed with her flighty (distant) cousin Jacques. When she thought he wanted to marry her, she was ecstatic. When she suspected he would marry someone else, she plunged into despair. Her happiness lay fragile in his slimy hands. When Beauvoir told a philosophy teacher that she was skeptical about conjugal love, the teacher responded anxiously, "Do you really believe, Simone, that a woman can find fulfillment without love and marriage?"[25]

Beauvoir took it as a challenge, deciding that she would have to pursue happiness sans Jacques. It was a good call: Jacques married someone else, had five or six children, and Beauvoir often saw him in bars, drunk, alone, and crying. When she ran into him twenty years later, he cried, "Oh! Why didn't I marry *you*!" He died, malnourished, at age forty-six.

* * *

Beauvoir's cousin clearly had many issues, and one of them was money, but money doesn't buy authentic happiness, which lies not in what we have or what we are, but in what we do. In her first philosophical essay, "Pyrrhus and Cineas," Beauvoir talks about the Hellenistic Greek general Pyrrhus. His advisor Cineas asks Pyrrhus what he will do after his next battle victory. Pyrrhus says he will fight another. And after that? Another. And then another, until eventually Pyrrhus will rest. Cineas asks why Pyrrhus doesn't just rest now. Cineas is an Epicurean, meaning that he is interested in maximizing tranquility and minimizing fear and pain. But war is neither serene nor painless. Cineas raises a good question: Why do anything?

Collecting possessions, friends, lovers, children, status, social media followers, money, and privilege can bring happiness. But they don't make us happy *in themselves,* and whatever happiness they do bring is often short-lived. People who win the lottery are thrilled for a while, but usually sooner rather than later, the elation fizzles. A gift can make us ecstatically happy, but soon it gets integrated into our lives, and we forget the initial exhilaration it ignited.

The same often happens with romantic love. "We have only five senses, and they become satiated so quickly," complains Beauvoir's character Henri in *The Mandarins*. Despite having an objectively good life—with a meaningful, high-profile, well-paying journalism job, beautiful women, and friends who love him—Henri has a desperate desire to rip apart the image of the beautiful blue sky and ocean he is looking at, along with his girlfriend's youthful skin. He doesn't. He is not a psychopath. He's just bored and disconnected. Once we get what we want, having it becomes the new normal, and we forget not to take it for granted.

Modern psychology calls this a "hedonic set point," which means that we have a stable level of happiness. Our feelings of happiness go up and down depending on things we procure, events, and circumstances, but generally we all return to our original level of content. Since existence precedes essence, Beauvoir would reject that there is such a thing as a predetermined set point, but she has her own explanation for the phenomenon. Happiness is not a fact of life, but it is a side effect of transcending toward goals:

> One cannot fulfill a man; he is not a vessel that docilely allows itself to be filled up. His condition is to surpass everything given. Once attained, his plenitude falls into the past, leaving that "constant emptiness of the future" . . . Since man is project, his happiness, like his pleasures, can only be projects.[27]

Fulfillment is a receding goal, and it's hard to know what path to set off on toward our quest. Aristotle's idea of eudaimonia suggests that we focus on who we are and what our talents are, and then put them to good use. Beauvoir provides no ready-to-wear solutions in the same way that Aristotle does. We can't achieve fulfillment in a static way because the pursuit is a never-ending quest toward a precariously precious end. But we can pursue meaningful activities which infuse our lives with authentic happiness. Anne in *The Mandarins* says that we can't give others packaged-up reasons for being, "But sometimes only trifles separate them from happiness."[28] Anne became a psychotherapist to help people raise their awareness about their possibilities for joy.

Beauvoir teaches us that we would do well to recognize that happiness lies not in the goals themselves, but in pursuing and surpassing them. This perspective shifts our focus from achieving to well-being. While there are significant ethical issues with Pyrrhus's conquering and pillaging, Pyrrhus's answer—that he will continue to embark on new quests—is an authentic one. Getting things won't bring happiness because we will always want more. Doing nothing won't bring happiness because wallowing in immanence is not really existing. Our best possibilities for authentic happiness prevail in embarking on quests toward destinations that stretch our imagination, in the ambiguities that lie in between mastering and succumbing to our world, and in the spaces where we create our essence.

* * *

When Beauvoir was a student, she desperately wanted a valuable, fruitful, and happy life, but she was also afraid of becoming too myopic about it. She worried that the pursuit of happiness would lure her into resignation and complacency and she would become numb. She was torn about whether happiness meant a peaceful and pleasant life, or one that was filled with achievements, or one where she lived knee-deep in profound suffering, or one brimming with depth and fervor and intoxication about being in control of her future. At one point she conjectured that happiness must be willed, and defined it as "ardent plenitude without *desire*—equilibrium and peace—an exaltation that isn't aware that it must come to an end."[29]

She also wondered if, given all the suffering in the world, happiness might be a privileged way of being. Perhaps it is only available to the select few who are deemed deserving of it, or those who pursue the right things in the right ways. Sometimes Beauvoir would throw her pen in exasperation: "If it comes, take it—it is only worthwhile if it is life—it is absurd to refuse it, absurd to seek it."[30]

Beauvoir came to believe that happiness involved a little of all of the above. In one of her later memoirs, Beauvoir said she never quite broke free from yearning for happiness, though she was aware that her obsession with happiness had initially distracted her from taking politics seriously.[31] This is what Beauvoir's notion of freedom warns against: letting the pursuit of happiness slide into self-interest, self-sacrifice, or short-termism.

Still, others' unhappiness doesn't preclude our own happiness. Beauvoir agreed with Albert Camus who told her that we shouldn't feel ashamed to snatch happiness wherever possible, even when we know about the miseries of the world because, "Happiness exists, and it's important; why refuse it? You don't make other people's unhappiness any worse by accepting it; it even helps you to fight for them."[32]

What also often gets overlooked is whether the pursuit of happiness is morally valuable or worthwhile, and whether it adds up to a good life overall. As mentioned in the introduction, Beauvoir pointed to the Marquis de Sade as an example of someone who found happiness in morally questionable ways, that is, in titillation, excitement, and arousal of the senses that he found while torturing people. Happiness, for him, was criminal excitement. Beauvoir rightly criticizes Sade for overgeneralizing his passions, such as assuming that everyone finds being bad to be a turn-on.

But Beauvoir takes important lessons from what she calls Sade's "black stoicism": that pain can, sometimes, be transformed into pleasure.[33] Defeats can be transformed into victories, depending on how you look at the situation. Sade's two characters, Justine and Juliette, are sisters and orphans who are both abused. Justine tries to live a virtuous life and is punished, tortured, and raped mercilessly. Juliette responds to her situation by becoming a nymphomaniac and murdering fearlessly. The brute facts of their situations were similar, but they gave their lives radically different meanings.

The intention with which one approaches an experience can vary significantly: Juliette embraced her situation, while Justine was devastated. Beauvoir is not suggesting that we take up libertinism, but Sade's characters show that the meaning we give life will be very different for different people in the same situations. Some people take pleasure and pride in being whipped, while others find it painful and humiliating.

Beauvoir is not suggesting that Justine would have been happier had she adopted the same attitude as Juliette. To claim that Justine just needed to put up with her situation would be victim-blaming. Beauvoir had a more important point to make: authentic happiness is not just about our own freedom, but others' freedom too. Our well-being and happiness are intimately linked with other people. We cannot expect oppressed people to be happy. Both sisters were in a dreadful situation and the solution is for people not to abuse or oppress anyone.

During World War II, Beauvoir looked for happiness in simple things, such as beautiful mornings, great weather, and writing, but most important, in community. She was happy to have authentic friends when she needed them and solitude when she wanted it.

Having both solitude and companionship reminded her how good it is that people exist, that we have a world in common, and that we are alive together. This was part of her motivation to work toward freedom for everyone to choose to fulfill their lives in their own ways but without oppressing others.

*   *   *

In addition to taking control of our lives in a way that's respectful of others, another path toward authentic happiness is to have a good understanding of our existence. While we can never fully know ourselves, Beauvoir wrote, "Self-knowledge is no guarantee of happiness, but it is on the side of happiness and can supply the courage to fight for it."[34]

Self-knowledge can help people to understand their situations, to consider what they want to do in life, to reflect on what they want out of life, and to explore possibilities for happiness. Beauvoir calls for us not to live like Monique, the woman destroyed, but to strive to live in lucidity, without illusions:

> No, really; what I like more than anything is not ardent faith . . . It is exhausted enthusiasms [élans], searches, desires, especially ideas. It is intelligence and criticism, lassitude, and defeat. It is the beings who cannot let themselves be duped and who struggle to live in spite of their lucidity.[35]

Beauvoir's existentialism helps us to clearly understand the truth of our situations. She motivates us to find the courage to face our existence sincerely. Ignorance and illusions can be comforting, but truth is vastly more fulfilling. Lucidity doesn't always bring happiness, but clarity can create the conditions for happiness. To become authentically happy, it's vital to free ourselves from other people's imposition of happiness, false idols, and commercial sadism that traps us into unnecessary consumption and disappointment. Freedom from such distractions primes us to take control of our own projects so that we can be free to create our own happiness. Happiness is a side effect of being actively engaged in our lives, throwing off our stifling and restrictive security blankets, and reaching outside our cozy cocoons to explore our existence and to rebel against injustices. Truth, not ignorance, is existential bliss.

REBELLION

Change your life today. Don't gamble on the future, act now, without delay.

—After The Second Sex

An authentically meaningful life is one that opens out into an endless and immense cosmos. Beauvoir wrote, "The spirit with all its riches must project itself in an empty sky that is its to fill."[1] Existentialism empowers us to leap out and fill our skies with our projects. But many people are bound in thousands of big and small ways that hold them back from becoming authentic creators of their lives. For Beauvoir, bonds that constrain our freedom are a moral emergency. These bonds constitute oppression.

As long as oppression exists, as long as our wings are clipped, none of us can genuinely fulfill ourselves in a morally authentic sense because, for Beauvoir, our freedom depends on the freedom of others. The goal of existential ethics is to eradicate oppression because, Beauvoir proposed, "Justice can never be created within injustice."[2]

The authentic response to oppression must be rebellion, meaning social and political struggle against unfair structures. Together we must work to create a new foundation of the world: on freedom instead of domination. Recreating the foundations of the world is in our power. Beauvoir came to believe that this transformation is the "real task of feminism."[3]

In an ideal world, we would see what Beauvoir called a "collective conversion" where oppressed people would rebel, oppressors would stop oppressing, and all freedoms would reconcile.[4] Rebellion would become unnecessary when all our freedoms are oriented toward efflorescing into an open sky.

But it's not quite so simple. When we rebel, we risk interfering with others' freedom, even when we don't intend to. How can we rebel ethically? And how can we act authentically *and* ethically, when our own cherished projects might not have anything to do with alleviating oppression?

There are even important objections to the idea of taking rebellion to be our goal: for many people, surviving, developing resilience, and being cautious are more crucial than rebelling.[5] Yet, tolerating awfulness perpetuates awfulness. And while many people are stuck in awful situations, unhappiness and suffering are not virtues in themselves.

Beauvoir realized that, as yet, humanity has not created a perfect political framework that solves all societal issues. Oppression can exist, and does exist, in all systems. So what do we do? Beauvoir's answer epitomizes the heart of existentialism: We must act in the midst of uncertainty. We can't wait until someone comes up with a perfect solution because there is no such thing. We need to start chipping away—sometimes sledgehammering—at changing our systems for the better despite not having all the answers at hand. In *The Mandarins*, one of Beauvoir's characters says, "If you wait until you meet absolute perfection before getting involved, you'll never love anyone and never do anything."[6] We need to jump in, act, do.

* * *

Early in her life, Beauvoir felt a moral obligation to rebel against injustices. She called herself a "dutiful" little girl, but would regularly disobey her parents for the pleasure of it. She would stick her tongue out in photos, which would sometimes entertain and sometimes frustrate her parents. The fact that she got away with so much mischief fired up her rebellious spirit.

Beauvoir's rebellion against her parents was a good training ground because she enjoyed challenging elitist values. She had grown up believing that the interests of the bourgeois were the same as those of other classes. When Beauvoir tried to fight for the interests of the lower classes, she was confused as to why her father chastised her and why her mother wailed that Beauvoir's soul needed to be saved.[7]

When Beauvoir shared her thoughts and concerns, her parents would be scandalized and tell her she was misunderstanding and overcomplicating life.[8] Beauvoir was also deeply frustrated with prominent authors such as Paul Claudel and André Gide who rebelled against their own family, their traditions, and inherited wisdom, but were fine with the status quo and had no interest in true revolt or societal solutions.

At age seventeen, Beauvoir had an epiphany. In an attempt to try to impress Jacques, her crush and cousin, she went to a lecture by Robert Garric. Garric was a French literature professor and founder of a group called Les Équipes Sociales, which organized exchanges between privileged students and young working-class people. The group aimed to mobilize friendship to overcome class divides, ignorance, and egoism.

Beauvoir was so inspired that she felt a clear call toward a life of advocacy. Upon returning home, she recalled, "I was stunned by the clear necessity of the call: innumerable tasks awaited me; it would need the whole strength of my being; if I allowed myself the slightest slackening of purpose, I would be betraying my trust and wronging humanity."[9]

Despite this early revelation, a couple of years later, Beauvoir wrote in her diary that she was more interested in the individual and reasons for being than society.[10] For many years she did focus on her inner world and building her career, but World War II changed her perspective.

*   *   *

Beauvoir highlighted a number of mystifications and tensions that she thought would be helpful to know as we embark on our quests to break oppressive bonds for ourselves and others. One mystification is that any action is futile. It's true that action often fails. For example, #WomenSupportingWomen was a chainmail-style movement that encouraged women to post flattering black and white selfies of themselves to celebrate women's empowerment. Millions of people including celebrities such as Gabrielle Union, Demi Lovato, Natalie Portman, Khloé Kardashian, Gal Gadot, and many others, joined in.

The problem is that no one really knows what the hashtag was meant to achieve. Was it celebrating women by encouraging each other to share photos with the expectation that there will be only positive comments about them? Was it to support cancer awareness? An excuse to post more shameless selfies? Or was it coopting a Turkish movement protesting femicide and domestic violence, with the goal of supporting the Istanbul Convention which aims to prevent violence, protect victims, and to hold murderers accountable? The hashtag could have been all or none of the above, and there were so many selfies that the chaotic avalanche drowned out whatever the original movement was.

This type of phenomenon is what has become known as "slacktivism," a portmanteau of slacking activism, that is, people doing enough to fit in but not enough to affect any meaningful change. They put in barely a soupçon of effort before moving on to the next fad.

These hashtag trends seem to be ultimately about self-promotion. They allow people to feel good about themselves, as though they are advocating for sexual or other justice, but in a way that centers their own reputation. Still, these movements allow people to generate awareness and to indicate where their allegiances lie. The critical thing is to move beyond slacktivism and turn awareness into advocacy.

To assume our actions will have no impact is inauthentic. Defeatism is a type of clairvoyance that decides in advance the meaning and outcome of our actions. Beauvoir wrote, "Whatever the given situation, it never necessarily implies one future or another since man's reaction to his situation is free. How can he decide in advance that peace, war, revolution, justice, happiness, defeat, or victory are impossible?"[11] Resignation is a choice, a choice that shapes and reinforces narratives that pull the future away from success. If we surrender before we've even tried, we kill options before possibilities have a chance to germinate.

"Immobile or in action, we always weigh upon the earth," Beauvoir wrote. "Every refusal is a choice, every silence has a voice. Our very passivity is willed; in order to not choose, we still must choose not to choose. It is impossible to escape."[12] Detaching, keeping aloof, being impartial and apolitical; these are all political stances and are flights from the truth and our lives. Being disengaged is inauthentic because we are responsible for our actions and nonactions alike. In doing nothing, we lose ourselves.

When Beauvoir visited the United States in 1947, she said of

Americans, "What is most striking to me, and most discouraging, is that they are so apathetic while being neither blind nor unconscious."[13] She observed that Americans condemned oppression, poverty, racism, and fascism. But despite America's global power, Beauvoir noticed that individuals in America felt demoralized, as though they had no power, and that they weren't responsible for ills in the world.

When we're overwhelmed with horrifying news, we become so desensitized that, with barely a quiver, we move to the next dreadful story. Witnessing orgies of hate every day desiccates our emotions. Beauvoir called this phenomenon "tetanus of the imagination," and, "That, perhaps, is the final stage of demoralization for a nation: one gets used to it."[14]

But putting or keeping others at risk makes us part of the problem; it makes us responsible for exacerbating collective human misery. Our well-being depends on the well-being of others. In *The Mandarins*, one of Beauvoir's characters says that we can't escape this history of our situations, but we need to look for ways to make the world a good place to live and "abstention isn't the answer."[15] Since we are interconnected, we have a moral obligation to take part in the struggle for freedom. In the face of oppression and morally flawed government policies, apathy makes us as guilty as if we were making the immoral decisions ourselves.

Let us believe that rebellion is possible. This is not simply wishful thinking. Rebellion has, in truth, been successful. Wildcat strikes in 1968, Occupy Wall Street, #BlackLivesMatter, #WomensMarch, #MeToo, #TimesUp, #TakeAKnee, and other movements are making real change. People are joining in and collectively making themselves heard. Our authenticity depends on being optimistic that rebellion will make a difference, but we need to balance our optimism with a healthy dose of realism that slacktivism is not nearly enough. To believe change for the better is possible is the first step toward making it possible.

* * *

Another mystification that people use to accept and justify oppression is, Beauvoir argued, to claim that inequality is "natural" and so we should not or cannot abolish unjust disparities.[16] You can't revolt against something natural like a pandemic, for example. This attitude acquiesces: sure, you can celebrate the small joys while life remains, but you can't rebel against a virus because, unlike humans, a virus is incapable of moral thinking (although of course you can protest policies that humans create in response to a pandemic).

When we adopt the idea that systems of oppression are likewise natural, we get similar results. Why try to change discrimination in hiring if women are "naturally" suited to unpaid housework? Why object to unfair wages and wealth distribution if an invisible hand will inevitably move free markets and put people in their "natural" place?

These kinds of complacent attitudes overlook key factors of our contexts, for instance, that many economic systems enable a few people to get rich at the expense of many people's exploitation. The attitude that oppression is natural also minimizes the power of our freedom, suggesting that humans don't have the ability to make different choices. The virus isn't a moral entity but our response to it is. We can rebel against fear and selfishness. Authentic action in the face of a non-compliant, faceless virus isn't complaining of the oppression of mask or vaccine mandates (as some have done) but keeping in mind the well-being of others and acting accordingly.

The American Dream is an example of this type of mystification. If you pull yourself up by your bootstraps hard enough, the natural law of the universe will reward you. You will rise to the top with wealth and success. If you don't, either you didn't try hard enough or you're not naturally good enough. The assumption that stark inequality is the inevitable result of people's choices ignores privileges and structural oppressions that prevent people from having access to the same possibilities. The belief overlooks that freedom is bound by circumstance.

In 1945, Beauvoir visited Portugal under Prime Minister António de Oliveira Salazar's nationalist dictatorship, where many people were undernourished and lived in extreme poverty. One night she dined on an outdoor terrace with a wealthy Portuguese man. Poor children surrounded them, and Beauvoir gave a child a coin.

Beauvoir's companion fumed and tried to get the money back. Through mouthfuls of prawns and mayonnaise, the man claimed that Beauvoir's generosity was wasteful because the children would spend it on cigarettes and candy. Beauvoir prevented him, later reflecting, "Each mouthful that I swallowed was an insult to their misery . . . They fear them, for they know very well that their fortune is the fruit of a shameful exploitation."[17]

One reading of this situation is that the man blamed the children's poverty on their supposedly "natural" tendency to spend frivolously. If this was the case, it's contemptibly paternalistic and arrogant to feel the need to dictate to less privileged people how to spend their money.

Even more than this, the man's violent and hateful response also reveals bad faith. He felt threatened because he feared being judged morally blameworthy for not mitigating the effects of poverty, despite having the means to do so. To avoid responsibility, he constructs the mystification that poor people deserve being poor, so their suffering is not his problem, and he can continue to indulge in his extravagant lunch amidst hungry children without feeling bad about his moral failure. If their poverty was natural and deserved, giving them money wouldn't threaten him; he'd know that the natural order would prevail. Beauvoir saw that his cruelty revealed that he knew the truth of the children's oppression and his own complicity.

A similar sentiment is at the heart of people who refuse to give homeless people money on the assumption that it's in their nature to spend it on alcohol or drugs, or to admonish younger generations for eating avocado toast instead of buying a home. Being unemployed, underpaid, or priced out of a home isn't natural. These situations can be a consequence of personal choices, but very often they are a consequence of the way society is regimented by more privileged people.

*   *   *

A third mystification Beauvoir pointed to was that when the oppressed become free, they will oppress their oppressors in retaliation.[18] Systemic racism is built on this underlying fear of revenge: the sense that white people are on the verge of being oppressed, and that when people of color claim their freedom, white people's freedom will be tethered.

Beauvoir saw the fear of revenge as starkly misplaced because, for one, the law is structured around protecting oppressors, sometimes licensing them to murder with impunity. When an oppressed person tries to defend themselves, they're often punished disproportionately for daring to challenge their situation.

Another reason that revenge is a mystification is that oppressors and oppressed are not distinct binary categories: that's what intersectionality is about. When we recognize the ways that identities intersect uniquely for different people, we can acknowledge that some people are more oppressed than others. And some people are both oppressed and oppressors.

When one group becomes less oppressed, they do sometimes

go on to oppress—but mostly they continue the oppression of the already-oppressed, and it's not out of revenge, but out of apathy and indifference. For example, many middle-class women and men free themselves from housework, childcare, and other mundane tasks when they earn enough to pay other people to do it for them. Outsourcing of domestic work isn't inherently exploitative but it is when people are undervalued and expected to work in deplorable conditions—which domestic workers often are.[19]

Some people are complicit in oppression not due to outright awfulness, but due to ignorance. Beauvoir argued that when a child cries "Heil, Hitler!" (today they're more likely to deliver racial slurs and homophobic insults on the playground or on social media), they're naïve, not guilty. Oppressors who mystified them, by inculcating them with hateful ideology, are responsible. Beauvoir also suggested that (white) women are often complicit in their own oppression. Though women may too be ignorant, Beauvoir classified them as willing victims. The difference between a child and a woman is that adults should know better.

Civil rights lawyer and scholar Kimberlé Crenshaw described the phenomenon of these complex intersections of oppression with the metaphor of a basement.[20] Everyone who is disadvantaged—whether in terms of race, gender, class, sexuality, age, ability, or other discrimination—is stacked on top of each other. Those at the bottom face multiple burdens and are the most oppressed. Those closer to the top are less encumbered.

The most privileged people escape through a hatch in the ceiling, becoming free, but usually only when they climb over more oppressed people, and people above the basement let those close to the top climb out. It's much harder for those at the bottom of the basement to get to the top, let alone escape it entirely. This image reflects the fact that many people are in ambiguous positions, because even though they're in the basement being oppressed, they are also oppressing Others lower down.

Beauvoir seemed aware of the beastly gamut of oppression and worried that her ideal of collective conversion was a utopian delusion. Even if there is a collective rebellion, there is no guarantee that people will behave well and stop blocking the hatches to freedom, or that situations will improve post-rebellion.

While Beauvoir observed extreme racism, classism, and sexism in 1940s America, such attitudes are still common today, evident in the disproportionate rates of police brutality against underprivileged people and the lenient criminal sentences for white people relative to people of color. It has taken too many years for white people to start caring about Black lives enough to come out to protest these deaths in any great numbers.

The term "Black Lives Matter" was coined in 2013 when Alicia Garza, Patrisse Cullors, and Ayọ Tometi formed a movement in response to the acquittal of the police officer who killed Trayvon Martin. But it wasn't until George Floyd's murder in 2020 that protests grew substantially—possibly because more people in the United States were plugged into social media during the COVID-19 pandemic and outraged about blatant racism, demagoguery, and pandemic mishandling.[21]

Oppressors' fear of becoming oppressed is part of the motivation for the #AllLivesMatter movement. #AllLivesMatter resists #BlackLivesMatter on the grounds that caring about Black lives oppresses white people in "reverse racism." Beauvoir noted that oppressors often fight to keep things the way they are, so that they can keep the freedom and power they already have to oppress and exploit. The #AllLivesMatter sounds like it is about protecting freedom for all, but this conceals a lie. The movement is concerned with freedom (for some) based on blocking freedom (for Others). For Beauvoir, there can be no such thing as an authentic fascist, since "a freedom which is interested only in denying freedom must be denied."[22]

*   *   *

Why is fascism, even when it curtails one's freedom, so very appealing to some? Well, for starters, it's easy—at least for its adherents. A fourth mystification that Beauvoir identified is idolizing reifications, like nationalism or tradition, that people resort to when they realize that defending the current system on the basis of freedom is impossible. Defenders of tradition want to conserve civilization, institutions, monuments, so-called "objective" values and virtues that fit with their world view.

In the United States, more than one thousand statues and symbols of the Confederacy still exist. Idolizing the Confederacy is based on the core belief that white supremacy is "natural and moral" (note the use of the term "natural" again). Since the #BlackLivesMatter protests, some structures are being removed. And protests have inspired international change.

After the #BlackLivesMatter protests, Belgians started paying more attention to their statues of King Leopold II. Leopold II was a notoriously brutal and sadistic exploiter who colonized the Congo in the nineteenth century to profit from ivory and rubber trading. His regime used slavery, rape, genocide, and torture to maintain their power. Though many Belgian people protested and vandalized the statues, many also signed petitions to defend the presence of the figures for a variety of reasons including preserving tradition and history.

Beauvoir pointed out that protectors of monuments defend them saying things like they are "beautiful and good in themselves."[23] Indeed, in 2017, after protesters targeted confederate statues, the then US president tweeted, "Sad to see the history and culture of our great country being ripped apart with the removal of our beautiful statues and monuments."[24]

Let's get real: What monument defenders value are not the statues themselves but what they represent. The statues are reminders of a system and society that made it possible for some people to be reduced to objects. Putting those who committed atrocities on pedestals and naming our streets and highways after them—instead of acknowledging the injustice of their atrocities and honoring their victims—is morally corrupt.

It is vital to acknowledge the past in a living and dynamic way, always linked to the future. Beauvoir proposed that the past is part and parcel of the human condition and, "If the world behind us were bare, we would hardly be able to see anything before us but a gloomy desert."[25] To understand our present, we must integrate the past into what we're doing now. We must learn from past mistakes and failures to inform our present actions and intentions. If we deny that the past matters, if we don't care what people before us cared about and were working toward, then we are setting a precedent that in the future, we can ignore what is now present. But our present actions spring from our hope for the future.

Beauvoir might have agreed with human rights activist and scholar Sir Geoff Palmer that the solution is not to tear down problematic statues because that would be to erase part of history.[26] A more honest approach might be to educate passers-by, for example, by labeling statues with information about the complex history of what the statues represented over time. Education has the power to remind us to disrupt exploitative habits, to help us to be honest in remembering history, to realize that no one—including memorialized figures—is all good or all bad, and that every one of us is a bundle of contradictions and ambiguities.

One way to think about this reckoning with history is like

coming to terms with trauma. In *Caste*, journalist Isabel Wilkerson recommended how to process the trauma involved in discovering the grim history of one's country:

> You don't ball up in a corner with guilt or shame at these discoveries . . . You educate yourself. You talk to people who have been through it and to specialists who have researched it. You learn the consequences and obstacles, the options and treatment . . . Then you take precautions to protect yourself and succeeding generations and work to ensure that these things, whatever they are, don't happen again.[27]

To face the future ethically calls for assuming the past bravely and truthfully, and taking precautions based on cumulative wisdom. If we don't, Wilkerson rightly noted, civilization becomes like a beautiful old house built on rotten foundations. The house might look fine on the outside, but peek behind the façade and you'll see that it's ready to crumble—and no one will want to take responsibility because they weren't around when it was built.

* * *

Happy ignorance is a fifth mystification that Beauvoir pointed to. Oppressors often convince themselves that oppressed people are doing just fine, so there is no need to free them or enlighten them about their situation. Oppressors argue that oppressed people are better off: they would become overwhelmed with freedom, it would disrupt the peace unnecessarily, and everyone would be miserable.[28]

This inane mystification is often at the root of behaviors such as gaslighting, when someone manipulates another person in order to undermine their perceptions, sanity, memories, and confidence in their own experience. Oppressed people often internalize these attitudes: they may be unaware of their submission, unaware of other options, or think their circumstances are natural and there's no point in rebelling. Sometimes people get so comfortable in their situations and so confused by mystifications that they don't see the bars of their enclosure or the sky that's open only to others.

A variation of this kind of deception is oppressors telling oppressed people that they have all the freedom and happiness they need. My friend Olivia's ex-husband told her that she should be happy in her "golden cage" (his words), and if she complained she was an ingrate. For many years, the sparkling bars of her confinement dazed her.

Oppressed people are often punished for pursuing happiness in the wrong way, creating a double bind. Do what your oppressor tells you, and you will not be punished and you will be happy; but if you do what your oppressor tells you and you are still not happy, then that is your fault. Such beliefs are not only duplicitous, but also flagrantly inauthentic. The message distorts and misrepresents oppressive situations.

When I witnessed Olivia's husband rain down a torrent of verbal abuse on her while she stood like a statue until it was over, I asked, "How is this water off a duck's back to you?" She shrugged with resignation and powerlessness. Olivia said it was habitual. The false accusations he threw at her incessantly were, she said, customary. Olivia's everyday hurt was, for her, normal. Olivia's husband fought against divorce, threatening to hide their savings and assets so that she would become homeless. He tried to silence her—by insisting she promise never to tell anyone about any of their exchanges, that is, the abuse and lies and conspiracy theories he hurled at her.

Later she told me, "I feel like a little moth in a dense sticky web that is his life. All I can do is flap my wings a little to show that I am still alive. My thoughts and feelings are drowned in his tsunami of self-righteous virtue. When I tell him I'm unhappy, he says it's my fault, I am a selfish bitch and having a mental breakdown."

Olivia said she attempted to leave her husband seven times, for many reasons including the sunk cost fallacy: They had been together for so long, why end it now? The force of inertia, like a kind of emotional asbestos, insulates us, make us feel safe, but also poisons us. When Olivia returned to her husband, she would sometimes ask me: "Do you think less of me?" I told her I was skeptical, but also reiterated that it was her choice and I respected her decisions. My distress for Olivia's situation did not make her well-being my authentic choice.

When an oppressed person does choose against their situation, Beauvoir said, "It is then that the movement of emancipation really begins."[29] Slowly Olivia built enough psychological and financial resilience to claw her way out of the miserable vortex permanently. Many years later, she still tells me: "It was a thousand percent the right decision. My only regret is not doing it years ago." Now she owns herself. Now she ventures on her own quests for fulfillment. Now she nurtures herself instead of her ex-husband's narcissism.

* * *

Olivia's situation presents an ambiguity of action, specifically, how to work toward freedom for others without becoming a white knight or white savior and making situations worse. Authentic rebelling— the kind that maximizes freedom—involves consciousness-raising: raising people's awareness of their complicity, tyrannical settings, mystifications, and oppressive assumptions about themselves such as self-sabotaging ideas of inferiority. Bringing people's attention to their submission is important. Consciousness-raising helps us to become aware of our freedom and teaches us about the power of our freedom. Consciousness-raising is a form of rebellion because oppression stifles the truth.

In Beauvoir's novel *The Mandarins,* Henri uses his literary magazine to educate working-class readers about class oppression. At the end of World War II, he surmises: "No more dictating opinions to them; rather teach them to judge for themselves."[30] For existential philosophers, the role of a teacher is not to dictate but to encourage students to think for themselves and make up their own minds. Similarly, the incarcerated students in my philosophy class didn't want or need to be saved. That would be to rob them of agency, which the carceral system was already doing. It was up to the teachers to be there to listen and to support their learning.

Is this attitude patronizing? Yes: it's not true that oppressed people don't or can't ever know they're being oppressed unless they're told so by those supposedly more enlightened. We're back to the problem of rebelling ethically: How can we rebel without doing more harm (and curtailing more freedom) than doing good?

Beauvoir was clear that it's up to oppressed people to choose against their maltreatment. To force them into freedom against their will pushes them into a new cycle of oppression. When my friend Olivia returned to her husband, she was doing what she needed to survive. As for my role, calling out her oppression, letting her know that she was experiencing abuse, but acknowledging her resignation with compassion, and lending her money and moral support, was enough—at least in that particular instance.

However, there are many instances where this kind of support isn't enough. Victims of human trafficking and police brutality, for example, do not have the power to stop their oppressors. In such cases, we have a moral responsibility to intervene to stop persecution.

In *Can the Subaltern Speak?* philosopher Gayatri Chakravorty Spivak provided an example that reveals how complex the tensions of intervention can be. Spivak wrote about how some Hindu people practiced sati—the tradition of widows throwing themselves on their husband's funeral pyre. Local tradition pushed women into it, British laws criminalized it, and women's voices were lost.

From Spivak we learn that we risk arrogance and white saviorism when we assume that elites and intellectuals can speak on behalf of oppressed people and should establish rules and laws to govern them. Traditions that force people to kill themselves are horribly oppressive because they rob people of their freedom. But we have to be careful not to patronize others, not to normalize oppression, and to be very careful not to speak *for* those who are underprivileged, but to make space to *hear* them and *speak with* them. We must act in some situations to remove external aspects of oppression, but we must also respect the freedom of people claiming and fighting for their own liberation. And sometimes that cause is served by keeping our silence and doing nothing.[31]

Beauvoir recognized that our intervention and our silence are both choices that will have consequences for other people. Her approach was in the spirit of Ursula K. Le Guin who said, "My job is not to arrive at a final answer and just deliver it. I see my job as holding doors open, or opening windows. But who comes in and out the doors, what you see out the window—how do I know?"[32]

*   *   *

Another tension inherent in rebellion is that there are multiple worthy causes to fight for. With our limited time and energy, how do we choose what to prioritize, what to do, especially when good causes conflict with each other? It is impossible to rebel against every injustice. It is hard to know where to start, and harder still to know how to do it in ways that do not make situations worse.

Since being engaged calls for political action, we have to pick a side. Being against the status quo is a start, but we also need an alternative to replace it with. We have to be *for* something. It's not always easy to know whose side to take. Beauvoir made mistakes.

For example, Beauvoir was an apologist for pedophiles in the 1970s. Along with Sartre, Michel Foucault, Roland Barthes, Jacques Derrida, Gilles Deleuze, Jacques Rancière, Jean-François Lyotard, and many others, she signed a petition against age-of-consent laws, stating that: "[French law] should acknowledge the right of children and adolescents to have relations with whomever they choose."[33] The petition was in response to three men incarcerated for non-violent sex offenses with twelve- and thirteen-year-old children.

In hindsight it seems obvious that *not*-pedophilia was the better choice. Beauvoir and Sartre intended to affirm children's freedom from their parents and the law. It seemed not to concern them that they were also fighting for the freedom of adult pedophiles to exploit vulnerable children. Freedom doesn't only mean freedom to engage in relationships; it means freedom to be a child, freedom from the pressure to consent to something you can't understand or imagine, freedom from an authority figure's abuse of power, and freedom from fear of retaliation. Later Beauvoir realized that she and Sartre had been narrow-minded about their conception of freedom.

Another of Beauvoir's missteps was that initially she supported Chairman Mao because she put her hopes in socialism, believing it to be the best chance for equal opportunities for the sexes, and that women would only get jobs if men were fully employed.

Over the course of decades, Mao murdered more than 45 million people. In hindsight, it seems that *not*-Mao was a better choice. Indeed, after discovering that socialist societies were just as oppressive as capitalist ones, Beauvoir realized that simply changing the ownership of the means of production from private to public isn't enough to change traditional gender roles and expectations. Nonetheless, she continued to believe that equal opportunity is impossible under capitalism.

Beauvoir's novel *The Mandarins* shows the difficulty in choosing sides. Two journalists, Henri and Robert, have a huge argument about whether to publish an exposé about the Russian gulags in the aftermath of World War II. Henri is torn because he knows it would be wrong to print something of which they have only fragmented evidence and limited capacity to fact-check; but it would also be wrong to hide the truth, however patchy.

Remaining silent makes Henri complicit. He becomes an accessory to the travesties. Turning away from the truth, even if a deeply problematic truth, is lying by omission. But in criticizing a communist regime, Henri would be perceived as supporting fascism. People would be outraged and feel betrayed no matter which stance he took. Some tell him that you have to break eggs to make an omelet, implying that the ends justify the means. Henri worries, "But in the end, who's going to eat all those omelets? The broken eggs will rot and fester in the earth."[34] It's an impossible calculation.

Robert tries to legitimize their silence by claiming that atrocities are everywhere. Robert's perspective doesn't make Henri feel any better, because if both sides are evil, then humanity is doomed. Henri decides to speak up because, "Either speaking out means something, or nothing means anything."[35] He is predictably accused of being fascist, but he made an authentic choice in doing what he thought was right—on personal and ethical levels because he was bringing attention to human rights atrocities. Henri's dilemma shows us that choices can be extremely difficult, but often it's the daring in itself that can make a decision authentic.

Sometimes one cause will be more urgent than others, and sometimes valid causes will get left behind. The clear danger with choosing one cause to the exclusion of others is that important causes get lost. Beauvoir thought it vital to avoid trading causes off against one another—which easily descends into tactics that trick people into compromising for trifling wins. When we have a choice, Beauvoir encourages us to choose the side that serves universal freedom and avoid positions that generate new separations and obsessiveness.[36]

Consider the case of vaccinations and concerns about whether to vaccinate or not to vaccinate. Applying Beauvoir's thinking, people should be free to make choices about their own bodies, but must also acknowledge that we coexist in a society and that we have a responsibility to others.

Adults who choose to vaccinate have a responsibility to respect individual choices and to advocate for collective health, well-being, and freedom. Vaccinations serve universal freedom because when most people are vaccinated, society becomes free from deadly viruses and individuals become free to socialize without fear of potentially fatal illnesses.

Adults who choose not to vaccinate (as opposed to vulnerable people who cannot vaccinate for health reasons) have a responsibility to recognize that viruses are contagious, to take care not to expose other people to risk, and not to force their bodies into spaces where transmission is possible. They must also accept the consequences of choosing not to vaccinate—such as keeping their distance or wearing masks properly. The responsibility of not vaccinating is even more critical when we take into account impacts such as the strains on health systems for avoidable illnesses.

Those who are most mystified, who have the least access to reliable information, will be the last ones to understand vaccines and the last ones to act to keep themselves and others healthy. Beauvoir acknowledged that the most oppressed are often the last to join the fight for collective freedom. Their livelihoods—and often their lives—depend on not risking even more than they already do. That means for those in privileged positions (Beauvoir included herself), it's crucial to recognize their own complicity and to take a stand, even if it risks security and ridicule, just as Henri did at his magazine.[37]

Beauvoir's vision for justice was clear: "We must end by abolishing all suppression."[38] This struggle can take many forms. Each person must choose how to commit themselves for themselves, which will depend on their opportunity, efficiency, and their unique situation.

*   *   *

If oppression must be rejected at any cost, then what do we do if people stand in the way of freedom? The best solution would be to use education to debunk mystifications. Other solutions include taking legal and political steps to reshape societal infrastructure.[39] Still other solutions include civic love, leading by example, taking the high moral ground, protesting peacefully, and behaving cordially. These are all excellent strategies. But the question is: What do you do when loving your oppressors doesn't free you? What if political and legal channels fail to relieve oppressed people because they are designed by oppressors to serve oppressors?[40]

While we have to be careful about letting our judgment become clouded, for Beauvoir, anger and indignation are sometimes necessary, sometimes even vital. Often rebellion cannot be peaceful, since oppressed people don't get heard until they disrupt the harmony of the status quo.

Beauvoir is not alone in her views about indignation. Philosopher Myisha Cherry argued that what she calls "Lordean rage"—a type of rage inspired by Audre Lorde that targets racism but incorporates compassion and empathy—"has a special power that is strong enough to combat some of the strongest forces and systems at work in the world."[41] And philosopher Judith Butler wrote, "Democracy requires a good challenge, and it does not always arrive in soft tones . . . When one has not been heard for decades, the cry for justice is bound to be loud."[42]

Nevertheless, Butler also makes the crucial argument that the problem with violence is that violence begets and licenses more violence. Fresh injustices create a more violent world, and our interdependence means that violence toward others is violence toward ourselves. While violence should be a last resort, Beauvoir proposed that in some situations it can be authentic to act on violence because freedom is discovered and tested in relation to and in tension with others.[43]

The implication of Beauvoir's view on violence is that people who stand in the way of freedom may have to be treated like objects, as means to a greater end. She wrote, "We are obliged to destroy not only the oppressor but also those who serve him, whether they do so out of ignorance or out of constraint."[44]

Using violence to rebel is a sticky question and one Beauvoir worried about at length. In endorsing violence, Beauvoir makes a kind of Machiavellian argument: oppressed people use force to get power, so that once they're in power, they can do good. The obvious problem, as with Machiavelli's ideas, is that using force to create moral liberation is a step toward the problematic view that "might makes right."

But in *The Ethics of Ambiguity* Beauvoir proposed that to deny other people their freedom is outrageous, so if outrageous violence is needed to combat it, then seizing whatever tools are available and fighting are justifiable options. Oppressed people have a right to claim their freedom, although they do not have a right to claim power over others. Encroaching upon others in the process of establishing freedom is a tragedy and a paradox, but one that sometimes can't be avoided.

Pacifists might object to Beauvoir's defense of violence, but in doing so they'd find themselves in interesting company. Oppressors are the first to declare that oppressed people shouldn't use violence to demand their freedom. Oppressed people are expected to justify violence in a way that oppressors aren't. Oppressors immediately call for civility as a way to try to ward off violence when the oppressed protest their condition. Often those calling for civility and nonviolence are oppressors who feel threatened and want to neutralize opposition, to blunt the teeth of dissent of people who are duly angry about injustices.[45]

* * *

Beauvoir's philosophy teaches us that we can't become authentic until everyone is free, because any freedom that relies on oppression is morally flawed. But she also teaches us how to live and become authentic in the midst of a complex and uncertain world. Every moment contains possibilities for grasping our situation, creating ourselves, and connecting with others as authentic friends. This is the process of authenticity: to continue creating our essence as we engage with others in a struggle to construct our shared world.

There is a huge amount of pressure to maintain the status quo. But, Beauvoir shows, we use many bad faith reasons to justify our unwillingness to fight oppression. Many of these justifications are based on mystifications. It's easy to slide into apathy, to go with the flow, to accept the just-so stories that tell us that our situation is destined by nature and tradition. These stories serve oppressors, reserving peace, harmony, and happiness for a select few. Yet to surrender our agency in the face of these lies violates our authenticity. It's important to recognize and understand these excuses, so that we can challenge people to reflect on their beliefs. To know and still to oppress—or be complicit—is to act inauthentically.

We always risk unintended consequences and failure. We cannot insulate ourselves from the ambiguity of action. Failure is a fact of life, but that is not a valid excuse to escape responsibility. "There is hardly a sadder virtue than resignation," Beauvoir wrote.[46] Actions always take place amidst a haze of ambiguity and risk, so we have to do what we can to become aware of the paradoxes of action, to look for alternate points of view, to listen to people who disagree, to stay open to changing our minds when we discover we've made mistakes, but to leap in and act anyway.[47] If we end up doing the wrong thing, then we do what we can to fix it and do better next time.

Beauvoir advised us not to beat ourselves up too much about this ambiguity. She describes the middle path we must take: "To suffer from these contradictions serves no good purpose; to blind oneself to them is mere self-deception."[48] The moment of existential rebellion is not defined by success or scope. It is realized when we reach beyond ourselves and our given situation to shape our world. This possibility exists at every moment. We live authentically in every moment we choose to rebel, against what is simply given, for the sake of freedom.

The path—not only toward rebellion against injustices, but also toward authenticity—is to try and fail and try again. Beauvoir advised:

> The lot of being torn apart [*déchirement*] is the ransom for his presence in the world, for his transcendence and for his freedom. If he tries to flee, he will be lost for good, because then he does nothing, or, what he does is nothing. He must give up any idea of finding rest; he must assume his freedom. Only at this price will he become able truly to surpass the given, which is the veritable ethics; truly to found the object in which he transcends himself, which is the only valid politics. At this price his action is concretely inscribed

in the world, and the world where he acts is a world endowed with meaning, a human world.[49]

James Baldwin expressed a similar sentiment when he urged us not to deny our complexity because "only within this web of ambiguity, paradox, this hunger, danger, darkness, can we find at once ourselves and the power that will free us from ourselves."[50]

While we can't expect those in power arbitrarily to give oppression up for equality, rebellion often creates new situations. This is how many civil rights have been won—though still we have a long way to go. History suggests that the struggle for equality won't be perfect, but situations can improve. Beauvoir was optimistic that we will be successful in achieving equal rights.[51] Persistence is essential. What's important for authentic living is to develop a rebellious spirit. The personal is political, our everyday lives are affected by politics, and engaging is the price of authentic existence.

Ideally, humanity would unite and create solidarities to fight oppression, led by a common guiding voice, to achieve peace and prosperity. But this is obviously far easier said than done. As activists and leaders like Greta Thunberg and the #BlackLivesMatter organizers are showing, creating a united voice is an epic challenge. Because each of us is free, people cannot be compelled to respect or care about others. Our freedom leads everyone to different goals, and so projects will often clash.

Nothingness gnaws away at all of us. We are all adrift in the world together, and we find ourselves in ambiguous situations. Life is a bit like bumper cars: we're all in the same arena that is the human condition. Our freedoms careen around, and our projects bounce into and off one another. We ricochet off the barriers around us, separate but interconnected, and fueled by the electric roof that is our ecosystem.

While Beauvoir supported violence and vengeance in some circumstances, she wholeheartedly agreed that education and forgiveness are better. Forgiving doesn't mean forgetting or letting people escape responsibility. It means trying harder to understand one another's situations and motivations, respecting one another, and upholding the dignity of humankind. Reciprocity and collaboration are strong steps toward intersubjectivity.

Justice requires reciprocal relationships—mutual respect for one another as free subjects—with others. While it's fine if you don't want to have anything to do with another person, Beauvoir would insist that given human and ecological interconnectedness, intersubjectivity is inevitable, important, and worthwhile for all of us. A basic level of respect that acknowledges the other people's freedom, even when we disagree, even when we are enemies, is a prerequisite for not only a just and proper society, but also authentic freedom.

Beauvoir argued we are like stones in the arch of society, our freedoms supporting one another.[52] Although we may never perfectly tesselate, respecting others is not mutually exclusive with respecting ourselves. It is the opposite: the sturdier the stones, the sturdier the arch. This is why becoming authentic also calls for fostering a rebellious spirit. We are not rebellious for the sake of being rebellious, but because our transcendent freedom gives us the power to positively engage in the world.

We are capable of rebellion, and rebellion is capable of transforming our individual and collective world for the better. But the responsibility to rebel falls on each of our individual shoulders. We can accept the role and rebel, or ignore it, but ignoring it is still a choice. Ideally, we wouldn't need to rebel because other people would be obstacles but not oppressors. But, Beauvoir noted, rebelling is freeing because

It attacks within each of us what is most intimate to us and what seems the most sure. It questions our very desires, the very forms of our pleasure. Do not back away from this questioning, for beyond the distress that it will perhaps provoke within us, it will destroy some of our shackles and open us to new truths.[53]

We don't know what these new truths are, but it's exciting—even if a little daunting—to face new possibilities. When we are free to act positively, effectively, and with creative daring, we will, Beauvoir's philosophy promises, become the poets of our own lives.[54]

GLOSSARY OF
KEY TERMS

bad faith: Self-deception which involves denying our own or others' freedom. We are in bad faith when we avoid the truth of our life and situation, when we deny we have choices, or when we reject responsibility for our actions.

being-for-itself / being-in-itself: Two modes of existence. A being-for-itself, such as a human, is conscious; a for-itself establishes being through exercising freedom, choosing, and acting. A being-in-itself is only what it is, like a rock; an in-itself cannot change itself and does not have the same possibilities available to it as a for-itself does.

facticity: The given—or unchosen—facts of our lives, including our parents, the bodies and brains we're born with, and other people.

immanence: The condition of being stuck in facticity, of being cut (or cutting ourselves) off from our freedom.

intersubjectivity: A reciprocal relationship where people mutually recognize and respect one another's freedom.

mystification: A form of oppression that creates and perpetuates myths and lies with the aim of taking advantage of people's trust, ignorance, or gullibility to keep them oppressed.

practico-inert: The human-made structures and systems that affect how we project ourselves into the world and which can create tensions between us, other people, and our environment.

projects: Self-chosen goals—including the concrete actions with which we propel ourselves toward those goals—which bring coherence, meaning, and justification to our lives.

transcendence (of facticity): The exercise of our freedom by striving toward self-chosen goals into an open future.

unrealizable: Our being as others see us, a view which we cannot see ourselves, and which shapes the context of our choices. Old age and death are key examples.

ACKNOWLEDGMENTS

I would like to acknowledge my deepest gratitude to a few of the very many people who joined and supported me on this book's quest: my brilliant editor Anna deVries and wonderful agent Tisse Takagi for their sharp edits, ideas, and for believing in this project; Alex Brown, Jonathan Bush, Alyssa Gamello, Eric Meyer, Danielle Prielipp, Sara Thwaite, Dori Weintraub, and the whole team at St. Martin's Press; Jamie Lombardi for her existential friendship and lucidity, for walking beside me on the dizzying crest, and for laughing with me at this unreasonably silent and absurd world; Alexandra Babin for her cheerleading since the beginning, her incredibly kindhearted first readings, and her friendship; Ji Kang for always being there with a glass of Prosecco whenever I needed it—and especially when I didn't know I needed it; my partner Nick and my son for their indomitable gorgeousness, duckiness, and love; my mum Julie, the strongest person I know; John Kaag, Heather Wallace, and Marine Rouch for their close readings and invaluable guidance; Gary Cox for our helpful existential correspondence; dear friends and colleagues for their intellectual generosity including Meryl Altman, Sofia Axelrod, David Bakis, Gracie Bialecki, Alison Cleary, Leon Garber, Barbara Greene, Samantha Rose Hill, Scott Barry Kaufman, Alycia LaGuardia-LoBianco, Alex Brook Lynn, Gordon Marino, Monica McCarthy, Caitlin Ochs, Katherine Spillane, means Regan Penaluna, Tanya Piacentini, Cai Pigliucci, Massimo Pigliucci, Robb Roby, Jennifer Sears, Richard Simonds, Nigel War-burton, Anne Waters, Grace Webber, Lucy, Olivia, and Sabina; the MacDowell Fellowship for the space to finish creating this book; Barnard Contingent Faculty-UAW Local 2110 for funding from the Adjunct Professional Development Grant; Sackett Street Writers; and my teachers Professor Robert Spillane, Ann-Maree Moodie, and Steven Segal at Macquarie University for educating, inspiring, and encouraging me in the earliest days of this adventure.

SELECTED BIBLIOGRAPHY AND SUGGESTED READING

Algren, Nelson. "The Question of Simone de Beauvoir." *Harper's Magazine,* May 1965: 134–36.

Altman, Meryl. *Beauvoir in Time.* Leiden & Boston: Brill Rodopi, 2020.

Appignanesi, Lisa. *Simone de Beauvoir.* London: Haus Publishing, 2005.

Arendt, Hannah. *On Violence.* San Diego, New York, London: Harvest/ HBJ, 1970.

———. *The Origins of Totalitarianism.* 1951. Cleveland: Meridian, 1962.

Arp, Kristana. *The Bonds of Freedom: Simone de Beauvoir's Existentialist Ethics.* Illinois: Open Court, 2001.

Ascher, Carol. *Simone de Beauvoir: A Life of Freedom.* Sussex: The Harvester Press, 1981.

Bair, Deirdre. *Simone de Beauvoir: A Biography.* New York: Summit Books, 1990.

Bakewell, Sarah. *At the Existentialist Café.* New York: Other Press, 2016.

Bauer, Nancy. *Simone de Beauvoir, Philosophy, and Feminism.* New York: Columbia University Press, 2001.

Beauvoir, Simone de. *Adieux: A Farewell to Sartre.* 1981. Trans. O'Brian, Patrick. New York: Pantheon Books, 1984.

———. *All Men Are Mortal*. 1946. Trans. Friedman, Leonard M. New York: W. W. Norton & Company, 1992.

———. *All Said and Done*. 1972. Trans. O'Brian, Patrick. New York: Paragon House, 1993.

———. *America Day by Day*. 1954. Trans. Cosman, Carol. Berkeley: University of California Press, 1999.

———. *The Blood of Others*. 1945. Trans. Moyse, Yvonne and Roger Senhouse. Victoria, Australia: Penguin Books, 1964.

———. *Brigitte Bardot and the Lolita Syndrome*. 1959. New York: Arno Press & *The New York Times*, 1972.

———. *Diary of a Philosophy Student: Volume 1, 1926–27*. Urbana and Chicago: University of Illinois Press, 2006.

———. *The Ethics of Ambiguity*. 1948. Trans. Frechtman, Bernard. Secaucus, New York: Open Road, 2018.

———. "Existentialism and Popular Wisdom." Trans. Timmermann, Marybeth. *Philosophical Writings*. 1945. Eds. Simons, Margaret A., et al. Urbana and Chicago: University of Illinois Press, 2004.

———. "An Existentialist Looks at Americans." *Philosophical Writings*. 1947. Eds. Simons, Margaret A., et al. Urbana and Chicago: University of Illinois Press, 2004.

———. "An Eye for an Eye." Trans. Arp, Kristana. *Philosophical Writings*. 1946. Eds. Simons, Margaret A., et al. Urbana and Chicago: University of Illinois Press, 2004.

———. *Force of Circumstance I: After The War*. 1963. Trans. Howard, Richard. New York: Paragon House, 1992.

———. *Force of Circumstance II: Hard Times*. 1963. Trans. Howard, Richard. New York: Paragon House, 1992.

———. *Inseparable*. Trans. Smith, Sandra. New York: Ecco, 2021

———. *Les inséparables*. Paris: L'Herne, 2020.

———. *The Inseparables*. Trans. Elkin, Lauren. London: Vintage, 2021.

———. "Introduction to *Women Insist*." Trans. Timmermann, Marybeth. *Feminist Writings*. Eds. Simons, Margaret A. and Marybeth

Timmermann. Urbana, Chicago, and Springfield: University of Illinois Press, 2015.

———. "It's About Time Woman Put a New Face on Love." *Flair,* 1950: 76–77.

———. "Jean-Paul Sartre." Trans. Timmermann, Marybeth. *Philosophical Writings.* 1946. Eds. Simons, Margaret A., et al. Urbana and Chicago: University of Illinois Press, 2004.

———. *Les Belles Images.* 1966. Trans. O'Brian, Patrick. New York: G. P. Putnam's Sons, 1968.

———. *Letters to Sartre.* Trans. Hoare, Quintin. New York: Arcade Publishing, 1992.

———. *The Mandarins.* 1954. Trans. Friedman, Leonard M. London and Glasgow: Fontana Books, 1960.

———. *Mémoires II.* Collection Bibliothèque de la Pléiade. Paris: Gallimard, 2018.

———. *Memoirs of a Dutiful Daughter.* 1958. Trans. Kirkup, James. New York: Harper Perennial, 2005.

———. *Misunderstanding in Moscow.* Trans. Keefe, Terry. *"The Useless Mouths" and Other Literary Writings.* 1992. Eds. Simons, Margaret A. and Marybeth Timmermann. Urbana: University of Illinois Press, 2011.

———. "Moral Idealism and Political Realism." Trans. Cordero, Anne Deing. *Philosophical Writings.* 1945. Eds. Simons, Margaret A., et al. Urbana and Chicago: University of Illinois Press, 2004.

———. "Must We Burn Sade?" Trans. Michelson, Annette. *The Marquis De Sade.* New York: Grove Press, 1953.

———. "My Experience as a Writer." Trans. Mann, Debbie. *"The Useless Mouths" and Other Literary Writings.* 1979. Eds. Simons, Margaret A. and Marybeth Timmermann. Urbana: University of Illinois Press, 2011.

———. *Old Age.* Trans. O'Brian, Patrick. London: Deutsch, Weidenfeld and Nicolson, 1972.

———. *Philosophical Writings.* Eds. Simons, Margaret A., et al. Urbana and Chicago: University of Illinois Press, 2004.

————. "Poetry and the Truth of the Far West." *Political Writings*. Eds. Simons, Margaret A. and Marybeth Timmermann. Chicago: University of Illinois Press, 2014.

————. *Political Writings*. Eds. Simons, Margaret A. and Marybeth Timmermann. Chicago: University of Illinois Press, 2014.

————. "Preface to *Divorce in France*." Trans. Timmermann, Marybeth. *Feminist Writings*. Eds. Simons, Margaret A. and Marybeth Timmermann. Urbana, Chicago, and Springfield: University of Illinois Press, 2015.

————. *The Prime of Life*. Trans. Green, Peter. Cleveland and New York: The World Publishing Company, 1962.

————. "Pyrrhus and Cineas." Trans. Timmermann, Marybeth. *Philosophical Writings*. 1944. Eds. Simons, Margaret A., et al. Urbana and Chicago: University of Illinois Press, 2004.

————. "The Rebellious Woman—an Interview by Alice Schwartzer." Trans. Timmermann, Marybeth. *Feminist Writings*. 1972. Eds. Simons, Margaret A. and Marybeth Timmermann. Urbana, Chicago, and Springfield: Illinois University Press, 2015.

————. *The Second Sex*. 1949. Trans. Borde, Constance and Sheila Malovany-Chevallier. New York: Vintage Books, 2011.

————. "The Second Sex: 25 Years Later: Interviewed by John Gerassi." *Society* 13.2 (1976): 79–85.

————. *She Came to Stay*. 1943. Trans. Moyse, Yvonne and Roger Senhouse. New York & London: W. W. Norton & Company, 1999.

————. *A Transatlantic Love Affair: Letters to Nelson Algren*. New York: The New Press, 1998.

————. "Two Unpublished Chapters from *She Came to Stay*." Trans. Gautheron, Sylvie. *Philosophical Writings*. 1979. Eds. Simons, Margaret A., et al. Urbana and Chicago: University of Illinois Press, 2004.

————. "The Urgency of an Anti-Sexist Law." Trans. Timmermann, Marybeth. *Feminist Writings*. Eds. Simons, Margaret A. and Marybeth Timmermann. Urbana, Chicago, and Springfield: University of Illinois Press, 2015.

———. *The Useless Mouths*. Trans. Stanley, Liz and Catherine Naji. *"The Useless Mouths" and Other Literary Writings*. Eds. Simons, Margaret A. and Marybeth Timmermann. Urbana, Chicago, and Springfield: University of Illinois Press, 2011.

———. *A Walk through the Land of Old Age: A Documentary Film*. Trans. Hertich, Alexander. *Political Writings*. 1974. Eds. Simons, Margaret A. and Marybeth Timmermann. Urbana, Chicago, and Springfield: University of Illinois Press, 2012.

———. *Wartime Diary*. 1990. Trans. Cordero, Anne Deing. Urbana and Chicago: University of Illinois Press, 2009.

———. "What Is Existentialism?" Trans. Timmermann, Marybeth. *Philosophical Writings*. 1947. Eds. Simons, Margaret A., et al. Urbana and Chicago: University of Illinois Press, 2004.

———. *When Things of the Spirit Come First*. 1979. Trans. O'Brian, Patrick. New York: Pantheon Books, 1982.

———. "Why I'm a Feminist: Interview with Jean-Louis Servan-Schreiber" *Questionnaire*. 1975. Accessed Jul 1, 2021. https://www.youtube.com/watch?v=c3u1A0Mrjjw.

———. *The Woman Destroyed*. 1967. Trans. O'Brian, Patrick. New York: Pantheon Books, 1969.

———. "Women, Ads, and Hate." Trans. Timmermann, Marybeth. *Feminist Writings*. 1983. Eds. Simons, Margaret A. and Marybeth Timmermann. Urbana, Chicago, and Springfield: University of Illinois Press, 2015.

Beauvoir, Simone de, Margaret A. Simons, and Jane Marie Todd. "Two Interviews with Simone De Beauvoir." *Hypatia* 3.3 (1989): 11–27.

Ben-Ze'ev, Aaron. *The Arc of Love: How Our Romantic Lives Change over Time*. Chicago: The University of Chicago Press, 2019.

Ben-Ze'ev, Aaron, and Ruhama Goussinsky. *In the Name of Love: Romantic Ideology and Its Victims*. Oxford and New York: Oxford University Press, 2008.

Bergoffen, Debra B. *The Philosophy of Simone de Beauvoir*. Albany, NY: SUNY Press, 1997.

Brison, Susan J. "Beauvoir and feminism: interview and reflections." *The Cambridge Companion to Simone de Beauvoir*. Ed. Card, Claudia. Cambridge and New York: Cambridge University Press, 2003.

Butler, Judith. *Gender Trouble*. New York: Routledge, 1990.

———. *The Force of Nonviolence*. New York: Verso, 2020.

Cacopardo, Max. *Jean-Paul Sartre and/et Simone de Beauvoir / Société Radio-Canada*. 1967. Brooklyn, NY: First Run/Icarus Films, 2005.

Card, Claudia. *The Cambridge Companion to Simone de Beauvoir*. Cambridge and New York: Cambridge University Press, 2003.

Cherry, Myisha. *The Case for Rage*. New York: Oxford University Press, 2021.

Coffin, Judith G. *Sex, Love, and Letters*. Ithaca: Cornell University Press, 2020.

Cooper, Anna Julia. *The Voice of Anna Julia Cooper*. 1892. Eds. Lemert, Charles and Esme Bhan. Lanham, MD: Rowman & Littlefield, 1998.

Cox, Gary. *How to Be an Existentialist*. London and New York: Continuum, 2009.

Daigle, Christine, and Jacob Golomb, eds. *Beauvoir and Sartre*. Bloomington: Indiana University Press, 2008.

Davidson, Maria del Guadalupe, Kathryn T. Gines, and Donna-Dale L. Marcano, eds. *Convergences: Black Feminism and Continental Philosophy*. Albany: SUNY Press, 2010.

Deurzen, Emmy van. *Psychotherapy and the Quest for Happiness*. London: SAGE, 2009.

Dœuff, Michèle Le. "Simone de Beauvoir and Existentialism." *Feminist Studies* 6.2 (1980): 277–89.

———. *Hipparchia's Choice*. Trans. Selous, Trista. Oxford: Blackwell, 1991.

Evans, Ruth, ed. *Simone de Beauvoir's The Second Sex*. Manchester: Manchester University Press, 1998.

Friedan, Betty. *It Changed My Life*. Cambridge: Harvard University Press, 1998.

Frye, Marilyn. *The Politics of Reality*. New York: Crossing Press, 1983.

Fullbrook, Edward, and Kate Fullbrook. *Sex and Philosophy*. London and New York: Continuum, 2008.

Garcia, Manon. *We Are Not Born Submissive*. Princeton, NJ: Princeton University Press, 2021.

Gines, Kathryn T. "Sartre, Beauvoir, and the Race/Gender Analogy: A Case for Black Feminist Philosophy." *Convergences: Black Feminism and Continental Philosophy*. Eds. Davidson, Maria del Guadalupe, Kathryn T. Gines and Donna-Dale L. Marcano. Albany: SUNY Press, 2010.

———. "Simone de Beauvoir and the Race/Gender Analogy in *The Second Sex* Revisited." *A Companion to Simone de Beauvoir*. Eds. Hengehold, Laura and Nancy Bauer. Hoboken: Wiley Blackwell, 2017.

Glass, Kathy. "Calling All Sisters: Continental Philosophy and Black Feminist Thinkers." *Convergences*. Eds. Davidson, Maria del Guadalupe, Kathryn T. Gines and Donna-Dale L. Marcano. Albany: SUNY Press, 2010.

Gothlin, Eva. "Simone de Beauvoir's Notions of Appeal, Desire, and Ambiguity and Their Relationship to Jean-Paul Sartre's Notions of Appeal and Desire." *Hypatia* 14.4 (1999): 83–95.

Gouges, Olympe de. "The Rights of Woman." Trans. Cole, John. *Between the Queen and the Cabby*. Ed. Cole, John. Montréal: McGill-Queen's University Press, 2011.

Hansberry, Lorraine. "Simone de Beauvoir and *The Second Sex*: An American Commentary." *Words of Fire*. Ed. Guy-Sheftall, Beverly. New York: The New Press, 1995.

Harari, Yuval Noah. *Sapiens*. New York: Harper Perennial, 2014.

Hecht, Jennifer Michael. *Stay*. New Haven: Yale University Press, 2013.

Heinämaa, Sara. "Simone de Beauvoir's Phenomenology of Sexual Difference." *Hypatia* 14.4 (1999): 114–32.

Hengehold, Laura, and Nancy Bauer, eds. *A Companion to Simone de Beauvoir*. Hoboken: Wiley-Blackwell, 2017.

Heter, T Storm. "Beauvoir's White Problem." *Hypotheses: Chère Simone de Beauvoir*. Jan 24, 2021. Accessed July 1, 2021. https://lirecrire.hypotheses.org/3404.

hooks, bell. *All About Love*. New York: HarperCollins, 2000.

———. "True Philosophers: Beauvoir and bell." *Beauvoir and Western Thought from Plato to Butler*. Eds. Mussett, Shannon M. and William S. Wilkerson. New York: SUNY Press, 2012.

Irwin, William. *The Free Market Existentialist*. West Sussex: Wiley Blackwell, 2015.

Kaag, John. *Hiking with Nietzsche*. New York: Farrar, Straus and Giroux, 2018.

Khader, Serene. *Decolonizing Universalism*. Oxford: Oxford University Press, 2019.

King, Deborah. "Multiple Jeopardy, Multiple Consciousness: The Context of a Black Feminist Ideology." *Signs* 14.1 (1988): 42–72.

Kirkpatrick, Kate. *Becoming Beauvoir*. London: Bloomsbury, 2019.

Kruks, Sonia. *Simone de Beauvoir and the Politics of Ambiguity*. New York: Oxford University Press, 2012.

———. "Simone de Beauvoir and the Politics of Privilege." *Hypatia* 20.1 (2005).

Leighton, Jean. *Simone de Beauvoir on Woman*. Rutherford: Fairleigh Dickinson University Press, 1975.

Lorde, Audre. *The Cancer Journals*. San Francisco: Aunt Lute Books, 1980.

Lundgren-Gothlin, Eva. *Sex and Existence*. Trans. Schenck, Linda. Hanover: Wesleyan University Press, 1996.

Mann, Bonnie, and Martina Ferrari, eds. *On ne naît pas femme: On le devient: The life of a sentence*. New York: Oxford University Press, 2017.

Manne, Kate. *Down Girl*. New York: Oxford University Press, 2018.

Marino, Gordon. *The Existentialist's Survival Guide*. San Francisco: HarperOne, 2018.

Marso, Lori Jo. *Politics with Beauvoir*. Durham: Duke University Press, 2017.

Moi, Toril. "Acknowledging the Other: Reading, Writing, and Living in *The Mandarins*." *Yale French Studies* 135–136 (2019): 100–115.

———. *Feminist Theory and Simone de Beauvoir*. Oxford & Cambridge: Blackwell, 1990.

————. *Simone de Beauvoir*. Oxford and Cambridge: Blackwell, 1994.

————. *What Is a Woman? And Other Essays*. Oxford and New York: Oxford University Press, 1999.

Mussett, Shannon M., and William S. Wilkerson, eds. *Simone de Beauvoir and Western Thought from Plato to Butler*. Albany: SUNY Press, 2012.

Nelson, George. "Angela Davis." *New York Times T-Magazine*, New York, Oct 19, 2020. Accessed Aug 27, 2021. https://www.nytimes.com/2020/10/18/t-magazine/angela-davis.html.

Nussbaum, Martha C., and Saul Levmore. *Aging Thoughtfully*. Oxford: Oxford University Press, 2017.

Okely, Judith. *Simone de Beauvoir*. London: Virago, 1986.

Penaluna, Regan. *How to Think Like a Woman*. New York: Grove Atlantic, forthcoming 2023.

Perel, Esther. *State of Affairs*. New York: HarperCollins, 2017: 39.

Rich, Adrienne. *Of Woman Born*. New York: W. W. Norton & Company, 1995.

————. "Women and Honor." *On Lies, Secrets, and Silence*. New York: W. W. Norton & Company, 1979.

Rodgers, Catherine. "Elisabeth Badinter and *The Second Sex*: An Interview." *Signs* 21.1 (1995): 147–62.

Rose, Jacqueline. *Mothers*. New York: Farrar, Straus and Giroux, 2018.

Rouch, Marine. "Le Deuxième Sexe: une publication en plusieurs étapes." *Hypotheses: Chère Simone de Beauvoir* 2019. Accessed Jul 2, 2021. https://lirecrire.hypotheses.org/1565.

————. "Vous Ne Me Connaissez Pas Mais Ne Jetez Pas Tout De Suite Ma Lettre. Le courrier des lecteurs et lectrices de Simone de Beauvoir." *Genre de l'archive. Constitution et transmission des mémoires militantes*. Ed. Blum, Françoise. Vol. 2–9517903–3-3. Paris: CODHOS, 2017. 93–108.

Ruddick, Sara. *Maternal Thinking*. Boston: Beacon Press, 1995.

Sanos, Sandrine. *Simone de Beauvoir*. New York: Oxford University Press, 2017.

Sartre, Jean-Paul. *Existentialism Is a Humanism*. 1946. Trans. Macomber, Carol. New Haven: Yale University Press, 2007.

Schwarzer, Alice. *After The Second Sex*. Trans. Howarth, Marianne. New York: Pantheon Books, 1984.

Shaw, Devin Zane. *Philosophy of Antifascism*. New York: Rowman & Littlefield, 2020.

Simons, Margaret A. *Beauvoir and The Second Sex*. Oxford: Rowman & Littlefield, 1999.

Simons, Margaret A., Jessica Benjamin, and Simone de Beauvoir. "Simone de Beauvoir: An Interview." *Feminist Studies* 5.2 (1979): 330–45.

Solomon, Robert C., and Kathleen M. Higgins, eds. *The Philosophy of (Erotic) Love*. Lawrence: University Press of Kansas, 1991.

Spivak, Gayatri Chakravorty. "Can the Subaltern Speak?" *Can the Subaltern Speak?* Ed. Morris, Rosalind. New York: Columbia University Press, 2010.

Srinivasan, Amia. *The Right to Sex*. New York: Farrar, Straus and Giroux, 2021.

Teresa of Ávila. *The Book of My Life*. Trans. Starr, Mirabai. Boston and London: New Seeds, 2011.

———. *The Interior Castle*. Trans. The Benedictines of Stanbrook. London: Thomas Baker, 1921.

Tidd, Ursula. *Simone de Beauvoir*. London: Routledge, 2004.

Vintges, Karen. *A New Dawn for The Second Sex*. Amsterdam: Amsterdam University Press, 2017.

———. *Philosophy as Passion*. Trans. Lavelle, Anne. Bloomington: Indiana University Press, 1996.

Webber, Jonathan. *Rethinking Existentialism*. Oxford: Oxford University Press, 2018.

Wilkerson, Isabel. *Caste*. New York: Random House, 2020.

Young, Iris Marion. *On Female Body Experience*. Oxford: Oxford University Press, 2005.

Zakaria, Rafia. *Against White Feminism*. New York: W. W. Norton & Company, 2021.

NOTES

INTRODUCTION

1. Beauvoir wrote that "essence does not precede existence" (Beauvoir, *The Second Sex*, 270). Jean-Paul Sartre coined the phrase in the format "existence precedes essence" (Sartre, *Existentialism Is a Humanism*, 20).

2. Beauvoir, *Old Age,* 601.

3. Beauvoir, *The Prime of Life*, 285.

4. Moi, *Simone de Beauvoir*, 23. Sanos, *Simone de Beauvoir*, 11–13.

5. Hansberry, *Simone de Beauvoir*, 129–133. Bakewell, *At The Existentialist Cafe*, 21. The quote and title of the article that appeared in *Le Nouvel Observateur* read, "Femmes, vous lui devez tout!" meaning, "Women, you owe her everything!" Badinter said it was a mistake and should have read, "Femmes, vous lui devez tant!" meaning, "Women, you owe her so much!" (Rodgers, "Elisabeth Badinter and 'The Second Sex,'" 147).

6. In an interview, Beauvoir said, "Anyhow, Sartre is a philosopher, and I am not, and I have never really wanted to be a philosopher. I like philosophy very much, but I have not created a philosophical work. My field is literature. I am interested in novels, memoirs, essays, such as *The Second Sex*. However, none of these is philosophy." (Simons, Benjamin, and Beauvoir. "Simone de Beauvoir: An Interview," 338).

7. Beauvoir, *The Prime of Life*, 178.

8. Beauvoir, "What Is Existentialism?," 324. Philosopher Nancy Bauer argued of Beauvoir's method in *The Second Sex* that "the main goal is not to 'get it right' but, rather, to understand the attractions and powers of philosophical abstraction as they bear on one's everyday life" (Bauer, *Simone de Beauvoir*, 10).

9. Beauvoir, *The Second Sex*, 3.

10. René Maheu, with whom Beauvoir was friends prior to meeting Sartre, gave her the nickname in 1929 because, he said, "Beavers like company and they have a constructive bent" (Beauvoir, *Memoirs of a Dutiful Daughter*, 323). Philosopher Kate Kirkpatrick suggested that Beauvoir and Maheu were romantically involved, although Beauvoir denied that it was a physical relationship (Kirkpatrick, *Becoming Beauvoir*, 86).

11. Beauvoir, *Force of Circumstance I*, 189.

12. Beauvoir, "The Second Sex: 25 Years Later," 79–80.

13. For an excellent analysis of the complexities between oppression and moral failure, see Manon Garcia's *We Are Not Born Submissive* (2021).

14. Beauvoir, *The Second Sex*, 283. In French, the sentence is: "On ne naît pas femme: on le devient." Kate Kirkpatrick pointed out that while Beauvoir's quote was original, the idea was inspired by Alfred Fouillée who wrote, "Man isn't born, but rather becomes, free," and that Beauvoir made other claims that were more revolutionary, such as that the relentless sexualization of women keeps them oppressed (Kirkpatrick, *Becoming Beauvoir*, 53).

15. Kirkpatrick, *Becoming Beauvoir*, 262. Beauvoir, "Why I'm a Feminist: Interview with Jean-Louis Servan-Schreiber. For a discussion of the sentence, "One is not born, but rather becomes, woman," see Mann and Ferrari's *On Ne Naît Pas Femme: On Le Devient* (2017).

16. Kristeva, Julia. *Beauvoir Présente*. Paris: Pluriel, 2016.

17. Beauvoir, *Force of Circumstance I*, 38.

18. As philosopher Gordon Marino proposed with respect to existential

advice: "The [existential thinkers] do not offer a step-by-step plan for coping with our feelings of inadequacy, or a checklist of behaviors to avoid. Instead of detailing some strategy for assuaging our depression, they might tender advice on how to keep our moral and spiritual bearings when it feels as though we are going under" (Marino, *The Existentialist's Survival Guide*, 31).

19. Authenticity is often associated with Heidegger's discussion of *Eigentlichkeit*—meaning being truly one's own—in *Being and Time* (1927), but many other philosophers had already discussed similar variations before this. In 390 AD, Saint Augustine popularized the idea of inwardness, urging people to introspect, to find God, and then to transcend: "Return within yourself. In the inward man dwells truth. If you find that you are by nature mutable, transcend yourself." In the nineteenth century, Max Stirner urged us to own ourselves, Friedrich Nietzsche incited us to "Become who you are!," and Søren Kierkegaard linked authenticity to self-government: "The world has perhaps always had a lack of what could be called authentic individualities, decisive subjectivities, those artistically permeated with reflection, the independent thinkers who differ from the bellowers and the didacticizers." (See Saint Augustine. *Of True Religion.* Trans. Burleigh, J. H. S. South Bend, IN: Gateway Editions, 1953: 69; Stirner, Max. *The Ego and His Own.* 1844. Trans. Byington, Steven T. Ed. Martin, James J. Mineola, New York: Dover Publications, Inc., 2005; Nietzsche, Friedrich. *Thus Spoke Zarathustra.* Trans. Kaufmann, Walter. New York: The Modern Library, 1995: 239; and Kierkegaard, Søren. *Concluding Unscientific Postscript Vol 1.* 1846. Trans. Hong, Howard V. and Edna H. Hong. Princeton: Princeton University Press, 1992: 66.)

20. hooks, *All About Love*, xxv.

21. Beauvoir, *All Said and Done*, 1.

22. In the words of philosopher and existential therapist Emmy van Deurzen, "authenticity in living is to 'own' life as it really is, to own up to our responsibilities as human beings, but more than that it is about not refusing life and its vagaries: daring to be 'engaged' with

life, a life where we are willing to connect and open our eyes to reality" (Deurzen, *Psychotherapy,* 158).

23. Philosopher Toril Moi, inspired by Beauvoir, suggested that writing is an appeal to others to join an intellectual journey: "A good reader remains herself—she doesn't abandon her own views, beliefs, and principles without careful consideration—but she is also willing to open herself up to the writer's vision, to try to see what she sees, to follow her on her adventure" (Moi, "Acknowledging the Other," 108).

EXISTENTIAL INFRASTRUCTURE

1. For example, Anke Samulowitz et al found that the perception that women are hysterical, emotional, and sensitive while men are stoic and tolerant is widespread and based on gendered norms rather than biological differences. (Samulowitz, Anke, et al. "'Brave Men' and 'Emotional Women': A Theory-Guided Literature Review on Gender Bias in Health Care and Gendered Norms Towards Patients with Chronic Pain." *Pain Research & Management* (2018).)

2. Beauvoir, *The Second Sex*, 266. I refer to women as "them" because I hope that women will not be the only readers of this book. I also aim to be careful about using "we" because I recognize that neither Beauvoir nor I speak for all women in all situations. Still, in the introduction to *The Second Sex*, Beauvoir notes that referring to women as "them" (and not "we" or "us") is a bad habit that reinforces women's secondary status to men because it discourages us (women) from using the language of subjectivity.

3. For example see: Libet, Benjamin. "Unconscious Cerebral Initiative and the Role of Conscious Will in Voluntary Action." *The Behavioral and Brain Sciences* 8.4 (1985): 529–39; Doidge, Norman. *The Brain That Changes Itself.* New York: Penguin Books, 2007.

4. Philosopher Karen Vintges argued that Beauvoir's analysis gives us a toolbox to analyze the patriarchy which Vintges likens to a hydra, a many-headed monster, because it's ugly, resilient, multifaceted, and

requires many different strategies to combat the varied manifestations of its power (Vintges, *A New Dawn,* 13).

5. Beauvoir, *The Second Sex,* 68.

6. Philosopher Gary Cox explained that authenticity is the acceptance that we are free and responsible, "The authentic person responds fully to the appeal to *get real* that pervades existentialism . . . That is, authenticity consists in embracing human reality for what it is and living in accordance with it rather than pretending it is something else: a nice fairytale reality where dreams come true without effort, where debts don't have to be paid back, where knights in shining armor ride to the rescue and we all live happily ever after" (Cox, *How to Be an Existentialist,* 82).

7. Beauvoir, *When Things of The Spirit Come First,* 6.

8. Beauvoir, *When Things of The Spirit Come First,* 33.

9. Beauvoir, *The Second Sex,* 756.

10. Beauvoir, *When Things of The Spirit Come First,* 212.

11. Beauvoir, *The Second Sex,* 6.

12. Inspired by Beauvoir, Manon Garcia argued that "patriarchy, like all structures of social domination, creates mechanisms to perpetuate itself, and women's submission is one of them" (Garcia, *We Are Not Born Submissive,* 204).

13. Sartre, Jean-Paul. "Huis Clos." Trans. Gilbert, Stuart. *Huis Clos and Other Plays.* 1944. London: Penguin Books, 2000. "Hell is other people" is one of Sartre's most famous statements, spoken by the fictional character Garcin. Sartre later said he meant that: "If our relations with others are twisted or corrupted, then others have to be hell . . . Fundamentally, others are what is most important in us for our understanding of ourselves." (Contat, Michel, Michel Rybalka, and Jean-Paul Sartre. *The Writings of Jean-Paul Sartre.* Trans. McCleary, Richard C. Vol. 1. Evanston: Northwestern University Press, 1974.)

14. Beauvoir, *The Second Sex,* 159.

15. Beauvoir, *The Second Sex,* 197. The "Eternal Feminine" is not Beau-

voir's term. Beauvoir pointed to writers including Goethe who, in *Faust*, refers to the Eternal Feminine as drawing men to heaven.

16. Beauvoir, *The Second Sex*, 213, 273.

17. Beauvoir, *Force of Circumstance I*, 187.

18. Beauvoir, *Force of Circumstance I*, 190.

19. Beauvoir, *Force of Circumstance I*, 186–187.

20. Hansberry, *Simone de Beauvoir*, 129–30.

21. Sylvie Le Bon de Beauvoir wrote that on July 14, 1956, the Vatican blacklisted *The Second Sex* and *The Mandarins* for creating a "destructive atmosphere" and spreading "subtle poison" (Beauvoir, *Mémoires II*, XIII, my translation).

22. For numbers of copies of *The Second Sex* printed, see Rouch, "Le Deuxième Sexe."

23. Beauvoir, *The Second Sex*, 72–73.

24. Beauvoir, *The Second Sex*, 46.

25. Beauvoir, *The Second Sex*, 42.

26. Lerner, Gerda. *The Creation of Patriarchy*. Oxford: Oxford University Press, 1986: 8, 221. There is some evidence to suggest that gender discrimination started emerging as early as the sixth millennium BC. Nodding to Beauvoir as part of their motivation, anthropologist Marta Cintas Peña and her team took up the challenge of seeing if there was archeological evidence for Lerner's claim. They analyzed graves in Spain that were up to eight thousand years old, and they found 50 percent more male than female graves, which indicates that women were less likely to be inhumed. They discovered more evidence of trauma on male remains and more weapons in male graves, suggesting that men participated in more violence than women. They also found more images of men than women in rock art. Overrepresentation of men in graves and art in Neolithic societies signifies that men were culturally more appreciated and valued than women and suggests an ideology of male power was already developing. If gender differences were only biological, there would be much less variation

in gender inequalities between societies throughout history. Pure biological differences wouldn't explain how women are now, since being given more freedom, achieving in the same ways as men (Cintas-Peña, Marta, and Leonardo García Sanjuán. "Gender Inequalities in Neolithic Iberia: A Multi-Proxy Approach." *European Journal of Archaeology* 22.4 [2019]: 499–522).

27. Beauvoir, *The Second Sex*, 12.

28. A much-cited 1996 *Psychological Science* article argued that, "There is literally nothing to be said, scientifically or therapeutically, to the advantage of the entire Freudian system or any of its component dogmas" (Crews, Frederick. "Review: The Verdict on Freud." *Psychological Science* 7.2 (1996): 63–68). While many people still idolize Freud, his legacy is more culturally provocative and imaginative than scientific. In *Freud: The Making of an Illusion* (2017), Crews argues that Freud was an unoriginal cocaine addict who was more obsessed with fame than academic rigor. See also Todd Dufresne in *Against Freud: Critics Talk Back* (2007). Even Freud was surprised at how popular his ideas were and on arriving in New York in 1909, he allegedly told his friend and colleague Carl Jung, "They don't realize we're bringing them the plague" (Lacan, Jacques. *Écrits*. Trans. Fink, Bruce. New York: W. W. Norton & Company, 1996: 336).

29. Harari, *Sapiens*, 172.

30. For example, Archer, John. "Sex Differences in Aggression between Heterosexual Partners: A Meta-Analytic Review." *Psychological Bulletin* 126.5 (2000): 651–80.

31. For example, Reardon, Sean F., et al. "Gender Achievement Gaps in U.S. School Districts." *Stanford Center for Education Policy Analysis.* 2018. Accessed July 20, 2021. http://cepa.stanford.edu/wp18–13; Voyer, Daniel, and Susan D. Voyer. "Gender Differences in Scholastic Achievement: A Meta-Analysis." *Psychological Bulletin* 140.4 (2014): 1174–1204; Bian, Lin, Andrei Cimpian, and Sarah-Jane Leslie. "Evidence of Bias against Girls and Women in Contexts That Emphasize Intellectual Ability." *The American Psychologist* 73.9 (2018).

32. A study of 1.6 million (mostly US) students found that both the variance and mean between men and women in STEM subjects, such as mathematics and science, was smaller than non-STEM subjects, such as humanities and social sciences. This means that if the variability hypothesis was correct, men should be overrepresented in non-STEM more than STEM careers, which is not the case. The researchers conclude that although girls' and boys' grades are equally as likely to be high enough for STEM careers, gendered beliefs such as stereotyping and backlashes threaten girls' paths to a greater extent than boys'. (O'Dea, R. E., et al. "Gender Differences in Individual Variation in Academic Grades Fail to Fit Expected Patterns for STEM." *Nature Communications* 9 [2018].)

33. Schwarzer, *After The Second Sex*, 45.

34. Beauvoir, *The Second Sex*, 10.

35. Beauvoir, *The Second Sex*, 270.

36. Beauvoir, *Misunderstanding in Moscow*, 226.

37. For a critique of elitist feminism, see Rottenberg, Catherine. *The Rise of Neoliberal Feminism*. Oxford: Oxford University Press, 2018.

38. "Scope of the Problem: Statistics (Analysis of the Department of Justice, Office of Justice Programs, Bureau of Justice Statistics, National Crime Victimization Survey, 2018)": Rape, Abuse & Incest National Network, 2019. Accessed July 20, 2021. https://www.rainn.org/statistics/scope-problem.

39. "Violence against Women Prevalence Estimates, 2018." Geneva and New York: World Health Organization, 2021. Accessed July 20, 2021. https://www.who.int/publications/i/item/9789240022256.

40. "Global Report on Trafficking in Persons 2018." Vienna: United Nations Office on Drugs and Crime, 2018: 10. Accessed July 20, 2021. https://www.unodc.org/documents/data-and-analysis/glotip/2018/GLOTiP_2018_BOOK_web_small.pdf.

41. "Global Study on Homicide 2019." Vienna: United Nations Office on Drugs and Crime, 2019: 11. Accessed July 20, 2021. https://www.unodc.org/documents/data-and-analysis/gsh/Booklet_5.pdf.

42. Boudet, Ana Maria Munoz, et al. *Gender Differences in Poverty and Household Composition through the Life-Cycle: A Global Perspective.* Washington, D.C.: UN Women and the World Bank, 2018. Accessed July 20, 2021. https://www.unwomen.org/en/digital-library /publications/2018/4/gender-differences-in-poverty-and-household -composition-through-the-life-cycle.

43. Coury, Sarah, et al. "Women in the Workplace 2021." LeanIn.Org and McKinsey, 2021. Accessed July 20, 2021. https://www.mckinsey.com /featured-insights/diversity-and-inclusion/women-in-the-workplace.

44. When people are asked to draw leaders, both men and women almost always portray men. There's also some evidence to suggest that young people are less likely than older people to believe men and women are equally capable of leadership. In 2020, female CEOs broke a new high record with representation of around seven percent on the list of Fortune 500 companies, even though research suggests that women are more effective leaders when people are asked to assess on the basis of what they identify as good leadership skills. In 1995, there were none, so . . . progress? Yet, in *Forbes* magazine's 2019 list of "most innovative leaders," it nominated ninety-nine men and one woman, Ross Stores CEO Barbara Rentler, in seventy-fifth place. A Twitter outcry prompted *Forbes* to review its methodology, which was exceedingly narrow and loaded with indicators that compounded biases that favor white men, such as being CEO of at least a $10 billion company. See Murphy, Heather. "Picture a Leader. Is She a Woman?" *The New York Times,* Mar 16, 2018. Accessed July 20, 2021. https://www.nytimes.com/2018/03/16/health /women-leadership-workplace.html; "The Reykjavik Index for Leadership 2020–2021." Kantar, 2020. Accessed July 20, 2021. https:// www.womenpoliticalleaders.org/wp-content/uploads/2020/11/The -Reykjavik-Index-for-Leadership-2020-Report-2–1.pdf; Zenger, Jack, and Joseph Folkman. "Research: Women Score Higher Than Men in Most Leadership Skills," *Harvard Business Review.* (Jun 25, 2019). Accessed July 20, 2021. https://hbr.org/2019/06/research-women-score -higher-than-men-in-most-leadership-skills; "*The Data on Women*

Leaders": Pew Social Trends (September 13, 2018). Accessed July 20, 2021. http://www.pewsocialtrends.org/fact-sheet/the-data-on-women -leaders/.

45. Black women have often been the ones fighting for freedom for all races and genders—despite the fact that they have often been left out. For example, philosopher Kathryn T. Gines highlighted that at the 1848 Seneca Falls Convention, the first women's rights convention in the United States, Black women were not included (Gines, "Sartre, Beauvoir, and the Race/Gender Analogy," 36). In the nineteenth century, activist Sojourner Truth spoke out against slavery and for women's rights, and philosopher Anna Julia Cooper argued that: "It is not the intelligent woman vs. the ignorant woman; nor the white woman vs. the black, the brown, and the red—it is not even the cause of woman vs. man . . . when race, color, sex, condition, are realized to be the accidents, not the substance of life . . . then woman's lesson is taught and woman's cause is won—not the white woman nor the black woman nor the red woman, but the cause of every man or woman who has writhed silently under a mighty wrong" (Cooper, *The Voice of Anna Julia Cooper*, 107–108).

46. Nelson, "Angela Davis."

47. hooks, "True Philosophers: Beauvoir and bell," 235.

48. Glass, *Calling All Sisters*, 228; Heter, "Beauvoir's White Problem."

49. Beauvoir, *The Second Sex*, 8.

50. Beauvoir, *The Second Sex*, 148, 343–344, 736.

51. Beauvoir, *The Second Sex*, 154.

52. Beauvoir, *The Second Sex*, 610.

53. Beauvoir, *The Second Sex*, 639.

54. Schwarzer, *After The Second Sex*, 71.

55. Altman, *Beauvoir in Time*, 128, 204.

56. According to historian Marine Rouch's estimates, there are 20,000 uncatalogued letters from general readers to Beauvoir in the Bibliothèque nationale de France archives. Historian Judith Coffin read

around one thousand of them and found that letters came from a diverse range of readers. Coffin wrote: "The letter writers were male as well as female, old and middle-aged as well as young, staid as well as rebellious. They wrote from all over the francophone world, including North and West Africa, from the Scandinavian countries, eastern Europe, Latin America, the United States, England, and from around the corner in Paris . . . Beauvoir's audience crossed boundaries of social class and educational capital as well as national borders: letters came from writers and writers in the making, teachers, university students, schoolgirls, social workers, factory workers, doctors, psychologists and psychoanalysts, and women at home." Of course, these letters didn't all agree with Beauvoir's analysis, and many of the letters she received have been lost since, but very few of the letters that survive are insulting, and the range of readers does suggest that Beauvoir challenged many people to reflect on their situations (Coffin, *Sex, Love and Letters*, 8–9; Rouch, "Vous ne me connaissez pas," 93).

57. Beauvoir, *The Second Sex*, 273.

GROWING UP

1. Sousa, Ronnie de. "Natural-born existentialists." *Aeon*. Dec 18, 2017. Accessed July 20, 2021. https://aeon.co/essays/how-evolutionary-biology -makes-everyone-an-existentialist.

2. Beauvoir, *The Second Sex*, 284.

3. For example, see Ferracioli, Luara. "Carefreeness and Children's Wellbeing." *Journal of Applied Philosophy* 37.1(2019): 103–17. Accessed July 20, 2021. https://onlinelibrary.wiley.com/doi/full/10 .1111/japp.12382?af=R.

4. Beauvoir, *The Ethics of Ambiguity*, 36.

5. Rothman, Barbara Katz. *The Tentative Pregnancy*. New York: Penguin, 1987: 129–130.

6. Rippon, Gina. *The Gendered Brain*. New York: Vintage Arrow, 2019: 153–55, 357.

7. Jonathan Webber explored Beauvoir's (and Franz Fanon's) views of

"sedimentation," which is the idea that we accumulate information and values from our environment like particles being deposited in a river over a long period of time. The analogy describes the way in which children are raised with different expectations that shape our goals, understandings, and attitudes and, as we grow older, nudge us toward gendered stereotypes. The more sediment we collect, the harder it is to shift to new paths. It's not impossible, but the choices we make cement our past and make us who we are—but not who we become. These imprints are often so subtle and gradual that we don't notice it happening to ourselves or when we impose it on others (Webber, *Rethinking Existentialism*, 4).

8. Beauvoir, *The Second Sex*, 311.

9. Beauvoir, *The Second Sex*, 311–12.

10. Macur, Juliet. "A Risky Move Only Biles Tries Is Little More Than Its Own Reward [Sports Desk]." *The New York Times*. May 25, 2021.

11. Beauvoir, *The Second Sex*, 200.

12. Tramontana, Mary Katharine. "Why Do We Still Have 'Girl Stuff' and 'Boy Stuff'?" The *New York Times*, Nov 18, 2020.

13. Barrett, Lisa Feldman. *How Emotions Are Made*. New York: Houghton Mifflin Harcourt, 2017: 228; *"Lisa Feldman Barrett Discusses 'Resting Bitch Face.'"* Washington, D.C.: Politics and Prose Bookstore, 2017. YouTube. Accessed July 20, 2021. https://www.youtube.com/watch?v=whWbVc6vUhg.

14. Philosopher Myisha Cherry reported that Black women who use their voices are often misperceived and mistakenly stereotyped as "overly aggressive, threatening, loud, and animalistic." Cherry, Myisha. "Gendered Failures in Extrinsic Emotional Regulation; Or, Why Telling a Woman to 'Relax' or a Young Boy to 'Stop Crying Like a Girl' Is Not a Good Idea." *Philosophical Topics* 47.2 (2019).

15. Beauvoir, *The Second Sex*, 3–4.

16. Beauvoir, *The Second Sex*, 724.

17. Beauvoir, *The Second Sex*, 345.

18. Beauvoir, *The Prime of Life*, 328; Beauvoir, *She Came to Stay*, 136. In *She Came to Stay*, the dialogue begins referring to the neighbor as "he" and then shifts to "she," highlighting that he/she gender categories are not a one-size-fits-all approach.

19. Building on Beauvoir, Judith Butler argued in *Gender Trouble* that the problem with the category of "woman" is that it implies that there is a "right" way to be one. This, in turn, legitimizes some experiences and leaves out others, such as those of queer and transgender women. Gender is not an essential, fixed, internal feature of a person's being. It's a social performance. It's something we *do,* repetitively and ritually which creates anticipations and expectations around us. This is consistent with Beauvoir's idea that existence precedes essence, however not everyone agrees with Butler's interpretation. One issue with Butler's reading is that classifying gender as a "performance" undervalues the lived experience of many people who do not fit into the traditional cis heterosexual binary. For example, transfeminist philosopher Julia Serano argued that "certain aspects of femininity (and masculinity as well) transcend both socialization and biological sex—otherwise there would not be feminine boys and masculine girls." Instead of empowering females, she proposed we should be empowering femininity to make the world a safer place for everyone, and for people to choose how to live their genders authentically (Serano, Julia. *Whipping Girl.* Emeryville: Seal Press, 2009: 18–20). Some philosophers highlight the limitations of applying the phrase, "one isn't born, but rather becomes, woman," to transgender identities. For example, philosopher Kathleen Stock wrote that, "The fact that in *The Second Sex* de Beauvoir was fairly obviously talking only about females and their involuntary encounters with a social system subjecting them to impossible ideals of femininity from birth seems mostly ignored" (Stock, Kathleen. *Material Girls.* London: Fleet, 2021: 296). Even if we do take Beauvoir's phrase to mean that people can choose their gender, then while that might feel liberating, it doesn't tell us much about the experience and meaning of transgender choices and perspectives. Philosopher Helga Varden argued that both Beauvoir's philosophy

and scientific determinism "struggle to get into focus the existential importance of the surgeries as well as the existential relief experienced when the process has been completed successfully" (Helga Varden, *Sex, Love, and Gender: A Kantian Theory,* Oxford, 2020: 126). Such ambiguities and disagreements are unsurprising given that Beauvoir did not address transgender identities in any detail.

20. Beauvoir, *The Second Sex,* 16–17.

21. Schwarzer, "The Rebellious Woman," 197; Beauvoir, *The Second Sex,* 4.

22. Beauvoir, *The Second Sex,* 287.

23. Beauvoir, *The Second Sex,* 348.

24. Beauvoir, *Memoirs of a Dutiful Daughter,* 99–101.

25. Beauvoir, *Memoirs of a Dutiful Daughter,* 121. Beauvoir's emphasis.

26. Beauvoir, *Memoirs of a Dutiful Daughter,* 111.

27. Beauvoir, *The Second Sex,* 369.

28. Beauvoir, *The Second Sex,* 366–67.

29. "Be a Lady They Said" by Camille Rainville Featuring Cynthia Nixon. Feb 26, 2020. Vimeo. McLean, Paul (Director) and Rothstein, Claire (Producer). Accessed July 20, 2021. https://vimeo.com/393253445.

30. Beauvoir, Simone de. "Observer Picture Archive: My Clothes and I, 20 March 1960 with Cynthia Judah." Ed. Whitmore, Greg: *The Guardian,* 2019. Accessed July 30, 2021. https://www.theguardian.com/theobserver/2019/mar/17/observer-archive-my-clothes-and-i-by-simone-de-beauvoir-20-march-1960.

31. Arefin, D. Sharmin. "Is Hair Discrimination Race Discrimination?" *American Bar Association-Business Law Today* (Apr 17, 2020). Accessed July 20, 2021. https://www.americanbar.org/groups/business_law/publications/blt/2020/05/hair-discrimination/; Koval, Christy Zhou, and Ashleigh Shelby Rosette. "The Natural Hair Bias in Job Recruitment." *Social Psychological & Personality Science* (Aug 2020). *The CROWN Research Study*: Dove, 2019. Accessed July 30, 2020. https://www.thecrownact.com.

32. Mader, Mary Beth. "The Second Sexuality." *A Companion to Simone de Beauvoir*. Eds. Hengehold, Laura and Nancy Bauer. Hoboken, NJ: Wiley-Blackwell, 2017.

33. Oluo, Ijeoma. *Mediocre*. New York: Seal Press, 2020: 6.

34. hooks, bell. *The Will to Change*. New York: Atria Books, 2004: 31.

35. Cassino, Dan, and Yasemin Besen-Cassino. "Of Masks and Men? Gender, Sex, and Protective Measures During COVID-19." *Politics & Gender* 16.4 (2020): 1052–62; Reny, Tyler T. "Masculine Norms and Infectious Disease: The Case of COVID-19." *Politics & Gender* 16.4 (2020): 1028–35; Palmer, Carl L., and Rolfe D. Peterson. "Toxic Mask-ulinity: The Link between Masculine Toughness and Affective Reactions to Mask Wearing in the COVID-19 Era." *Politics & Gender* 16.4 (2020): 1044–51.

36. Lahren, Tomi. "Might as well carry a purse with that mask, Joe." Twitter. Oct 5, 2020. Accessed July 30, 2021. https://twitter.com /TomiLahren/status/1313312828670046208?s=20.

37. Beauvoir, *The Second Sex*, 312.

38. Beauvoir, *Pyrrhus and Cineas*, 123.

39. Beauvoir, *Les Belles Images*, 223.

FRIENDSHIP

1. Beauvoir, *The Second Sex*, 160.

2. Beauvoir, *The Second Sex*, 159.

3. Beauvoir, *She Came to Stay,* 302.

4. Hegel, G. W. F., *Phenomenology of Spirit*. 1807. Trans. Miller, A. V. Oxford: Clarendon Press, 1981: 114.

5. Beauvoir, *The Mandarins*, 43.

6. Beauvoir, *She Came to Stay,* 291.

7. Fullbrook and Fullbrook, *Sex and Philosophy*, xiii.

8. Beauvoir, *A Transatlantic Love Affair*, 208.

9. Beauvoir, *The Prime of Life*, 24.

10. Beauvoir, *The Prime of Life*, 183.

11. Rowley, *Tête-à-Tête*, 60.

12. Beauvoir, *The Prime of Life*, 209.

13. Gerassi, John. *Talking with Sartre: Conversations and Debates*. New Haven & London: Yale University Press, 2009: 221.

14. Rowley, *Tête-à-Tête*, 337–338.

15. Sartre wrote, "I haven't felt Nausea, I'm not authentic, I have halted on the threshold of the promised lands. But at least I point the way to them and others can go there. I'm a guide, that's my role." (Sartre, Jean-Paul. *War Diaries: Notebooks from a Phoney War 1939–1940*. Trans. Hoare, Quintin. London & New York: Verso, 1984: 62.) For Sartre's views on lying, see Sartre, Jean-Paul. *Being and Nothingness*. 1943. Trans. Barnes, Hazel E. New York: Washington Square Press, 1992: 89.

16. Beauvoir, *Force of Circumstance I*, 270.

17. The US government estimates the cost of loneliness is almost $7 billion per year due to the pressure on the health system. "The Health Impact of Loneliness: Emerging Evidence and Interventions." Washington, DC: The National Institute for Health Care Management, 2018. Accessed Jan 16, 2021. https://www.nihcm.org/categories/the-health-impact-of-loneliness-emerging-evidence-and-interventions; Meisters, Rachelle, et al. "Does Loneliness Have a Cost?: A Population-Wide Study of the Association between Loneliness and Healthcare Expenditure." *International Journal of Public Health* 66.581286 (2021).

18. "The Loneliness Epidemic." Rockville, MD: Health Resources & Services Administration, 2019. Accessed Jan 16, 2021. https://www.hrsa.gov/enews/past-issues/2019/january-17/loneliness-epidemic.

19. Renken, Elena and Lydia Denworth. "Survival of the Friendliest: How Our Close Friendships Help Us Thrive." *NPR* (February 22, 2020). Accessed Jan 16, 2021. https://www.npr.org/sections/health-shots/2020/02/22/807742275/survival-of-the-friendliest-how-our-close-friendships-help-us-thrive.

20. Onishi, Norimitsu. "A Generation in Japan Faces a Lonely Death." *The New York Times,* Nov 30, 2017. Accessed Jan 16, 2021. https://www.nytimes.com/2017/11/30/world/asia/japan-lonely-deaths-the-end.html.

21. Beauvoir, *All Said and Done*, 215.

22. Like Beauvoir, Hannah Arendt also acknowledged that loneliness can hold people back from living fully, but a danger that Arendt emphasized that Beauvoir did not was the political risk of loneliness. Arendt proposed that loneliness is different from isolation and solitude. To be isolated is to be severed from human companionship, whereas loneliness is to be severed from connection with others, meaning that one can still feel lonely even if surrounded by people. Drawing on Arendt, philosopher Samantha Rose Hill argued that organized loneliness is a prime breeding ground for tyranny and totalitarianism because it blurs people's ability to make judgments: "In loneliness, one is unable to carry on a conversation with oneself, because one's ability to think is compromised. Ideological thinking turns us away from the world of lived experience, starves the imagination, denies plurality, and destroys the space between men that allows them to relate to one another in meaningful ways." Loneliness clears the way for totalitarian leaders to offer tyrannical solutions and communities to "cure" our loneliness. Hill, Samantha Rose. "Where Loneliness Can Lead." *Aeon,* October 2020. Accessed Aug 28, 2021. https://aeon.co/essays/for-hannah-arendt-totalitarianism-is-rooted-in-loneliness.

23. Beauvoir, *Memoirs of a Dutiful Daughter*, 92.

24. Beauvoir, *Memoirs of a Dutiful Daughter*, 94.

25. Beauvoir, *Memoirs of a Dutiful Daughter*, 143; Schwarzer, *After The Second Sex*, 120.

26. Tannen, Deborah. *You're the Only One I Can Tell*. New York: Ballantine Books, 2017: xii. Although women share more than men, this does not mean that they "gossip" more, which is a criticism that often aims to try to keep women from talking to one another. See

Robbins, Megan L., and Alexander Karan. "Who Gossips and How in Everyday Life?" *Social Psychological and Personality Science*, 11.2 (2020): 185–195.

27. Beauvoir, *Diary of a Philosophy Student Vol 1*, 311.

28. Beauvoir, *Memoirs of a Dutiful Daughter*, 258.

29. Almaatouq, Abdullah, et al. "Are You Your Friends' Friend? Poor Perception of Friendship Ties Limits the Ability to Promote Behavioral Change." *PLoS One* 11.3 (2016).

30. It's probably not a coincidence that the character Sylvie shared a name with another of Beauvoir's close friends, Sylvie Le Bon. Beauvoir dedicated her autobiography *All Said and Done* to Sylvie, and wrote of her, "I loved her enthusiasms and her anger, her gravity, her gaiety, her horror of the commonplace, her uncalculating generosity" (Beauvoir, *All Said and Done*, 63).

31. Letter partly published in Lecarme-Tabone, Éliane, and Jean-Louis Jeanelle, eds. *Simone de Beauvoir*. Paris: L'Herne, 2013: 127. My translation. Extract via Beauvoir, Simone de. "Importante correspondance à Violette Leduc." Sotheby's, 1945–1972. Accessed Aug 27, 2021. https://www.sothebys.com/en/buy/auction/2020/livres-et-manuscrits/importante-correspondance-a-violette-leduc.

32. Plath, Sylvia. *The Bell Jar*. New York: Buccaneer Books, 1971: 36.

33. Beauvoir, *The Second Sex*, 355.

34. Gandhi, Leela. *Affective Communities*. Durham & London: Duke University Press, 2006: 31.

35. As a condition of teaching, I am not allowed to say which prison or share the incarcerated students' names, but I am allowed to write about the experience.

36. Plato. *Symposium*. Trans. Gill, Christopher. New York: Penguin, 1999: 49.

37. Plato. *Symposium*, xiv.

38. Plato, *Symposium*, 47.

39. Beauvoir, *The Second Sex*, 511.

40. Most studies find a clear inverse correlation between education and recidivism. For example, see Hall, Lori L. "Correctional Education and Recidivism: Toward a Tool for Reduction." *Journal of Correctional Education* 66.2 (2015): 4–29; Gerber, Jurg, and Eric J. Fritsch. *Prison Education and Offender Behavior: A Review of the Scientific Literature.* Huntsville, TX: College of Criminal Justice, Sam Houston State University, 1993.

41. Tolokonnikova, Nadya. *Read and Riot: A Pussy Riot Guide to Activism.* San Francisco: HarperOne, 2018: 173.

42. Beauvoir, *The Ethics of Ambiguity*, 91.

43. Beauvoir, *The Second Sex*, 66.

ROMANTIC LOVE

1. Beauvoir, *A Transatlantic Love Affair*, 208.

2. Beauvoir, *Letters to Sartre*, 183; Beauvoir, *The Second Sex*, 511.

3. Beauvoir, *The Second Sex*, 706.

4. Beauvoir, *The Prime of Life*, 252.

5. Sweaty T-shirt dating is based on research that suggests some molecules released in body odors influences our mate choices. See Wedekind, Claus, et al. "MHC-Dependent Mate Preferences in Humans." *Proceedings: Biological Sciences* 260.1359 (1995): 245–49.

6. Emanuele, Enzo, et al. "Raised Plasma Nerve Growth Factor Levels Associated with Early-Stage Romantic Love." *Psychoneuroendocrinology* 31.3 (2006): 288–94; Marazziti, Donatella, and Domenico Canale. "Hormonal Changes When Falling in Love." *Psychoneuroendocrinology* 29.7 (2004): 931–36.

7. Beauvoir, *Memoirs of a Dutiful Daughter*, 89.

8. Beauvoir, *The Ethics of Ambiguity*, 65.

9. Perel, *State of Affairs*, 39.

10. Beauvoir, *The Mandarins*, 194.

11. Beauvoir, *The Second Sex*, 696.

12. Beauvoir, *The Ethics of Ambiguity*, 67.

13. Beauvoir, *The Useless Mouths*, 70–71.

14. Algren, "The Question of Simone de Beauvoir," 136.

15. Amia Srinivasan doesn't mention Beauvoir, but presents an apt argument in "Sex as a Pedagogical Failure." *The Yale Law Journal* 129.4 (2020).

16. Schwarzer, *After The Second Sex*, 53.

17. Beauvoir, *Letters to Sartre*, 389.

18. Beauvoir, *Force of Circumstance I*, 125.

19. Schwarzer, *After The Second Sex*, 84, 113.

20. Avery, Daniel. "71 Countries Where Homosexuality Is Illegal." *Newsweek* (2019). Accessed Aug 27, 2021. https://www.newsweek .com/73-countries-where-its-illegal-be-gay-1385974.

21. Ruiz, Michelle. "The Young Women of Hollywood Are Single and Loving It." *Vogue* 2019. Accessed Aug 29, 2021. https://www.vogue .com/article/emma-watson-ariana-grande-selena-gomez-celebrate -being-single.

22. Smith, Janet Farrell. "Possessive Power." *Hypatia* 1.2 (1986): 103–20.

23. Beauvoir, *The Second Sex*, 261.

24. Beauvoir, *Brigitte Bardot*, 17, 20.

25. Beauvoir, *The Useless Mouths*, 81.

26. Beauvoir, *The Second Sex*, 566.

MARRIAGE

1. Kreider, Rose M., and Renee Ellis. *Number, Timing, and Duration of Marriages and Divorces: 2009*. Washington, DC: U.S. Census Bureau, 2011: 11. Accessed Aug 27, 2021. https://www.census.gov/prod /2011pubs/p70-125.pdf. More recent research suggests people are waiting longer to get married or not marrying at all. See Barroso, Amanda, Kim Parker, and Jesse Bennett. "As Millennials near 40, They're Approaching Family Life Differently Than Previous Generations." Washington, DC: Pew Research Center, 2020. Accessed Aug 27, 2021. https://www.pewresearch.org/social-trends/2020/05/27/as -millennials-near-40-theyre-approaching-family-life-differently-than

-previous-generations/; Horowitz, Juliana Menasce, Nikki Graf, and Gretchen Livingston. "Marriage and Cohabitation in the U.S.": Pew Research Center, 2019. Accessed Aug 27, 2021. https://www .pewresearch.org/topics/marriage-and-divorce/.

2. Beauvoir, *Diary of a Philosophy Student Vol 1*, 246.

3. Beauvoir, *The Useless Mouths*, 50.

4. Beauvoir, *The Useless Mouths*, 66.

5. Beauvoir, *Diary of a Philosophy Student Vol 1*, 246.

6. Hegel, G. W. F. "A Fragment on Love." *The Philosophy of (Erotic) Love*. Eds. Solomon, Robert C. and Kathleen M. Higgins. Lawrence: University Press of Kansas, 1991: 120.

7. "Defense of Marriage Act: Update to Prior Report." Washington, DC: U.S. Government Accountability Office, 2004. Accessed Aug 27, 2021. https://www.gao.gov/products/GAO-04-353R.

8. Aristotle. *Politics*. Trans. Jowett, Benjamin. New York: Random House, 1943: 75–77.

9. Beauvoir, *All Said and Done*, 458.

10. Beauvoir, *The Blood of Others*, 140.

11. Beauvoir, *The Second Sex*, 510.

12. Beauvoir, *The Woman Destroyed*, 246.

13. Sabbia, Lorna, and Maddy Dychtwald. "Women & Financial Wellness: Beyond the Bottom Line." Merrill & Age Wave, 2019: 20. Accessed January 2, 2019. https://mlaem.fs.ml.com/content/dam/ML /Registration/Women-Age-Wave-White-Paper.pdf.

14. Beauvoir, *The Second Sex*, 522.

15. There is some evidence to suggest that young adults' perceptions about the roles of the sexes are more conservative and less egalitarian than in the late twentieth century. In a 2014 study, around half of men (and a third of women) aged eighteen to twenty-four surveyed believed that "it is better for women to take care of the home and for men to be the achievers in the outside world." Fate-Dixon,

Nika. "Are Some Millennials Rethinking the Gender Revolution? Long-Range Trends in Views of Non-Traditional Roles for Women." University of Texas at Austin: Council on Contemporary Families, 2017. Accessed Aug 27, 2021. https://contemporaryfamilies.org/7 -fate-dixon-millennials-rethinking-gender-revolution/.

16. Lachance-Grzela, Mylène, and Geneviève Bouchard. "Why Do Women Do the Lion's Share of Housework? A Decade of Research." *Sex Roles* 63 (2010): 767–80; Mixon, Bobbie. "Chore Wars: Men, Women and Housework." Virginia: National Science Foundation, 2008.

17. Collins, Caitlyn, et al. "COVID-19 and the Gender Gap in Work Hours." *Gender, Work and Organization.* 28.S1 (2020): 101–12.

18. Ramey, Valerie A. "Time Spent in Home Production in the 20th Century: New Estimates from Old Data." Cambridge, MA: National Bureau of Economic Research, 2008: 56–58.

19. Beauvoir suggests that cooking can be less infernal because there's greater scope for creativity: discovering, negotiating, and procuring ingredients; invention in recipes, methods, and presentation; and perfecting complex creations that call for skill, patience, trials, and errors, especially with baking and pastry-making. Nevertheless, as long as cooking is a chore, as long as it is an unpaid requirement, it is repetitive and monotonous, and drags one back into the Manichean skirmish as swiftly as housework does. (Beauvoir, *The Second Sex,* 476–80.)

20. Thebaud, Sarah, Sabino Kornrich, and Leah Ruppanner. "Good Housekeeping, Great Expectations: Gender and Housework Norms." *Sociological Methods & Research* (2019): 1–29.

21. Beauvoir, *The Second Sex,* 734.

22. Collins, Patricia Hill. *Black Feminist Thought.* New York: Routledge, 2000: 46.

23. Wollstonecraft, Mary. *Vindication of the Rights of Women.* London: The Remnant Trust, 1792.

24. Solomon and Higgins, *The Philosophy of (Erotic) Love,* 52.

25. Beauvoir, *The Second Sex,* 465.

26. Beauvoir, *The Second Sex*, 467.

27. Beauvoir, *The Second Sex*, 457.

28. Beauvoir, *The Second Sex*, 511.

29. Beauvoir, *Diary of a Philosophy Student Vol 1*, 78.

30. Beauvoir, *A Transatlantic Love Affair*, 128.

31. Beauvoir, *The Prime of Life*, 21–22. A morganatic marriage is one between people of different classes, usually with the husband of a higher social rank than the wife. Beauvoir doesn't explicitly state what she meant by the term, but it is possibly based on the fact that Beauvoir was born to a higher social ranking than Sartre, although her family lost their money and left Beauvoir and her sister without a dowry.

32. As Susan J. Brison pointed out, this idea is in tension with Beauvoir's idea that lovers are free to change themselves and their relationship: "So how is a love that is both 'essential' (necessary, permanent, and unchangeable) *and* authentic possible?" (Brison, "Beauvoir and Feminism: Interview and Reflections," 201).

33. Beauvoir, *The Prime of Life*, 67.

34. Beauvoir, *Les Belles Images*, 82–83.

35. Beauvoir, *Les Belles Images*, 138.

36. Coontz, Stephanie. *Marriage, a History*. New York: Viking, 2005, 31. Some of these examples might seem absurd, but there are risks in imposing western values—independence and individualism, such as choosing partners without parents' approval or involvement and both partners working—on the rest of the world. Philosopher Serene Khader argued that we should be careful about ethnocentrism and culture-washing because western and northern societies have not relieved women of oppression and are not models of justice. In some societies, being part of a family through marriage is important to women for religious, cultural, and protective reasons. For Khader, independence is not the only path to well-being. *Personhood* individualism—being free from oppression and free to choose from

a range of options—is vital. For most people around the world, work is grueling, exploitative, and horribly paid and it's absurd to do it if you don't have to, and some people don't have the choice (Khader, *Decolonizing Universalism,* 59).

37. Beauvoir, *The Prime of Life*, 24.

38. Gouges, "The Rights of Woman," 36.

39. Gouges, "The Rights of Woman," 37.

40. A few days after Gouges's execution, a French newspaper reported: "Olympe de Gouges, born with an exalted imagination, believed her delusions were inspired by nature. She wanted to be a Statesman; it would seem that the law has punished this plotter for having forgotten the virtues suitable to her own sex." Not everyone was so sexist though. An anonymous Parisian wrote that, "She attempted to unmask the villains through the literary productions which she had printed and put up. They never forgave her, and she paid for her carelessness with her head" (Mousset, Sophie. *Women's Rights and the French Revolution*. New York: Routledge, 2017: 97–99). Almost two hundred years later, her exalted imagination, virtues wholly suitable to her sex, and carelessness have been appreciated for what they really were: extraordinary courage. Her ideas have been incorporated into the United Nations' Declaration on the Elimination of Discrimination against Women, and her ideas on marriage are a real option for many people. More recently, philosopher Elizabeth Brake argued for a similar structure to what Gouges imagined. Brake calls her own version "minimal marriage," based on contracts between consenting and caring adults (Brake, Elizabeth. *Minimizing Marriage*. New York: Oxford University Press, 2012). Problems remain even with minimal marriages: they discriminate against those not in conjugal relationships and care can be a slippery term. After all, traditional marriage was structured to "care" for women, but in effect kept them oppressed and uneducated. Philosopher Brook J. Sadler argued against marriage—even minimal ones—and for civil unions on the grounds that civil unions would be more flexible because they

allow for individualized arrangements, less government interference into sexual orientation and activities, and shake off the patriarchal burden that marriage, in its traditional form, carries (Sadler, Brooke J. "Re-thinking Civil Unions and Same-Sex Marriage." *The Monist* 91.3/4 [2008]: 578–605).

41. Beauvoir, *The Second Sex*, 511.

42. Beauvoir, "Preface to *Divorce in France*," 248.

43. Rich, "Women and Honor," 188.

44. Butler, Judith. "Judith Butler on Rethinking Vulnerability, Violence, Resistance." Verso Blog Mar 6, 2020. Accessed Aug 28, 2021. https://www.versobooks.com/blogs/4583-judith-butler-on-rethinking-vulnerability-violence-resistance.

45. Beauvoir, *Letters to Sartre*, 472. The English edition translates *petit* from French as "little." I have changed "little" to "dear" to emphasize that *petit* is more likely to be a term of endearment rather than a reference to Sartre's stature.

MOTHERHOOD

1. Cacopardo, "Jean-Paul Sartre and/et Simone de Beauvoir."

2. Ruddick, *Maternal Thinking*, xii.

3. Rose, *Mothers*, 78.

4. Arendt, *The Origins of Totalitarianism*, 473. Although Arendt's thinking lends itself to the experience of caregiving, Arendt was specifically talking about Nazism and how totalitarian thinking does not concern itself with the miracle of newness.

5. Rich, *Of Woman Born*, 35–36.

6. Beauvoir, *The Second Sex*, 192.

7. Beauvoir, *The Second Sex*, 541.

8. Stadlen, *What Mothers Do*, 1.

9. Stadlen, *What Mothers Do*, 15.

10. Schwarzer, *After The Second Sex*, 54, 76.

11. Simons, "Two Interviews with Simone de Beauvoir," 18–19.

12. For example, see Gines, "Sartre, Beauvoir, and the Race/Gender Analogy" and King, "Multiple Jeopardy, Multiple Consciousness."

13. The "second shift" was coined after Arlie Hochschild's book first published in 1989 (Hochschild, Arlie Russell, and Anne Machung. *The Second Shift*. New York: Penguin Books, 2003). French cartoonist Emma coined the term "mental load" in 2019 (Emma. "Do You Want Me to Do It? (No)." Jan 17, 2019. Accessed Jan 16, 2021. https://english.emmaclit.com/2019/01/17/do-you-want-me-to-do-it-no/).

14. Rose, *Mothers*, 77.

15. Patmore, Coventry. *The Angel in the House*. 1891. Ed. Morley, Henry. London, Paris & Melbourne: Cassell & Company, 2014. www.projectgutenberg.org. Accessed Jun 22, 2021. https://www.gutenberg.org/files/4099/4099-h/4099-h.htm.

16. Woolf, Virginia. *Killing the Angel in the House*. New York: Penguin, 1995: 3–5; Woolf, Virginia. *The Pargiters*. New York: New York Public Library & Readex Books, 1977: xxix-xxx.

17. Inspired by a Facebook rant (Friedberg, Sarah Buckley. "Society to Working Moms." Facebook. Apr 18, 2019. Accessed Aug 27, 2021. https://www.facebook.com/sarah.buckleyfriedberg/posts/10100880594353836).

18. Beauvoir, *The Second Sex*, 523.

19. Aristotle. *The Basic Works of Aristotle*. New York: Random House, 1941: 1092.

20. Kant, Immanuel. "Friendship." Trans. Infield, Louis. *Lectures on Ethics*. London: Meuthen & Co., 1930: 204.

21. Nietzsche, Friedrich. *Beyond Good and Evil*. 1886. Trans. Zimmern, Helen. Auckland: The Floating Press, 2008: 217.

22. Nietzsche, *Thus Spoke Zarathustra*, 116.

23. Hoffman, Kelly M., et al. "Racial Bias in Pain Assessment and Treatment Recommendations, and False Beliefs About Biological Differ-

ences between Blacks and Whites." *PNAS* 113.16 (2016). Accessed Aug 27, 2021. https://doi.org/10.1073/pnas.1516047113; Kiesel, Laura. "Women and Pain: Disparities in Experience and Treatment." *Harvard Health Blog* Oct 9 2017. Accessed Aug 26, 2021. https://www.health.harvard.edu/blog/women-and-pain-disparities-in-experience-and-treatment-2017100912562.

24. "Severe Maternal Morbidity in the United States." Centers for Disease Control and Prevention, 2014. Accessed Jan 12, 2019. https://www.cdc.gov/reproductivehealth/maternalinfanthealth/severematernalmorbidity.html; Martin, Nina, and Renee Montagne. "U.S. Has the Worst Rate of Maternal Deaths in the Developed World." (2017) *NPR*. Accessed May 2, 2019. https://www.npr.org/2017/05/12/528098789/u-s-has-the-worst-rate-of-maternal-deaths-in-the-developed-world; MacDorman, Marian F., et al. "Recent Increases in the U.S. Maternal Mortality Rate." *Obstetrics & Gynecology* 128.3 (2016): 447–55. These and other researchers noted that there has been a trend of underreporting maternal mortality in the US.

25. "Infant Mortality." Centers for Disease Control and Prevention, 2016. Accessed Feb 28, 2019. https://www.cdc.gov/reproductivehealth/maternalinfanthealth/infantmortality.htm; "Pregnancy-Related Deaths by Race/Ethnicity." Centers for Disease Control and Prevention, 2017. Accessed Feb 28, 2021. https://www.cdc.gov/reproductivehealth/maternal-mortality/pregnancy-mortality-surveillance-system.htm.

26. Kendall, Mikki. *Hood Feminism*. New York: Penguin, 2020: 233.

27. Even wealth, fame, education, and status do not protect Black women. Beyoncé and Serena Williams both faced life-threatening complications during childbirth. Meghan Markle was pilloried by the British media for touching her pregnant belly when Kate Middleton was earlier glorified for exactly the same gesture. A *Daily Mail* headline gushed, "Pregnant Kate tenderly cradles her baby bump," and then one year later, "Why can't Meghan Markle keep her hands off her bump? . . . Is it pride, vanity, acting—or a new age bonding technique?" When sociologist Tressie McMillan Cottom was four months pregnant she had abdominal pain,

sought medical advice three times over the course of a couple of days, and was dismissed. Doctors told her that it was normal spotting for an overweight person, then constipation, and then food poisoning. She had been in labor for three days and delivered her daughter who died shortly thereafter. Nurses scolded her with comments such as, "You should have said something," and "Just so you know, there was nothing we could have done, because you did not tell us you were in labor." Cottom noted that such victim-blaming is pervasive: "When the medical profession systematically denies the existence of black women's pain, underdiagnoses our pain, refuses to alleviate or treat our pain, healthcare marks us as incompetent bureaucratic subjects. Then it serves us accordingly" (Cottom, Tressie McMillan. *Thick: And Other Essays*. New York: The New Press, 2019, 82–86). In 2019, Black medical doctor Susan Moore sought medical care for COVID-19 in Indiana and a white male doctor and staff allegedly made her wait hours for medication, made her feel like a drug addict, and attempted to discharge her early. Before she died of the disease, she said, "This is how Black people get killed. When you send them home and they don't know how to fight for themselves" (Nirappil, Fenit. "A Black Doctor Alleged Racist Treatment before Dying of COVID-19." *The Washington Post*, Dec 24, 2020).

28. For an excellent philosophical defense of complaining, see Norlock, Kathryn J. "Can't Complain." *Journal of Moral Philosophy* 15.2 (2018): 117–35.

29. Beauvoir, *The Second Sex*, 566.

30. Beauvoir, *Memoirs of a Dutiful Daughter*, 190.

31. Beauvoir, *Force of Circumstance I*, 191.

32. Beauvoir, Simone de. "Pourquoi Nous Avons Signe." *Le nouvel observateur*. April 1971: 43.

33. "The World's Abortion Laws." Center for Reproductive Rights, 2021. Accessed Aug 27, 2021. https://reproductiverights.org/worldabortionlaws.

34. Lyons, Joseph D. "Justin Humphrey Is the Oklahoma 'Hosts' Lawmaker." *Bustle*, Feb 14, 2017. Accessed Aug 27, 2021. https://www

.bustle.com/p/who-is-justin-humphrey-the-oklahoma-lawmaker
-made-waves-for-his-hosts-comment-37966.

35. Rivkin-Fish, Michele. "Conceptualizing Feminist Strategies for Russian Reproductive Politics: Abortion, Surrogate Motherhood, and Family Support after Socialism," *Signs* 38.3 (2013): 573.

36. Beauvoir, *The Second Sex*, 525.

37. Beauvoir, *The Second Sex*, 568.

38. Lawler, Opheli Garcia. "Michelle Obama Is Done with the Gospel of 'Lean In.'" *The Cut,* Dec 2, 2018. Accessed Feb 28, 2019. https://www.thecut.com/2018/12/michelle-obama-lean-in-becoming-book-tour.html. There is some evidence to back up Obama's skepticism of "lean in" philosophy. Leonora Risse published a study in 2020 based on surveys with 7,500 Australians and found that the central indicators associated with leaning in—confidence, ambition, boldness, extraversion, and an internal locus of control—increased the likelihood of promotion for men but not women. Risse concluded despondently: "Collectively these findings point to a disturbing template for career success: be confident, be ambitious . . . and be male" (Risse, Leonora. "That Advice to Women to 'Lean in', Be More Confident . . . It Doesn't Help, and Data Show It." *The Conversation* 2020. Accessed Aug 27, 2021. https://theconversation.com/that-advice-to-women-to-lean-in-be-more-confident-it-doesnt-help-and-data-show-it-146998).

39. Schwarzer, *After The Second Sex*, 73.

40. Sandberg, Sheryl. "On Mother's Day, We Celebrate All Moms." Facebook. May 6, 2016. Accessed Aug 27, 2021. https://www.facebook.com/sheryl/posts/10156819553860177?fref=nf&pnref=story.

41. Beauvoir, *The Second Sex*, 568.

42. Luthar, Suniya S. and Ciciolla, Lucia. "What It Feels Like to Be a Mother: Variations by Children's Developmental Stages." *Developmental Psychology* 52.1 (2016): 143–54.

43. Beauvoir, *The Second Sex*, 765.

AGING

1. Beauvoir, *Old Age*, 604.

2. Beauvoir, *Old Age*, 315.

3. Beauvoir, *All Said and Done*, 463; Beauvoir, *Old Age*, 8.

4. Beauvoir, *Old Age*, 319.

5. Beauvoir, *Force of Circumstance II*, 378.

6. Beauvoir, *Old Age*, 323–24.

7. Beauvoir, *Old Age*, 324. Beauvoir's emphasis.

8. Beauvoir, *Old Age*, 320.

9. Beauvoir, *Force of Circumstance II*, 377–78; Schwarzer, *After The Second Sex*, 83.

10. Beauvoir, *Old Age*, 244.

11. In Romania, around 93 percent of grandmothers provide some care for grandchildren. In the US, UK, China, Sweden, the Netherlands, Denmark, France, Hungary, and other countries, over 50 percent provide care (Janta, Barbara. *Caring for Children in Europe*. European Union: RAND Europe, 2014: 11. Accessed Sep 4, 2021. https://www.rand.org /content/dam/rand/pubs/research_reports/RR500/RR554/RAND _RR554.pdf); Ko, Pei-Chun, and Karsten Hank. "Grandparents Caring for Grandchildren in China and Korea." *The Journals of Gerontology* 69.4 (2014): 646–51. Accessed Sep 4, 2021. https://academic.oup .com/psychsocgerontology/article/69/4/646/616809; Chamie, Joseph. "Increasingly Indispensable Grandparents." *YaleGlobal Online* Sep 4, 2018. Accessed Sep 4, 2021. https://archive-yaleglobal.yale.edu /content/increasingly-indispensable-grandparents.

12. Beauvoir, *Old Age*, 13.

13. Beauvoir, *Old Age*, 415.

14. Beauvoir, *Old Age*, 465. There is research that backs this up: a study of British voting choices between 1964 to 2010 found a correlation between growing older and voting conservatively, that is, for parties that uphold the status quo. Tilley, James, and Geoffrey Evans.

"Ageing and Generational Effects on Vote Choice." *Electoral Studies* 33 (2014): 19–27. Accessed Aug 27, 2021. https://www.sciencedirect .com/science/article/abs/pii/S0261379413000875.

15. Beauvoir, *Old Age*, 425.

16. There is some empirical evidence to support the notion that the subjective perception of time speeds up as people age, although it is unclear as to whether this is caused by biological aging or shaped by cultural and social factors. Wittmann, Marc, and Sandra Lehn-hoff. "Age Effects in Perception of Time." *Psychological Reports* 97.3 (2005): 921–935. Accessed Aug 27, 2021. https://doi.org/10.2466 /pr0.97.3.921–935.

17. Beauvoir, *Force of Circumstance II*, 1.

18. Beauvoir, *Force of Circumstance II*, 7.

19. Beauvoir, *All Said and Done*, 34.

20. Beauvoir, *Old Age*, 409.

21. Beauvoir, *Old Age*, 103, 124, 134.

22. Beauvoir, *Old Age*, 104; Ptah-hotep. *The Instruction of Ptah-Hotep*. 2414–2375 BCE. Trans. Gunn, Battiscombe. London: John Murray, 1912: 41.

23. Beauvoir, *Old Age*, 112, 136.

24. Beauvoir, *Old Age*, 309.

25. Franck, Thomas. "Human Lifespan Could Soon Pass 100 Years Thanks to Medical Tech, Says BofA." *CNBC* 2019. Accessed Aug 27, 2021. https://www.cnbc.com/2019/05/08/techs-next-big-disruption -could-be-delaying-death.html.

26. Beauvoir, *Old Age*, 604.

27. Beauvoir, Simone de. "Observer Picture Archive: My Clothes and I, 20 March 1960 with Cynthia Judah." Ed. Whitmore, Greg: *The Guardian*, 2019. Accessed Jul 30, 2021. https://www.theguardian .com/theobserver/2019/mar/17/observer-archive-my-clothes-and-i -by-simone-de-beauvoir-20-march-1960.

28. As of 2016, the plastic surgery market was worth over $16 billion annually in America. "More Than $16 Billion Spent on Cosmetic Plastic Surgery." American Society of Plastic Surgeons, April 12, 2017. Accessed Aug 27, 2021. https://www.plasticsurgery.org/news/press-releases/more-than-16-billion-spent-on-cosmetic-plastic-surgery.

29. It is still a common trope that men age like wine but women have an expiration date. In a 2016 comedy skit called "*Last F**kable Day*," Amy Schumer, Julia Louis-Dreyfus, Tina Fey, and Patricia Arquette picnic by a river in idyllic California woods. They are celebrating Louis-Dreyfus reaching an age where she will be put out to Hollywood pasture. Louis-Dreyfus explains that now that she is a middle-aged woman the media will stop portraying her as a desirable and sexual being. She means that she will never again be offered roles in which she will be a love interest, but rather asexual roles in films with titles such as *Whatever It Takes* or *She Means Well*. "Last F**kable Day (ft. Tina Fey, Julia Louis-Dreyfus, and Patricia Arquette)." *Inside Amy Schumer*. Comedy Central, 2015. Accessed Aug 27, 2021. https://www.youtube.com/watch?v=XPpsI8mWKmg.

30. Beauvoir, *Force of Circumstance II*, 378.

31. Spar, Debora L. "Aging and My Beauty Dilemma." *The New York Times*, Sep 25, 2016. Accessed Aug 27, 2021. https://www.nytimes.com/2016/09/25/fashion/aging-plastic-surgery-feminism.html.

32. I adore the bravery of actor Justine Bateman, who is normalizing women's aging and exposing sexist implications of the notion that men's aging implies more power and women's aging implies less power. Not being dubbed as young and pretty is, Bateman wrote, a "pernicious distraction that has permeated seemingly every female fiber," and, "It felt like a ploy to somehow shut me down, to get me to hide, to be quiet, to erase myself, all at the exact moment in my life when I had gained the most intelligence, the most wisdom, and the most confidence. What an easy way to try to make sure that I stopped accomplishing anything further." (Bateman, Justine. *Face*. New York: Akashic Books, 2021.)

33. This is not only an American phenomenon. Breast augmentation, liposuction, and tummy tucks are popular in Brazil, for example, and eyelid surgeries are in demand in Japan. "ISAPS International Survey on Aesthetic/Cosmetic Procedures Performed in 2017." International Society of Aesthetic Plastic Surgery, 2019. Accessed Nov 1, 2020. https://www.isaps.org/wp-content/uploads/2019/03/ISAPS_2017 _International_Study_Cosmetic_Procedures_NEW.pdf

34. Nussbaum, *Aging Thoughtfully*, 20–21, 120.

35. Beauvoir, *Old Age*, 323.

36. Beauvoir, *Old Age*, 330.

37. Beauvoir, *The Second Sex*, 619, 625.

38. Beauvoir, *The Second Sex*, 619.

39. Beauvoir, *Old Age*, 542.

40. "A Translation of Sappho's 'Old Age Poem' by J. Simon Harris." *The Society of Classical Poets*, Jul 6, 2018. Accessed Aug 27, 2021. https://classicalpoets.org/2018/07/06/a-translation-of-sapphos-old -age-poem-by-j-simon-harris/.

41. Beauvoir, *Old Age*, 601.

42. Nussbaum, *Aging Thoughtfully*, 196, 207.

43. Beauvoir, *After The Second Sex*, 89.

44. Beauvoir, *Adieux*, 188.

45. Beauvoir, *Old Age*, 547.

DEATH

1. Beauvoir, *Memoirs of a Dutiful Daughter*, 138. Beauvoir's emphasis.

2. Beauvoir, *Force of Circumstance II*, 379.

3. Beauvoir, *A Walk Through the Land of Old Age*, 363.

4. Beauvoir, *The Ethics of Ambiguity*, 127; Beauvoir, *Pyrrhus and Cineas*, 114.

5. Beauvoir, *The Ethics of Ambiguity*, 127.

6. Beauvoir, *All Men Are Mortal*, 26.

7. Beauvoir *All Men Are Mortal*, 22.

8. Beauvoir, *A Very Easy Death*, 91.

9. Beauvoir, *Memoirs of a Dutiful Daughter*, 239.

10. Weil, Simone. *The Notebooks of Simone Weil*. 1956. Trans. Wills, Arthur. London: Routledge, 2003: 492.

11. Weil, Simone. *Gravity and Grace*. 1947. Trans. Crawford, Emma and Mario von der Ruhr. London and New York: Routledge, 2003: 153.

12. Beauvoir, *Force of Circumstance I*, 110.

13. Beauvoir, *The Ethics of Ambiguity*, 57.

14. Beauvoir, *The Mandarins*, 360.

15. Beauvoir, *The Mandarins*, 359, 607.

16. Beauvoir, *The Mandarins*, 607.

17. McGinty, Jo Craven. "The Numbers: Around the World, Suicides Rise in Spring." *Wall Street Journal*, Apr 20, 2019.

18. In her excellent in-depth philosophical analysis of the arguments for and (mostly) against suicide, philosopher Jennifer Michael Hecht comes to the same conclusion. Hecht quotes David Hume to argue that, "'There are an infinite variety of secret connections and associations in the vast system of things,' and no one can know what he or she might be able to do sometime in the unforeseeable future" (Hecht, *Stay*, 138).

19. Beauvoir, *All Said and Done*, 97.

20. Beauvoir, *The Mandarins*, 610. There is research to suggest that mothers with dependent children are less likely to die of suicide—perhaps because their love for their children, or at least their sense of responsibility toward them, can give mothers a compelling reason to stay alive (Hecht, *Stay*, 153).

21. Beauvoir, *Force of Circumstance I*, 271.

22. Beauvoir, *All Said and Done*, 119.

23. Beauvoir, *My Experience as a Writer*, 297.

24. Abrutyn, Seth, Anna S. Mueller, and Melissa Osborne. "Rekeying

Cultural Scripts for Youth Suicide: How Social Networks Facilitate Suicide Diffusion and Suicide Clusters Following Exposure to Suicide." *Society and Mental Health* 10.2 (2020): 112–35.

25. Beauvoir, *Adieux*, 127.

26. Beauvoir, *The Mandarins*, 234.

SELF-SABOTAGE

1. Beauvoir, *The Second Sex*, 740–41.

2. Mercer, Christia, "Descartes' Debt to Teresa of Ávila, or Why We Should Work on Women in the History of Philosophy." *Philosophical Studies* 174 (2017): 2539–2555.

3. Beauvoir, *The Second Sex*, 712–13.

4. Teresa of Ávila, *The Book of My Life*, 225.

5. Saint Teresa pointed to two kinds of love that are sometimes impossible to distinguish: purely spiritual and, "The other is also spiritual, but mingled with it are our sensuality and weakness; yet it is a worthy love, which, as between relatives and friends, seems lawful" (Teresa of Ávila, *The Way of Perfection*. Trans. Peers, E. Allison. Grand Rapids, MI: Christian Classics Ethereal Library, 1964: 31).

6. Teresa of Ávila, *The Interior Castle*, 26–28.

7. Catherine of Siena, *Catherine of Siena: An Anthology*. Ed. Noffke, Suzanne. Vol. 1. Arizona: Arizona Center for Medieval and Renaissance Studies, 2012: 231.

8. Scudder, Vida D., ed. *Saint Catherine of Siena as Seen in Her Letters*. New York: E. P. Dutton & Co., 1906: 305.

9. Beauvoir, *The Second Sex*, 659. Equality of salvation was one of Christianity's appeals in its inception. For example, Galatians 3:28 states: "There is neither Jew nor Gentile, neither slave nor free, nor is there male and female, for you are all one in Christ Jesus."

10. Vintges, *A New Dawn*, 99–101.

11. Ahmed, Leila. "Feminism and Cross-Cultural Inquiry." *Coming to Terms*. Ed. Weed, Elizabeth. London: Routledge, 1989: 149.

12. Beauvoir, *The Second Sex*, 667.

13. Beauvoir, *The Second Sex*, 669.

14. hooks, *All About Love*, 72.

15. Beauvoir, *The Second Sex*, 668.

16. Beauvoir, *The Second Sex*, 219–220.

17. Beauvoir, "Women, Ads, and Hate," 275.

18. Beauvoir, "The Urgency of an Antisexist Law," 266.

19. Beauvoir, *The Second Sex*, 671.

20. Beauvoir, *The Second Sex*, 677.

21. Teresa of Ávila, *The Interior Castle*, 26.

22. Beauvoir, *Force of Circumstance II*, 184–85; Beauvoir, *The Prime of Life*, 251–52.

23. Beauvoir, *My Experience as a Writer*, 291.

24. Beauvoir, *The Prime of Life*, 445.

25. Bioethicist Rosemarie Garland-Thomson found that Beauvoir's notion of identity and becoming a woman was helpful in understanding her identity as a woman with disabilities: "The idea that culture, discourse, and social relations—rather than the rightness or wrongness of our bodies—make us who we are and who we are understood to be was an intellectual lightning bolt for me . . . Suddenly, what had been wrong with me all my life became what was wrong with the social order. I became disabled, then, similarly to the way I had become a woman. Although woman was an identity I had always claimed and which had claimed me, disabled was an identity . . . from which I fled" (Garland-Thomson, Rosemarie. "The Story of My Work: How I Became Disabled." *Disability Studies Quarterly* 34.2 [2014]). However, as discussed in Part I, some women of color have found Beauvoir's analysis unhelpful. For example, see Oyewumi, Oyeronke. "Family Bonds/ Conceptual Binds." *Signs* 25.4 (2000): 1093–98.

26. Beauvoir, *Memoirs of a Dutiful Daughter*, 142.

27. Coffin, *Sex, Love and Letters*, 242.

28. Bair, *Simone de Beauvoir*, 197.

29. Kirkpatrick, *Becoming Beauvoir*, 190, 212, 396.

30. Beauvoir, *Memoirs of a Dutiful Daughter*, 343–344.

31. Beauvoir, *The Prime of Life*, 61.

32. Beauvoir, *Adieux*, 300.

33. Beauvoir, *Wartime Diary*, 187.

34. Beauvoir, "The Rebellious Woman," 198.

35. Beauvoir, *The Prime of Life*, 62.

36. Beauvoir, *Force of Circumstance II*, 377.

37. Beauvoir, *Memoirs of a Dutiful Daughter*, 343.

38. Beauvoir, *Memoirs of a Dutiful Daughter*, 345.

39. Beauvoir, *The Prime of Life*, 478–79.

40. Beauvoir, *Wartime Diary*, 176–77.

41. Beauvoir, *All Said and Done*, 131.

42. Beauvoir, *Letters to Sartre*, 170.

HAPPINESS

1. Beauvoir, *The Ethics of Ambiguity*, 13. Beauvoir's emphasis.

2. Beauvoir, *Jean-Paul Sartre*, 230–32.

3. Beauvoir, *The Ethics of Ambiguity*, 135.

4. Beauvoir, *All Said and Done*, 462–63.

5. Beauvoir, *The Ethics of Ambiguity*, 87.

6. Beauvoir, *America Day by Day*, 387.

7. Beauvoir, *The Ethics of Ambiguity*, 25.

8. Beauvoir, "An Existentialist Looks at Americans," 303, 310–311.

9. Beauvoir, *Les Belles Images*, 51.

10. Beauvoir, "Poetry and Truth of the Far West," 36; Beauvoir, *America Day by Day*, 64.

11. "Kate Raworth on economics in the time of an environment and climate emergency." BBC Newsnight, May 2, 2019. Facebook. Accessed

June 19, 2021. https://www.facebook.com/bbcnewsnight/videos /2335084250106026/.

12. Danner, Deborah D., David A. Snowdon, and Wallace V Friesen. "Positive Emotions in Early Life and Longevity." *Journal of Personality and Social Psychology* 80.5 (2001): 804–813.

13. Fredrickson, Barbara L., et al. "Open Hearts Build Lives: Positive Emotions, Induced through Loving-Kindness Meditation, Build Consequential Personal Resources." *Journal of Personality and Social Psychology* 95.5 (2008): 1045–62.

14. Jobin, Joelle, Carsten Wrosch, and Michael F. Scheier. "Associations between Dispositional Optimism and Diurnal Cortisol in a Community Sample: When Stress Is Perceived as Higher Than Normal." *Health Psychology* 33.4 (2014): 382–91.

15. Huffman, Jeff C., et al. "Effects of Optimism and Gratitude on Physical Activity, Biomarkers, and Readmissions after an Acute Coronary Syndrome." *Circulation: Cardiovascular Quality and Outcomes* 9.1 (2016): 55–63.

16. Beauvoir, *A Very Easy Death*, 101.

17. Psychologists Heather Barry Kappes and Gabriele Oettingen found that positive fantasizing can sap energy, meaning that people lose the ambition to pursue their dreams. Their solution is what they call the "WOOP" strategy: Wish, Outcome, Obstacle, Plan—meaning that it is fine to make wishes, but it is just as important to consider possible hurdles, ways to overcome them, and to map out action. See Kappes, Heather Barry, and Gabriele Oettingen, "Positive Fantasies About Idealized Futures Sap Energy." *Journal of Experimental Social Psychology* 47.4 (2011): 719–29; Oettingen, Gabriele. *Rethinking Positive Thinking*. New York: Current, 2015.

18. Byrne, Rhonda. *The Secret*. Atria Books, 2006: 28.

19. Beauvoir, *America Day by Day*, 241–2.

20. Ahmed, Sara. *The Promise of Happiness*. Durham and London: Duke University Press, 2010, 2.

21. Philosopher Marilyn Frye agreed with Beauvoir: "It is often a requirement upon oppressed people that we smile and be cheerful. If we comply, we signify our docility and our acquiescence in our situation" (Frye, *The Politics of Reality*, 2).

22. Lorde, *The Cancer Journals*, 75.

23. Beauvoir, *The Woman Destroyed*, 140.

24. Beauvoir, *The Woman Destroyed*, 252.

25. Beauvoir, *Memoirs of a Dutiful Daughter*, 224.

26. Beauvoir, *Memoirs of a Dutiful Daughter*, 348.

27. Beauvoir, *Pyrrhus and Cineas*, 98.

28. Beauvoir, *The Mandarins*, 53.

29. Beauvoir, *Diary of a Philosophy Student Vol 1*, 164.

30. Beauvoir, *Diary of a Philosophy Student Vol 1*, 165.

31. Beauvoir, *The Prime of Life*, 288.

32. Beauvoir, *Force of Circumstance I*, 162.

33. Beauvoir, "Must We Burn Sade?," 87.

34. Beauvoir, *Force of Circumstance I*, 192.

35. Beauvoir, *Diary of a Philosophy Student Vol 1*, 241–42.

REBELLION

1. Beauvoir, *The Second Sex*, 749.

2. Beauvoir, *The Second Sex*, 759.

3. Schwarzer, *After The Second Sex*, 116.

4. Beauvoir, *The Ethics of Ambiguity*, 96.

5. Srinivasan, *The Right to Sex*, 179; Zakaria, *Against White Feminism*, 95.

6. Beauvoir, *The Mandarins*, 584.

7. Beauvoir, *Memoirs of a Dutiful Daughter*, 192.

8. Beauvoir, *Memoirs of a Dutiful Daughter*, 193.

9. Beauvoir, *Memoirs of a Dutiful Daughter*, 181.

10. Beauvoir, *Diary of a Philosophy Student Vol 1*, 264.

11. Beauvoir, "Moral Idealism and Political Realism," 180.

12. Beauvoir, *Pyrrhus and Cineas*, 180.

13. Beauvoir, *America Day by Day*, 94.

14. Beauvoir, *Force of Circumstance II*, 88–89.

15. Beauvoir, *The Mandarins*, 585.

16. Beauvoir, *The Ethics of Ambiguity*, 81.

17. Beauvoir, *Political Writings*, 26.

18. Beauvoir, *The Ethics of Ambiguity*, 90.

19. Schwarzer, *After The Second Sex*, 74.

20. Crenshaw, Kimberlé. "Demarginalizing the Intersection of Race and Sex: A Black Feminist Critique of Antidiscrimination Doctrine, Feminist Theory and Antiracist Politics." *University of Chicago Legal Forum*. 1 (1989): 151–152.

21. Demby, Gene. "Why Now, White People?" *NPR: Code Switch*. June 16, 2020. Accessed Sep 1, 2021. https://www.npr.org/2020/06/16 /878963732/why-now-white-people.

22. Beauvoir, *The Ethics of Ambiguity*, 91.

23. Beauvoir, *The Ethics of Ambiguity*, 91.

24. Trump, Donald J. "Sad to See the History and Culture of Our Great Country . . ." Twitter. August 17, 2017. Accessed Jun 1, 2020. https:// twitter.com/realDonaldTrump/status/898169407213645824?s=20.

25. Beauvoir, *The Ethics of Ambiguity*, 91. Philosopher Cécile Fabre also argued that we have a responsibility to choose to honor and remember the right people and the right things in the right ways (Fabre, Cécile and Nigel Warburton, "Philosophy Bites." *Cécile Fabre on Remembrance*. 2016. https://philosophybites.libsyn.com/cecile-fabre -on-remembrance).

26. "Call for Plaques on Scotland's Statues with Links to Slavery." *BBC News* June 8, 2020. Accessed February 28, 2021. https://www.bbc .com/news/uk-scotland-edinburgh-east-fife-52965230.

27. Wilkerson, *Caste*, 14.

28. Beauvoir, *The Ethics of Ambiguity*, 84.

29. Beauvoir, *The Ethics of Ambiguity*, 87.

30. Beauvoir, *The Mandarins*, 26.

31. Philosopher Sonia Kruks argued that when the underprivileged can't speak or act for themselves, or can't do so effectively, then it can be helpful and responsible for an ally to use their advantages or platform to amplify the message—but otherwise it's often better to stay out of it—to say and do nothing (Kruks, "Simone de Beauvoir and the Politics of Privilege," 185). Philosophers Maria Lugones and Elizabeth Spelman advise white women to join the community in the spirit of openness, friendship, reciprocity of care, and especially humility: "So you need to learn to become unintrusive, unimportant, patient to the point of tears, while at the same time open to learning any possible lessons" (Lugones, Maria C., and Elizabeth V. Spelman, "Have We Got a Theory for You! Feminist Theory, Cultural Imperialism and the Demand for 'the Woman's Voice.'" *Women's Studies International* 6.6 [1983]: 580).

32. Phillips, Julie. "Ursula K. Le Guin Was a Creator of Worlds." *Humanities* Winter 2019. Accessed Aug 26, 2021. https://www.neh.gov/article/ursula-k-le-guin-was-creator-worlds.

33. "Lettre ouverte à la Commission de révision du code pénal pour la révision de certains textes régissant les rapports entre adultes et mineurs." Archives Françoise Dolto 1977. Accessed Mar 1, 2021. http://www.dolto.fr/fd-code-penal-crp.html.

34. Beauvoir, *The Mandarins*, 358.

35. Beauvoir, *The Mandarins*, 397.

36. Beauvoir, *The Ethics of Ambiguity*, 89–90.

37. Beauvoir, "The Second Sex: 25 Years Later," 80.

38. Beauvoir, *The Ethics of Ambiguity*, 89.

39. In *The Bonds of Freedom*, philosopher Kristana Arp criticized Beauvoir's stance on violence because you can't fully negate another per-

son's freedom unless you kill them; however, you can limit their power by, for example, imprisoning them to prevent further oppression.

40. Philosopher Amia Srinivasan argued that getting angry is a vital way of registering and communicating injustices beyond simply knowing them. In Srinivasan's view, telling people not to be angry is about social control. Opposing anger, even if sympathetic to injustices, suggests not only that the victim is responsible but also that the injustice was not a big deal, since the implication is that it's not worth getting upset about. An example of this, Srinivasan noted, is when women are given advice about not getting raped, which puts the moral responsibility for rape on victims and not perpetrators of rape. This is a function of reverse oppression. In this case, the flawed logic is that some people's freedom *from* being raped impinges on other people's freedom *to* rape. (Srinivasan, Amia. "The Aptness of Anger." *The Journal of Political Philosophy* 26.2 [2018]: 123–44.)

41. Cherry, *The Case For Rage*, 5.

42. Ferber, Alona. "Judith Butler on the Culture Wars, JK Rowling and Living in 'Anti-Intellectual Times.'" *New Statesman* Sep 22, 2020. Accessed Sep 5, 2021. https://www.newstatesman.com/international /2020/09/judith-butler-culture-wars-jk-rowling-and-living-anti -intellectual-times.

43. Beauvoir, *The Second Sex*, 343.

44. Beauvoir, *The Ethics of Ambiguity*, 97–98; Beauvoir realized that by virtue of being French, she was complicit in France's colonialism. She asked, "I wanted to stop being an accomplice in [the Algerian] war, but how?" (Beauvoir, *Force of Circumstance II*, 91). She helped Algerian torture victims, but felt generally powerless until lawyer Gisèle Halimi asked her to help launch a campaign to release activist Djamila Boupacha, a member of a militant Algerian independence group who was arrested, then tortured and raped for weeks, for a crime she said she didn't commit and that there was no evidence of her committing. Beauvoir transcribed Boupacha's story and published it in the national newspaper *Le monde,* with the view to shifting public opinion about

the war toward Algerian independence. After Boupacha was released, the militant group she was a part of forcibly sent her back to Algeria but Beauvoir refused to get involved because she didn't want to speak out against a rebellion she supported. Philosopher Sonia Kruks argued that Beauvoir objectified Boupacha—because Beauvoir decided how to share Boupacha's story and used it to advocate for a greater cause—but Beauvoir was probably not wrong to do so because, at least in this case, even though the choice was harrowing, the means justified the ends (Kruks, "Simone de Beauvoir and the Politics of Privilege," 194).

45. There is much philosophical support for fighting with rhetoric instead of violence. For example, Hannah Arendt proposed that, "politically speaking, it is insufficient to say that power and violence are not the same. Power and violence are opposites; where the one rules absolutely, the other is absent" (Arendt, *On Violence*, 56). The suggestion is that power flows through reason which should counter the need for violence. The problem with this logic is that if oppressed people use violence, then it becomes their fault, not the oppressor's fault, even though the oppressors used violence to create the oppressive situation. Indeed, when members of oppressed groups use violence to counter violence, they are often the ones who are punished. Domestic violence is tolerated, if not acceptable or legal—such as in Russia, where domestic violence was decriminalized in 2017—and standing up to it is shunned or ignored. While police brutality in the US is acceptable, violence by protesters against police brutality is condemned and any hint of violence is countered with more police violence. When CeCe McDonald, a Black trans woman, was attacked in a racist altercation outside a bar and after a woman smashed a glass in her face, McDonald protected herself with a pair of scissors and killed one of the attackers. McDonald said, "For all of my life I was conditioned to believe that I'm supposed to get abused or accept violence because I was trans . . . This white man was getting off on seeing me beg for my life . . . seeing the fear in me that made him validate his white supremacy." She took a plea bargain for manslaughter and was sentenced to forty-one months

in a men's prison, including three months in solitary—punishment even worse than imprisonment—under the guise of protecting her (Gares, Jacqueline. *Free CeCe!* Jac Gares Media, Inc., U.S., 2016).

46. Beauvoir, *The Ethics of Ambiguity*, 28.

47. Inspired by Beauvoir, Sonia Kruks employed the term "an ambiguous humanism," to refer to a self-critical and well-intentioned humanism that combats oppression and dehumanization, acknowledges tensions in political action, accepts responsibility for failures, and focuses on continually reconstructing itself (Kruks, *Simone de Beauvoir and the Politics of Ambiguity*, 33).

48. Beauvoir, *Force of Circumstance II*, 375.

49. Beauvoir, "Moral Idealism and Political Realism," 190–191.

50. Baldwin, James. *Notes of a Native Son*. 1955. Boston: Beacon Press, 2012: 15.

51. Beauvoir, *The Second Sex*, 764.

52. Beauvoir, "Pyrrhus and Cineas," 140.

53. Beauvoir, "Introduction to *Women Insist*," 251.

54. In *The Second Sex*, Beauvoir nodded to Arthur Rimbaud who wrote that when women become free from servitude, they will become poets.

INDEX

of Sartre, 205–6
self-knowledge and, 222
women and, 216
Harari, Yuval Noah, 18
Harper's Magazine, 90
Hecht, Jennifer Michael, 300n18
Hegel, Georg Wilhelm Friedrich, xvii,
56–59, 69, 84, 103
Heidegger, Martin, xvii, xxii, 165,
269n19
Héloïse, 110–11
Hill, Samantha Rose, 283n22
Holtzclaw, Daniel, 26
homeless people, 232
Homer, 154
homo economicus, 16, 17
homosexuality, 93–94
hooks, bell, xxiii, xxvii, 26, 48, 191
Horace, 154
housework, 106–10, 230, 233,
288n19
humanism, ambiguous, 310n47
Hume, David, 300n18
Hurtado, Luchita, 151

immanence, 5, 148, 253
inauthenticity, *see* bad faith
indignation, xi–xii
inertia, 149, 150, 239
Inseparables, The (Beauvoir), 66
intersubjectivity, xii, 55–56, 75–77, 89,
250
defined, 253
Istanbul Convention, 227

Joan of Arc, 189
Jollivet, Simone, 200
Jung, Carl, 273n28
justice, 250

Kafka, Franz, 135
Kant, Immanuel, 134
Kappes, Heather Barry, 304n17
Kendall, Mikki, 135
Khader, Serene, 289n36
Kierkegaard, Søren, xvii, 127, 269n19
Kirkpatrick, Kate, 195, 199, 268n14
Kosakiewicz, Olga and Wanda, 60–62, 79
Kristeva, Julia, xxi
Kruger, Barbara, 191
Kruks, Sonia, 307n31, 309n44, 310n47

Lacoin, Elizabeth ("Zaza"), 64–67, 77, 177
Lanzmann, Claude, 93, 152
Lao Tzu, 153
leadership, 275n44
Lean In (Sandberg), 141
Le Bon, Sylvie, 123, 284n30
Leduc, Violette, 67
Legally Blonde, 157
Le Guin, Ursula K., 241
Leopold II, King, 235
Lerner, Gerda, 16, 272n26
Little Mermaid, The (Andersen), 164
Little Women (Alcott), 82–83
Lizzo, x, 94
loneliness, 62, 63, 105, 282n17, 283n22
Lorde, Audre, xxiii, 215, 245
Louis-Dreyfus, Julia, 298n29
love
authenticity in, 131
in marriage, 104–5
maternal, 130–31
narcissism and, 191
romantic, *see* romantic love
self-love, 191
Teresa of Ávila on, 301n5
Lugones, Maria, 307n31
Lyotard, Jean-François, 242